Moore's writing has appeared in the *Observer*, the *Daily Telegraph*, *Sunday Times* and *Esquire*. His first book, the important travel-*Frost on My Moustache*, was published in three languages, g Norwegian. He lives in West London with his wife and e children.

Also by Tim Moore

FROST ON MY MOUSTACHE
The Arctic Exploits of a Lord and a Loafer

Continental Drifter

Taking the Low Road with the
First Grand Tourist

TIM MOORE

An *Abacus* Book

First published in Great Britain in 2001 by Abacus

The Route of the European Tour (p.vii) © Oxford University Press 1962.
Reprinted from *The Life and Adventures of Thomas Coryate* by Michael Strachan
(1962) by kind permission of Oxford University Press.

A CIP catalogue record for this book
is available from the British Library.

ISBN 0 349 11464 1

Typeset in Bembo by Palimpsest Book Production Limited,
Polmont, Stirlingshire
Printed and bound in Great Britain by
Clays Ltd, St Ives plc

Abacus
A Division of
Little, Brown and Company (UK)
Brettenham House
Lancaster Place
London WC2E 7EN

www.littlebrown.co.uk

TO T. C.

Acknowledgements

Thanks to: my family; Thordis Olafsdottir; Paul Sadka; Ferny and Peter; Donald Grey; Simon Tillotson; Ian Hunter; Professor Edward Chaney; the lady from Odcombe who sent me the tape. Oh, and the bloke who bought the Rolls.

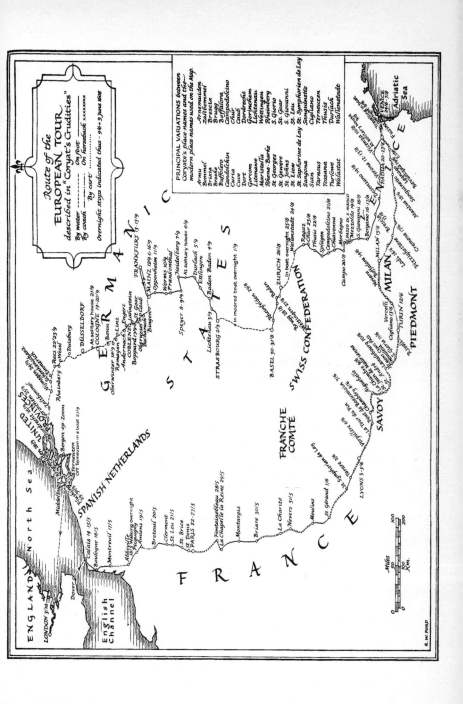

Introduction

Back in 1982, a company called Magic Bus used to operate non-stop coaches between London and places far, far too far away for anyone except especially tight-arsed students to consider travelling by coach from. So it was that at the fag-end of that summer I found myself in Athens with four dozen like-minded young Britons, boarding an unventilated fifty-footer commanded by two *Midnight Express* jailers.

Before we'd even left I was already beginning to suspect that the next seventy-three hours would incorporate more notable discomforts than the brief and simple distress endured in spending an extra £19 on a plane ticket. As I spread my unsightly belongings about the adjacent seat to deflect the likes of me shambling up to share my life for three days, vigorous bouzouki music blurted scarily from a speaker dangling above my head. After an hour, the tape ended, was ejected, inverted and replayed. This was the start of a process which did not stop.

Shortly after crossing into Yugoslavia, we spent six hours completely stationary in astonishing heat awaiting removal of the bounteous fatalities resulting from contact between a coach once indistinguishable from our own and the heavily stoved-in carcasses of a trio of Zastavas. At the Italian border, customs officers unearthed a huge trove of Marlboro cartons in the luggage holds – there were protracted negotiations with the drivers, presumably resolved success-fully as after we'd driven a further four or so miles the coach pulled into a side road where a team of enthusiastic gangsters ferried the cigarettes into the boots of their Mercedes.

Somewhere in the middle of the second night – in Italy? Austria? Germany? – I was heaved off the salami-scented vinyl by an emer-gency stop on the hard shoulder of a rainy autostrada/bahn. Picking myself up, I watched blearily through the back window as our two drivers dragged a protesting silhouette out of the car behind and, presumably on the pretext of some perceived breach of motoring etiquette, contrived a Tarantino-esque scene which melded a lengthy and systematic beating to the wittily incongruous bouzouki backbeat.

This was the last straw for the quintet of pixie-booted Scottish Goths on the back seat just behind me, who immediately opted to consume the forty-eight cans of Greek lager they had laboriously carried aboard. In doing so they successfully blotted out the awful-ness of their predicament, but at a price. As dawn broke and their bladders became almost audibly distended, heart-rending moans and winces rose above the music, every pluck and strum of which I had by now accepted would forever occupy a small but important part of my brain. (Ask me to name five varieties of apple or the head of the Tracy family in *Thunderbirds* and I'll tilt my head, smile gently, then jump messily to my feet with clawed hands aloft and Zorba the Greek bursting from my throat in a tortured ululation.)

After perhaps two hours of accelerating distress, one fluid-filled young Braveheart rushed suddenly up the aisle to request an unscheduled roadside halt, returning almost in tears at the ferocity of his rebuttal. Minutes later, with no indication of an impending comfort stop, strange noises emerged behind me: metal being punctured and torn; tinny, echoing trickles; soft, despairing, self-revolted oaths. When we finally did pull into a service station, the Scots trooped dismally past, the dark circles on the seats and crutches of their black drainpipes telling of the varying success with which they had voided themselves into the sawn-off beer cans sloshing in their sticky, disgusted grasps.

What was noticeable through all these trying incidents was the complete lack of solidarity between the passengers. We were broken men, dispirited and divided, frightened, hungry and stripped of both dignity and humanity. As we pulled away up the sliproad after a twenty-six-second stop at a German autobahn service station, one of the Scots mumbled beerily to his friend that we'd left someone behind. Then another spotted him in the distance, and as I squinted through the seatbacks I could see a little figure peering randomly about the coach park in the early stages of what, as I watched, blossomed into a magnificent panic. 'Yeah,' came an almost bored Caledonian murmur. 'It's that Irish guy from up the front, him with the books. He was on the phone outside the bogs.'

'Oh, right,' said his colleague, turning to examine the shrinking yet impressively animated speck. 'Mr Voyage of Discovery. Mr Grand Tour.' Neither mentioned the possibility that we should alert the drivers, and I wasn't about to. The evidence showed that only by keeping your head down and obeying orders might you be spared.

No one spoke for an hour. Then, as I heard another beer can being laboriously bisected, a sad and tiny voice said: 'Some fucking Grand Tour.'

I didn't really know too much about the Grand Tour beyond a vague image of a load of baggy-shirted aristos going off to Pompeii to paint watercolours, write poetry and generally hone their sense of melancholy, but even so it was suddenly and humiliatingly apparent that the British holidaymaker had lost his grip on the top rung of the Continental tourism ladder some time ago, and was still falling. The Grand Tour had been about travelling in style and coming back a man of the world. They returned well read; I returned . . . well, red. Luxury and learning had been strangers to me in the previous month, just as ouzo and youth hostels had become unwanted but somehow unavoidable associates. The sum total of knowledge garnered during what had at least partially been intended as a voyage of understanding was (a) that man cannot live by cream crackers and basil-flavoured tomato puree alone; and (b) that German vending machines accept 5p coins as Deutschmarks.

Sixteen years is a long time to wait, especially if after seven of them the Royal Mint cruelly renders half that painfully acquired knowledge obsolete with a new generation of 'poxy little' coinage. But then it's also a long time to plan. My subsequent sorties into Continental Europe were only small, shy steps up the travel-in-style scale: France and Spain in an ex-GPO Morris Minor van; Scandinavia in a very old and very orange Saab that thoughtfully deposited pieces of itself at regular intervals on the road in case I got lost on the way home. But I was biding my time, preparing the single, glorious odyssey that would at a stroke atone for decades of personal and national cheapskate slovenliness and boorish stupidity.

Could a tour of the Continent still improve the tourist, even in an age when the rich tapestry of Europe was being shrunk by high-speed travel, its boundary seams unstitched by harmonising EU legislation? I supposed the Antipodeans driving for months round Europe still thought so, during the short breaks between blowing up condoms over their heads and spraying 'Muff Divers On Tour' on the back doors of their camper vans. But them and the year-out students aside, the concept of a long journey round the hotspots of Continental culture seemed an anachronism. Maybe we didn't need to visit the places to feel the benefit; maybe a couple of hours of Classic FM followed by *Dangerous Liaisons* on video would do the trick. Though come to that, what in fact was the benefit? Could I enhance my qualities as a human being by knowing more about flying buttresses or *chiaroscuro*? Is the tourist standing still with wonder before the Duomo in Florence wiser or better than the one haggling with a grubby tart down the next alley?

Answer: he is the same man. When I actually got around to reading up about the Grand Tour, I soon discovered that my initial perceptions had been some way wide of the mark. Yes, the Tour had been intended to educate and civilise the future leaders of a backward little country, teaching them the Continental languages, manners and aesthetic sophistication that would be needed if Britain was ever to be taken seriously as a major European power. But by the time of its rampant Byronic finale, the Tour was no longer a sort of mobile finishing school for Britain's privileged youth – or rather it was, but with a lot more going on round the bike sheds. What had been intended as a gilded academy of cultural betterment had somehow descended into every gondolier's worst nightmare – millionaire InterRailers on laudanum; Lambrusco louts; the Club 18–30 of the 1830s.

Even a cursory glance at the literature unearthed depravity on a scale to shame the worst excesses of today's 'ere-we-go Brits on the piss. On Christmas Eve 1827, a drunken mob of Englishmen blocked the entrance to the Cordeliers church in Paris and swore at the Midnight Mass worshippers who tried to get past. In 1787, Adam Walker's stay in Milan was spoilt by the activities of a small party of fellow countrymen sharing his inn – on the morning after their noisiest performance, he learnt that ten of them had drunk 'thirty-six bottles of burgundy, claret and champaign'. An Austrian news-paper report from July 1786 detailed a road-rage incident between three 'English gentlemen of distinction' in a phaeton and a Viennese cabbie: 'one of the gentlemen jumped out of the carriage, and, to the astonishment of the multitude, attacked the driver with his fists; who, after a good thrashing, lost several of his teeth'. And so it went on. The Earl of Crawford threw a French marquis into a pond at Versailles; the Duke of Kingston shot someone's prize pigeons; Lord Leven's son knocked out a postilion in Lille. They peed off balconies and even, I'm afraid, crapped in churches.

And then there was the whoring. In 1792, Thomas Brand bemoaned the English community in Vienna: 'They are of the two-idea sort – The Bottle is one.' The other idea finds expression in perhaps the most disturbing verse I have ever encountered, including that limerick about the young lady called Blunt. It was penned by the Earl of Buckinghamshire, after hearing via his brother-in-law, writing from Naples in 1754, about the lurid effects of the pox contracted by his noble travelling companions. It begins:

In flannel were his limbs array'd
With spittle smear'd and snot;
Attended by a nurse-like shade
That held a spitting pot.
Feebly the specter took his stand,
All withered, wan and sick,

Supporting, in a shrivled hand,
His oozing shankered prick.

Good God. There's one for Poems on the Underground. What's actually worse about this is that it was apparently composed during a 'masturbatory reverie', which speaks volumes about the good Earl's psyche, as well as explaining the erratic handwriting.

So while those who went off on the Grand Tour promised mater and pater they would be good boys and spend all their time in museums, for every one that came home with the inspiration for a classical revival, there were ten others who came home with the clap. Early eighteenth-century Britain had a reputation for philistine parochialism; the Grand Tour had been about encouraging us to learn from European culture rather than ridicule it, but the low-brow temptations soon proved irresistible. That reputation returned, and three centuries on it hadn't gone away.

In a crushing blow for those with a fondness for national stereotyping, it was left to the Americans to restore some erudition and respectability. Perhaps the last cultural trend to cross the Atlantic the other way, the Grand Tour became an essential part of an American gentleman's education. The influence is most apparent in the country's Classical architecture: Thomas Jefferson, having been the US ambassador in Paris, travelled the Continent in the 1780s and was heavily influenced by the Palladian villas he saw in Italy – his home, Montebello, is a straight copy of Palladio's Villa Rotonda. Benjamin Latrobe's designs for the White House and the Capitol had their roots in a teenage Grand Tour around France and Germany near the end of the eighteenth century. Many Southern plantation houses were similarly influenced, evidence for which I am indebted, for the first and only time, to my wife's life-blighting fixation with *Gone*

With the Wind. The apparently saint-like Ashley Wilkes, I am told, honed his sensitive aestheticism during a 'three years Grand Tour in Europe', returning so elegantly refined that Scarlett O'Hara immediately fell in love with him.

By the time Ashley set off to be spruced up, his British Grand Touring counterparts had long since dumbed down. Sex tourism, package trips, the first Cook's Tour − in short, travel as we recognise it today. They barrelled down to Dover, stuck their coaches on ride-on, ride-off ferries to Calais, whisked through France moaning about the garlic and rudeness, drank their way around Italy with a courtesan on each arm and came home sunburnt and broke. Then they bored the neighbours to death by having them all round to look at their holiday watercolours. If nothing else, the Grand Tour spawned the first tourists.

This was no good at all. I had been looking for someone to follow, someone whose foreign experiences I could compare and contrast to my own. It seemed now that to find an appropriate model for my own trip, I needed to go back to the Tour's roots, back to its noble origins of cultural curiosity and the earnest quest for self-improvement. I needed, in fact, to find out who started the bloody thing. By the eighteenth century it was already an institution − in 1786, there were an estimated 40,000 Englishmen on the Continent; the following year, 3,760 visited Paris in six weeks. The phrase 'Grand Tour' first appeared in print in 1670. Before that, travel was generally associated purely with trade or a royally commissioned quest to invent Japan or befriend the mango or something. Then, of course, there were crusades and pilgrimages: theologically inspired desires to behold St Derek's mummified buttocks and/or decapitate Arabs. As far back as the 1550s, British scholars were studying at the universities of Bologna and Padua, bringing the

Renaissance to England but not really travelling in any way that could be described as tourism (a word not in fact coined until 1800, but there you go).

More in-depth research was clearly needed, and I eagerly set about the task of finding someone else to do it for me. It's astonishing how easy it is for a stupid person, as might be me, to telephone a clever person, as might be Professor Edward Chaney, and receive a succinct yet thoughtful answer to a childlike request of towering crassness. 'Who invented the Grand Tour?' repeated the author of *England and the Continental Renaissance* steadily, in the manner of an electronics engineer asked what he feeds to the little people inside the radio. 'Should we phrase that as "Who was the first British traveller to write an account of an extended trip around Continental Europe undertaken for non-commercial purposes?"?' With as much dignity as possible I agreed that we should. 'Well. It's obviously difficult to . . . Are you familiar with *Coryats Crudities*?'

'Oh yes! Yes . . . That's the . . . wasn't it a . . .' I said, meaning, 'Who's asking the bloody questions round here?'

It took a month of J. R. Hartleyism to track down a 1905 reprint of *Coryats Crudities*, having established this to be a book rather than pretentious stripagram agency. Its full title:

CORYATS CRUDITIES
Hastily gobled up in five Monthes travells in France, Savoy,
Italy, Rhetia commonly called the Grisons
country, Helvetia alias Switzerland, some parts of high
Germany and the Netherlands; Newly digested in
the hungry aire of Odcombe in the County of Somerset,
and now dispersed to the nourishment of the

travelling Members of this Kingdome
By
THOMAS CORYAT

This was good in terms of the unexpected absence of words like 'digefted' and 'difperfed', but bad in so far as it suggested that my initial determination to pursue a Tour characterised by elegant connoisseurship was likely to be severely compromised by posthumous association with the author of this work. As well as sounding really very mad, the whole thing was clearly an extended fart analogy.

This initial suspicion was confirmed when I did what any competent historian would do, and looked at the pictures. There were only nine, all handsome early seventeenth-century engravings, but the themes and content of the frontispiece illustration alone told the whole sorry story. Before I'd even started reading his book, I had already witnessed the small, bearded figure of Thomas Coryate (that's 'corry-ert') being pelted with eggs, pursued by a knife-wielding man in a turban and, finally and most arrestingly, copiously vomited upon by a topless woman with a beer barrel on her head.

The implications of these images were disturbing, particularly when a footnote on the frontispiece informed me that the flyblown rags in the top right corner I had taken to be a scarecrow were in fact Coryate's suit of clothes as it appeared at the end of his journey. I had wanted posh, not scary; IQ, not BO. This wasn't the urbane travelogue of a gentleman abroad. This was Baldrick Does Europe.

But when I got back to the drawing board, I found a note written on it. 'You blew £115 on that book, you daft arse,' it read. Indeed so: £115 – more than I thought I would ever spend on any single publication, except maybe 'How to Save £116'. And that took no account of the £25 invested in a copy of the only book written

about him, Michael Strachan's *The Life and Adventures of Thomas Coryate*, published in 1962 and never reprinted. (Why had that final 'E' been added to his name? I wouldn't want history meddling with my vowels. Having said that, 'Time Moore' has an enigmatically epic ring to it.)

Perhaps, given this financial commitment, I was in too deep to get out. The only way to resolve the issue was a no-holds-barred internal conflict, pitching the forces of aestheticism and scholarship against those of depravity and ignorance. As host, I was according to tradition given the honour of nominating their prospective champions: for the latter, a giant invisible leopard; for the former, a drugged postman tied to a chair.

So it was that almost immediately I found myself driving through cold autumn sun to the Somerset village of Odcombe, from where Coryate had set off on his five-month return trip to Venice in May 1608. As I sat in the car park at Tesco's in Yeovil with Strachan's book on one knee and a Party Snack Pack on the other, I rather belatedly got to know the man I would be going on holiday with.

Strachan's was a work of sober scholarship, its tone and content encapsulated in a foreword that began: 'One Spring day years ago I was trying to keep pace with my friend Enoch Powell during a walk from Shrewsbury to Hereford . . .' (the banks of the River of Blood are lovely at that time of year), and ended: 'I have throughout received splendid assistance from Miss V. J. Ledger.'

But at least Mr Strachan had done his homework properly. By the time I was crumpling up empty cellophane and brushing processed matter from my chin, it was clear that inadequate forethought had recently led me into making two major errors. The lesser of these was that last picnic egg.

George Coryate was the rector of Odcombe, and in 1577 his

wife Gertrude gave birth to their only child, Thomas. George was an obsessive but unambitious amateur scholar, who during a stolid thirty-seven-year tenure as parson secretly translated the entire Book of Psalms into Latin, the literary equivalent of making a matchstick model of a cathedral and then – as he made no attempt to preserve the fruits of his labour – stamping on it. At nineteen he had been chosen to deliver an oration to Queen Elizabeth during her visit to the Oxford college where he was reading Divinity, and while sinking slowly from this high-water mark of achievement endeavoured to ensure that his son would succeed where he had failed. Despite a minimal income, the Coryates somehow paid Thomas's way through Winchester College and then Oxford, where he apparently excelled at Latin and Greek. But the money ran out before he could take a degree – a shame, as in those days even finals were oral examinations of minimal complexity. Sometimes held in pubs, sometimes on horseback, they typically consisted of two· questions. Lord Eldon reported the following exchange as an account of how he earnt his Bachelor's degree in Hebrew and History:

Examiner: What is the Hebrew for the Place of a Skull?
Lord E: Golgotha.
Examiner: Who founded University College?
Lord E: King Alfred.
Examiner: Very well, sir, you are competent for your degree.

And that was in 1770. In Coryate's day they'd probably have let you go fifty-fifty and ask the audience.

Nonetheless, when Thomas returned to Odcombe in 1599 he immediately set about succeeding where his father had failed in the twin arenas of showing off and sucking up. George had been wise

13

enough to name his son after the local squire, Thomas Phelips of Montacute, who was sufficiently flattered to accept the position of godfather. Not even Michael Strachan knows quite how the young Thomas occupied the following seven years back at Odcombe after his curtailed education, but much of his time seems to have been spent using this connection to ingratiate himself with all aristocrats in a generously broad radius. During these visits he honed his 'act', a series of convoluted after-dinner speeches combining lengthy classical quotations with his own improvised phrases, usually in praise of the host. It doesn't sound particularly enthralling by today's standards — I find myself being uncomfortably reminded of the master of ceremonies on *The Good Old Days* (played, I believe, by Manuel's dad) and his awful introductions: 'Ladies and gentlemen, I present the crantambulous ['Oooh!'], the crestophanescing ['Aaaah!'], the crimpompudanulent ['Oh, sod off'] . . .' And it doesn't seem to have been particularly enthralling by yesterday's standards, either. Coryate had to wait seven years for his first booking, and that was the local church fair.

I read Strachan's account of the 1606 Odcombe parish fundraising pageant with growing unease. Here was the final confirmation that the endearing hooligan depicted in those bare-breasted food-fights was clearly a different Thomas Coryate altogether. Having rounded up the merrymakers, Coryate mounted the stage, sword aloft, and embarked upon an endless oration which, in Strachan's words, 'made no concession to the limited education of most members of his audience'. But it wasn't so much the thought of Odcombe's ruddy-faced straw-chewers exchanging sideways looks during the 'allusions to Homer and Xenophon' that dampened my spirits. It was his theme: that the time had come to clamp down on the 'drunkennesse, gluttonie, swearing and lasciviousnesse' traditionally associated with such events. This wasn't what I wanted to hear at all. Pretentious, pompous, sycophantic, priggish . . . Served me right, I supposed. Things had already come full circle. I would, after all, be taking a Grand Tour with a grand bore.

It had occurred to me as I drove past Stonehenge and Salisbury Plain that beyond the tarmac I could have been looking through Thomas Coryate's eyes. The population of Britain at the start of the seventeenth century was about five million, with the fertile hills of Somerset among the most densely populated regions in the land. Now, of course, it's one of the emptiest – still largely agricultural, the landscape here has changed less than almost anywhere else in England. It was easy, on this basis, to imagine what Odcombe would look like on a comatose Saturday afternoon in October: a cold but well-kept church; a sub-post office with odd and unhelpful opening hours; a small, lumpy village green ringed by scarecrow thatch, a mobile library and a doomed pub; not a soul anywhere in sight.

Well, I was right about the church. And the souls. In recent years, Odcombe has almost become a suburb, its Barrett borders snaking down Ham Hill towards Yeovil. Aiming for the church spire, I drove through a rather dispiriting swathe of houses of the type the sergeants might have lived in on a Fifties barracks, up a street labelled 'Odcombe Speed Control Area' in type so brash and proud it was a wonder the signwriters hadn't started with 'Welcome To'.

I parked in a hilltop cul-de-sac of windy inglenook bungalows and crossed over to the church. It was better up here. There was an ancient yew sheltering well-tended graves; the strangely pleasing whiff of dung and woodsmoke wafted up from unseen farms. A muddy football scattered crows from a treetop before dropping back into a disembodied Mick Channon chorus. And beyond it all stretched an enormous and timelessly rustic panorama, lavishly gilded with dying foliage.

Inside, the church was empty and tall and whitewashed, with a faded British Legion banner, plaques to the dead from two world wars, horrid crazy-paved modern stained glass and all the usual church stuff. I nosed around the priest's hole, or whatever you call the room where he makes tea and gets the head choirboy to press his cassocks. When I emerged, I was no longer alone – a man with a slight limp was fussing about a camera tripod by the end wall. Realising this was the first Odcombian I had encountered, I quickly replaced the vicar's kettle and strode down the echoing aisle to question him. But he beat me to it. 'Do you mind sticking a hand behind this?' he said pleasantly, indicating a framed inscription propped precariously against the end pew. 'Just taking some snaps for the village website.'

If this was unexpected, what followed was more so. As I bent to assume control of the inscription-balancing process, my gaze passed to the wall behind the small thicket of human and mechanical limbs. There were two further frames alongside the dust-outlined blank where the one in my hands had been positioned, and the central, unmistakably, was a rather crude enlargement of the *Crudities* frontispiece. Then an explosive burst of light blotted everything out. 'Sorry! Thought I'd turned the flash off,' said a figure looming among the interesting green and purple shapes burnt into my retinas.

Blinking hugely, I squinted down at the inscription. Dated 1967, it commemorated the collection of £350 for Indian famine relief on the 350th anniversary of the death of Thomas Coryate. This, the frontispiece and the two other framed inscriptions formed a modest but heartfelt Coryate shrine. Looking at the many representations of his features – standard Tudor beard, wavy hair swept back from a high forehead, gaunt cheeks, close-set eyes – I noted for the first time how much he resembled a sort of composite of every British pioneering traveller from Sir Walter to Sir Ranulph.

Having thanked me for my assistance, the jolly photographer began lugging his tripod up the aisle. 'Trying to finish up before the bell-ringers get here. Coachload from the Cotswolds,' he said, setting up a shot of the British Legion banner. I was still reading the inscription in my hands with no small amount of awe when he turned back to me.

'Oh, sorry. Do you need a hand with poor old Tom?'

'No, no, he's . . . it's fine,' I said, before lifting the hefty frame and realising it wasn't.

'Um . . . why poor old Tom?' I asked after we'd eased it up on to its hook.

'Well . . . I don't know. He died.'

Except as an expression of general sympathy for the human condition this seemed inadequate. But it was intriguing all the same, intriguing enough for me to find myself ten minutes later amid the teetering piles of books in this cheery gentleman's sitting room as his equally hospitable wife placed a florally decorated cup of coffee in my cold hands. Donald Grey was his name, and though he happily admitted knowing almost nothing about poor old Tom, the bullet-point biography he delivered after I'd explained what I was doing did much to restore my faith.

'Well, he's our most famous son. After his European trip he came back and hung his shoes up in the church – they were there for years. And he's credited with introducing the fork to Britain. I think they gave him a nickname for it at the time.'

'Fork wit?'

'Mmm – no. No, I don't think that was it. It's on the website, anyway. And then when he got home he went off and walked to India, except when he got there he dropped dead.' Having read only the first two chapters of Strachan's biography, these were significant and arresting developments to me. 'Don't suppose you'd be interested in your own website?' I contemplated the twin accuracies of this as a literal statement. 'I'm always open to a deal. See our new uPVC windows? Spot of bartering with the glaziers in exchange for doing their website.'

It's awful, but apart from the limp I now remember nothing about Donald Grey's physical appearance. I had him down in my bouzouki-addled memory as a big bloke with Two Ronnies specs and wet lips, until I realised that was the head of drama at my school. All I can say to justify this baseless confusion is that neither man displayed the twitchy vigour of thrusting media pioneers – particularly not the head of drama, who in a distant era of more traditional global communication fell down some stairs and died, which would have been more sad had he been a slightly less enthusiastic paedophile.

'He *walked* to India?'

'That's the reason for the famine charity plaque in the church. Are you on email?'

Having eventually put my signature beneath a prepared statement agreeing that the Internet was the voice of the future and that those who did not heed that voice would fall down some stairs and die, I thanked the Greys for their kindness and drove away over Ham Hill into a half-hearted sunset.

Five minutes later I pulled up in front of the locked gates of Montacute, built by Thomas's godfather's son and the place he'd spent most time hanging out with the big nobs. Forks, India, indefinable pathos. I'd started the day looking for a laughing cavalier and by lunchtime had found a sour-faced puritan. He wasn't naughty, and he wasn't nice. But now I didn't know who he was, or why he'd been depicted in his own book as a lecherous oaf, or what inspired him to walk away from the church fêtes and not stop walking for ten years.

Montacute's splendid golden façade was intimidating despite the diminishments of twilight and a long, tree-flanked drive. Coryate's godfather Thomas Phelips was a comparatively humble squire, but Phelips's son, Edward, moved and shook. As a lawyer and politician he acquired the enormous wealth and influence that was symbolised in this vast house, which the young Coryate would have watched rising slowly out of the Somerset fields. When the Gunpowder plotters came to trial, it was Phelips who led the prosecution of Guy Fawkes (though I think even I could have secured the conviction of a bloke found crouching next to thirty-six barrels of explosives with a lit match while his mates waited round the corner with their fingers in their ears. Mind you, it was quite clever of them to do it on 5 November, what with all the fireworks distracting everyone). To any normal person of Coryate's modest position, even the thought of crunching up that white gravel to meet such a man would have inspired painfully graphic distress.

George Coryate died in April 1607. There was no will, and Thomas and his mother couldn't even scrape together enough for an immediate funeral. At least I hope that's the reason why his father's corpse was left in a cave for six weeks before being buried. I suppose after a month and a half above ground you wouldn't need such a big coffin. A particularly mild Easter and you could have got away with a bucket.

A new parson was appointed, and at the age of thirty Thomas found himself homeless and unemployed. Unable to agree with his mother on a joint plan of action, he set off over Ham Hill, walked up the Montacute drive, knocked on the door and boldly asked for a large favour. It was a wise move. Gertrude Coryate ended up in an Odcombe hovel; after a couple of Phelips words in the right ears, Thomas found himself immediately installed in the London court of the Prince of Wales.

Coryate accepted this sudden and alarming social upgrade with nonchalance. It was quickly becoming obvious that here was a man whose life was spent running around after his ego. There were 500 courtiers, all far grander than Coryate, but within months the parson's son had made a name for himself as a sort of unofficial court jester.

Henry, the Prince of Wales, was only thirteen, and so should by rights have been adequately entertained by vigorous flatulence and watching stuff melt. But it is not every thirteen-year-old who carries a swear box around with him and prefers learning Greek to maiming small animals. One might describe such a youth as precocious and sober, or perhaps as a ghastly little shit (whoops – that's another groat in the slot). As such, his evenings were spent presiding over a battle of wits, a battle into which Coryate made a typically kamikaze charge.

'Sweetmeats and Coryate made up the last course at all entertainments,' noted one contemporary. Question: how could nightly variations on the awful-sounding routine he had developed in Odcombe possibly have impressed a room full of vicious wits and braying aristocratic drunks? Answer: by providing endless opportunities for them to egg Coryate on before abruptly turning on him. 'He was the courtiers' anvil to try their wits upon,' is the same contemporary's diplomatic phrase. It would have taken an especially sharp tongue to puncture Coryate's thick skin and burst that inflated ego. Whether it was a single verbal assault or the cumulative effect of all those nightly insults, after less than a year he had already decided on a drastic course of action. I am fortunate enough to have located a transcript of his final evening at court. As the last honey-glazed swan's head is spat out and slung into the fire, Mr Coryate rises . . .

Thomas Coryate: Your Highness is the most gracious Hyperaspist, refocillating us as it were with the sevenfold shield of Ajax or the aegis of Pallas.

Vicious wit: Howbeit that is so, sire. But, Mr Coryate, might not a corollary observation be that if his majesty is the aegis of Pallas, then you yourself are Zeus's own escathatripmotist.

TC (uncertainly): . . . Your lordship is too generous.

VW: Not so, Mr Coryate, not so! The like implication is that you are a man with rich experience of the very basest types of solitary lust. To wit, a drainscrote.

Braying aristocratic drunk: And a chuffjuggler!

Prince Henry: Tuppence in the box, Lord Dudley.

BAD: Oh, come on! He called him a drainscrote!

PH: A statement of fact, Lord Dudley. The man Coryate is an impoverished rural type of abysmal stock and minimal education. One might justly encapsulate these manifold inadequacies in such a phrase.

VW: If I may be so bold, your Highness, despite the deepness of his potations, Lord Dudley has some substance to his argument. If Coryate is a drainscrote, he must reasonably a chuffjuggler be also.

PH (after brief reflection): Very well. Let it be recorded that drainscrote and chuffjuggler are to be added to the catalogue. Lord Stafford, might you refresh the court's memory?

Lord Stafford (riffling about some scrolls): One moment, your majesty . . . (*small cough*) Here follow the profanities that may be acceptably applied to Mr Coryate without fiscal penalty.

Slagprannet, sowfiddle, wankfriar, flaptwat, widdleprick, shagbatter, 'Old Gravyhole', poncelady, gobbleturd . . . (*the scratch of
quill on parchment*) . . . chuffjuggler . . . and . . . drainscrote.
PH:Very good, Lord Stafford. Hey! Where do you think you're
going, shagbatter?
TC (*distantly, and followed by a slammed door*):Venice.

I always find this sort of puppy-kicking nastiness painfully tragic,
though I can't imagine why. Anyone would think it was me who
begged the tall girl in Miss Woodward's class to sing 'Save All Your
Kisses For Me' on the feigned pretext that only she knew all the
words, when actually it was because her rendition was memorably
coloured by a severe hearing impairment. Coryate's plight in finding
himself on the wrong side of the laughing at/laughing with divide
recalls the opening scene in Disney's masterful interpretation of *The
Hunchback of Notre-Dame*, when, as part of the celebrations marking
the revered festival of Topsy-Turvy Day, the cruel Parisian mob
pretends to elect the eponymous cripple as their king, waiting until
he is utterly and joyfully convinced of this fact before erupting in
a great civic guffaw at the risibility of anyone doing anything for a
big ugly freak like him. (It is touching to note that Topsy-Turvy
Day is still celebrated across Paris throughout the tourist season.)

At Odcombe, Coryate had been a big fish in a small pond. But
at court, the pond was rather larger, with pretty coloured gravel on
the bottom and a whole load of those decorative bubbling shipwreck
features, and the fish were sleek and predatory and hunted provin-
cial small fry in packs. His social and intellectual inferiority complexes
were being exposed, and it must have been clear that he needed a
specialist subject, something on which he could hold forth without
being shouted down. Prince Henry was always entranced by the tales

of diplomats and soldiers returning from abroad. A foreign trip would provide Coryate not only with a healthy stock of Prince-impressing anecdotes, but also the material for the first travel book, a sort of *Ruff Guide to Europe*. By showcasing his academic credentials, this unique work would silence the after-dinner bully boys. His prototype Grand Tour was indeed to be about self-improvement, but not of the mind or spirit. He wanted more concrete benefits: an eager but respectful silence when he next addressed the court, a spine with his name embossed on it in the royal library and, who knows, maybe a title and a country estate.

Soon it was all set up. Although I still can't quite believe it, he had somehow managed to finance his trip with a convoluted bet – depositing £40 with a Yeovil linen draper at odds of around 7/2 that he would return safely, and obtaining from the draper letters of credit for £122 6*s* 8*d* which he would use to procure cash from British merchants around Europe. If he didn't make it back he was ruined; but then if he didn't make it back he was dead anyway. It was the definitive double-or-quits wager.

The loudmouthed, jumped-up parson's son from Somerset had given them all plenty to poke fun at, but, as he set off for Dover on 14 May 1608, in his thirty-second year, he was sure that the last laugh would be his. Providing that laugh was postponed until Calais, when he had finished 'varnishing the exterior parts of the ship with the excrementall ebullitions of my tumultuous stomach'.

ONE

The Channel

Coryate wasn't the first Briton to cross the Channel with a view to broadening his horizons in all senses, but never before had anyone regarded Continental travel as an end in itself, let alone set off with the intention of writing a personal account of the experience. It would be 100 years before it became common for well-bred young men to head for France and Italy as part of their education, and a further half-century before such trips acquired a consistent structure.

A tutor – usually a bumbling, ignorant clergyman – would be employed as chaperone by the Grand Tourist's parents, along with a governor and perhaps the odd servant. In 1714, the Earl of Burlington managed to assemble a travelling twelve-man entourage, including an artist, accountant and three liveried footmen; fifty years later, Lord Baltimore waltzed into Vienna with an even more eclectic party that boasted a doctor, two black eunuchs and eight women. (He died in Naples in 1771, leaving 'a whole seraglio of white, black etc to cater for'.)

Rather than risk carrying too much gold, the finances were sorted out with variants of Coryate's letters of credit, essentially post-dated cheques drawn up by a London bank with links to merchants and other bankers across the Continent. On the occasions when this system broke down – and that it apparently rarely did even in Coryate's time still astonishes me – they borrowed from British envoys or other Grand Tourists. And because a tour generally lasted at least six months, the sums involved could become considerable – while James Burges got by on less than £2 a week during a long summer in the Loire in 1771, the Earl of Huntingdon somehow blew almost six grand in 1754 and 1755, roughly £350,000 at today's prices.

The trouble for most of the tourists was that being grand, they had no idea what things cost in England, let alone abroad. For many, the coach ride down to Dover would have been their first experience of the world that existed outside London or their own county town – they might never have stayed or dined at an inn, and if they had, they'd certainly have been isolated from the payment process. In fact, food and accommodation were generally cheaper on the Continent – one experienced traveller reckoned £100 in Italy could last five times longer than in England.

The main expense, besides the usual holiday rubbish like souvenir portraits and kiss-me-quick velvet breeches (Charles James Fox once went all the way to Lyon just to get waistcoat patterns), was travel. If you took your own coach, the long distances involved soon took their toll on the wheels and axles; repair charges were extortionate. Those who hired coaches and horses could reckon to pay over £1 a day, and public transport could be even more expensive. In the 1770s, the stagecoach trip from Lille to Paris – barely 150 miles – cost £2 5s single. The average wage at the time wasn't much more than £1 a month.

✦　✦　✦

The Channel crossing could last thirty-five hours; Coryate's crossing took seven; and though these days it's less than two I very nearly contrived to inaugurate my trip with an authentic baptism by vomit. Slowly raising my Dairylea face from the deck railings, I reflected that a mid-October departure date left much to be desired. It was sunny and clear – halfway across I had timeless, Coryate-evoking views of both Dover and Calais – but it was not anything else nice. Sailors would have described the conditions as 'fresh', in the same way that police would have described having your car stolen by incontinent thieves and used to ramraid the teddy bears' playroom at a children's hospice as 'disappointing'.

In fact, however, the nausea had begun boiling up long before the white cliffs got on their seesaw. Long before I got on the boat, in fact. Its source was a decision I had made as I distantly surveyed Montacute's manicured topiary and glowing ashlar, a determination to replicate somehow the cocky, deluded grandeur that had fuelled Coryate on his trip. His had been a Grand Tour in his mind alone; if I was to lay the Magic Bus ghost to rest, I would need some authentic props. One of these was the purple velvet suit that now flapped and billowed preposterously in the brine-flavoured gale. The other lay somewhere below me, filling a space and a half on car deck B. This, the true origin of my nervous disorder, was a 1980 Rolls-Royce Silver Shadow 2.

'A lot of flash for not much cash.' A latent ponce streak combined with a keen sense of economy was always likely to render me vulnerable to such an advertised claim. Having blundered across it in a local paper ad, I succumbed to an instant and irresistible obsession. If you're going to do a Grand Tour, you need a grand tourer. And the grandest of them all is a Rolls-Royce.

Actually, and it is an important distinction, I wouldn't be looking for a Rolls-Royce, but a Roller. There comes a point in every Silver Shadow's life when it becomes a Roller, promptly ceasing to be of interest to anyone but fat publicans and wedding-hire firms with names intended to guarantee alphabetical prominence in the Yellow Pages. Rust gnaws wheelarches, engines gulp vast petrochemical cocktails. Prices tumble, as, mysteriously, do mileages. The cheapest I saw with an MOT was £3,750, and was advertised with unique and disarming honesty: '90,000 miles (probably wrong), if you want a new one, please don't phone.'

But making a decision that you knew in advance to be stupidly imprudent and very probably disastrous has its own seductive comfort. Fact: I was going to buy a clapped-out Rolls-Royce and ponce about in it round Europe. Practicality and common sense be damned – I was simply not at home to Mr Reason, or indeed Mrs Insurance Excess.

For two weeks I roamed the south-east, accompanying desperate vendors on the 50-foot hike entailed in circumventing their Silver Shadows. A big man in a vest hoping I wouldn't notice the confetti rotting in the footwells; a scarily yellow example drooling fluids all over the crazy paving ('They all do that,' said the Asian owner. 'It's called . . .' – and here I detected the slightly shifty wince of a good man forced by economic duress into an idiotic untruth – '. . . wetting themselves').

It was hopeless. A week later, following some forgotten chain of recommendation, I found myself on the phone seeking advice from Lufford, who was said to service slightly tired old Bentleys and Rollers in a railway-arch yard in Wandsworth. A man called Lufford should by rights be issued with a cravat at birth, but a fondness for the words 'bollocks' and 'shafted' marked this one out as a different sort of man. He breathed very loudly during the small gaps in his long and rapid sentences, all of which ended with my first name. Having promised to send his 'top boy' to inspect any vehicle I might be interested in, he warmly signed off with: 'I just don't want you to buy a piece of shit, Tim.'

These words did not shatter a lifelong ambition of mine. Some days later, Lufford's top boy and I were driving through the Kent countryside, en route to my second appointment with the man who had dictated these words to the classified department of the *Thames Valley Auto Trader*. 'SHADOW 2 1980 £5,750 Moorland green over pewter, green interior, MOT August 2000'. It was a no-frills ad, and my telephonic encounters with Mr David Baldock's clipped and rather tetchy military diction marked him out as a no-frills man. But the moment I saw his car, presiding over an orchard flanked with semi-abandoned MGs and stacks of radiator grilles, it was clear that here, at last, was class, a Rolls that stood head and pewter shoulders above the tarted-up wrecks I had seen.

For a start it was filthy, its considerable bonnet covered in the pawprints of cats attracted by the astonishing thermal aftermath of eight fat pistons hammering about in an engine block the size of a wardrobe. Not the most immediately obvious indicator of pedigree, perhaps, but in the preceding month I had discovered an infallible correlation between cleanliness and bodily decay – an almost incandescent polish was always counterpointed by leprous corrosion. I had begun to find this somehow revolting, like lipstick on a corpse, or the visual equivalent of a sickly squirt of Haze in a stinking latrine.

And sure enough, there was nary a single bubbling scab beneath the feline paws and liberal splodges of what the makers of car-care products refer to as 'bird lime'. (It's interesting, though clearly not surprising, how many commercial euphemisms exist in this area. My parents once engaged a plumber who spent an unhappy afternoon removing improbable quantities of what he called 'toby' from a blocked soil pipe.)

The interior was the same, unmarked olive hide and walnut concealed beneath a carpet of cobwebs, crumbs and the lifeless carapaces of a squadron of outsized hornets. 'Did it as a part-exchange on a Silver Spirit,' said Mr Baldock carelessly, scratching a grey temple and addressing himself to his apple trees. He had been in the trade for many decades, but now operated on an occasional basis, buying and selling the odd Rolls or Bentley from his pleasantly rural front drive. 'Just drove it about in the summer with the fridge on,' he continued, referring, as I realised some weeks later, to the air-conditioning unit. 'But now it's got to go.' Not that you'd have guessed from his manner. It was oddly refreshing to deal with a car dealer, albeit a casual one, who seemed to have no interest in selling you a car. 'Well, there it is,' he muttered briskly, wandering back indoors. 'I'll just leave you to it.'

He hadn't mentioned a service history, considered essential with capricious cars of advanced years, particularly those with a recorded mileage of 185,000, but on the passenger seat I found a thick ring-bound archive of JPM 455V's life. The signatures of all the engineers and craftsmen who had built her (I'm sorry, that just slipped out — is it all right if I promise never to refer to any car in that unutterably sickmaking way again?) were there, along with the factory-fitted accessories specified by the Sheffield company director who placed the order. Among these was a little chrome flagstaff mast, designed to fit over the silver lady. It was when I read an explanatory note in the file that I felt fate's hot and heavy hand slap jarringly against my buttocks. 'Pennant for ceremonial use by Master Cutler of Sheffield.' Thomas Coryate had introduced the fork to Britain, and here was the big, fat car owned by a big, fat man who had made a fortune from forks, a symbol of the wealth and social standing that had ganged up on Coryate and effectively driven him away. This was my car.

'Slats', the aforementioned top boy, did his best to deter me when we returned the next day. He lifted up the carpet and exposed a floor pan the colour and consistency of wet bark, and detected large areas of temporary plastic filler which would soon flake away and bring an ugly oxidised autumn to the moorland green. He pumped the brake pedal and soon had big red warning lights flashing on the fascia. He started the engine and immediately informed me that it was running on seven cylinders.

Mr Baldock accepted these revelations with characteristic equanimity. 'Well, if you were to offer me five two and a half . . .' he murmured peripherally as Slats emerged from under the lambswool over-rugs with another handful of rust. I said nothing; Slats thoughtfully crumbled bits of dead car in his oily hands. There was a very quiet sigh as Mr Baldock launched into plan B: making friends with Slats.

'D'you know Gordon from Merricks over at Gravesend?'

Slats brightened. 'Yeah – actually he gave me a bell last week about a Cloud 2 he wanted sorted.' The clapped-out Roller community was clearly a small one, and, as with any close-knit family, disagreements occasionally got out of hand. 'Hear about Paddy from Doohans in Bexhill?' reciprocated Slats.

'Yes – bit of a nasty business. Something to do with his son?'

'That's right. His boy got in a bit of bother, and Paddy wades in and winds up knifing this feller dead. Next morning someone torches his workshop and he scarpers. No one's seen him for three months.' (All names changed to protect the frightened.)

On that invigorating note Slats and I made our excuses and left.

I was now very depressed, and Lufford's top boy sensed it. 'Make him a silly offer,' he said as we looped back round the M25. 'He'll take it, believe me. That floor has pissed him off. He's dropped a monkey before we've even started.' A passing familiarity with the work of Dennis Waterman spared me from interpreting this as an account of butterfingered cruelty. 'Phone him up early doors and offer him four.'

I didn't want to do that. This was clearly a buyers' market, but to swipe almost a third off the advertised price seemed morally offensive. And that was before Slats suffered a sudden crisis of confidence just as we turned into Lufford's yard. 'Now I'm thinking threenarf. Trade value three,' he said, shaking his head. Then the final damning judgement: 'It's just the wrong car.'

Lufford turned out to be a comfortably built man with Frank Butcher glasses and haphazard dentistry. He listened to Slats's candid analysis, then began scanning his yard. 'What about this, Tim. I've got a couple of cars here that could do with a run – you could, y'know, rent one for a couple of months. Tim.'

This seemed a decent suggestion. 'Won't you be needing them?'

'Well, no. They're not *mine*,' he said, with a slight twang of irritation at having this irrelevance brought to his attention. 'We did some work on them, and . . . well, y'know, I'm owed.' I wasn't sure what this meant, but it didn't sound at all good. Lufford, however, was now on a roll. 'That green Corniche – Rackstraw's car.' I followed his gaze to a terrifyingly immaculate coupé.

'Isn't that a bit too . . . nice?' I mumbled. Next to it was a far more homely looking grey Shadow with a flat tyre. 'What about that one?'

Lufford squinted at it. 'I wouldn't even let you fucking drive that one,' he said. 'Wouldn't get that to fucking Dover.' He had dropped the Tims and there was a new stridency to his voice that I found disturbing. Raising a half-cupped hand to his mouth, Lufford turned and bellowed to an unseen assistant inside the railway-arch office. 'Get on to Rackstraw in Holland. And George about his Bentley. Say we might have a proposition.'

I was becoming a pawn in a very ugly-sounding game, a game whose final round would feature George angrily lashing me to the sails of Rackstraw's windmill. Half an hour later I was at home, hurriedly dialling Mr Baldock's number. 'Four seven fifty,' he repeated twelve seconds into our conversation. There was a long pause. 'Oh, go on then.'

The first week of my association with JPM 455V was not a happy one. It is perhaps least painful to condense it to diary form:

Mon. Meet Mr Baldock and car at Haines & Hall, a recommended workshop in suitably downmarket south London suburb of Merton. Exchange much cash for keys and documents.

Tues. Arrange with Mick Hall of aforementioned establishment to conduct minimal patch-up likely to sustain car for two months of light Continental motoring.

Wed. Receive first of many progress reports from Mr Hall.

Thur. Mr Hall informs me that my 'bollocks are on the block'.

Fri. Mr Hall drops toolbox on aforementioned block-positioned genitalia. Final bill is £2,186.

Sat. Set off for Merton with tears of impotent rage burning cheeks.

I arrived at Haines & Hall a shell of a man. What had I got myself into? Who did I think I was? Why, why, why? It was all made worse because Mick Hall was actually a decent sort – the bollocks/block analogy had merely been a misguided icebreaker.

He talked me gently through the bill, adopting the placatory whisper of an undertaker explaining to a recently bereaved widow why, in mistaking a hedge trimmer for his electric toothbrush, her husband had inadvertently guaranteed that cosmetic preparations for his funeral would be a little more labour intensive than usual. No single item seemed exorbitant or unnecessary – sundry brake bits, a reconditioned carburettor, a new distributor cap – but the bill just went on and on and on, as long as a fat family's fortnightly food shop.

As he continued, my silent glazed nods became ever tinier, prompting him at length to delve into a drawer and pull out a yellowed fax roll.

'Look, this might help. It's a bill sent me by a feller who'd taken his Shadow in to an official Rolls garage to sort out a squeaky boot hinge, and made the mistake of asking them to sort out any other niggles they came across. They stung him for 23 grand.'

I looked at him like the man in the bad news/good news joke when he's told that though both his legs have been mistakenly amputated, the bloke in the next bed wants to buy his slippers.

Mick persevered. 'What you have to remember is that these are cars which have always cost the same new as a three-bed semi. I think the latest one is 150-odd grand in the showroom. They're not cheap to buy when they're new and they're not cheap to run when they're old.'

He gave up in the end, and it was only when I found myself alone at the wheel that I realised in failing to utter any sound, I had also failed to request any tips on driving this overblown monstrosity. After heaving the door closed with a dungeon clunk, I vaguely centralised myself in the Chesterfield driver's seat and placed my hands at ten-to-two on a Bakelite hoop the diameter of a cartwheel. In front of me yawned a tapering bonnet topped by the Spirit of Ecstasy and flanked by little nascent fins (*fins* on a car made in 1980? Dear oh dear). Behind was a dark and leathery railway compartment, beyond which an enormous boot sloped unhelpfully out of sight.

I stuck the key in a hole in the slab of over-glossed walnut from which the dashboard had been hewn, twisted it and unleashed a terrible roar, which soon subsided to a phlegmy tugboat burble. For a moment I sat there, marooned in this enormous, ancient machine, feeling like a Lancaster pilot awaiting clearance. Then, with a random flick on the steering-column gearstick, I fishtailed terrifyingly down Haines & Hall's muddy entrance lane and was off.

I had learnt a lot more about the car and a little more about myself by the time I drove off the ramp at Calais two days later. Naturally, my car had its inevitable idiosyncratic failings – all the air-conditioning fluid had leaked into the carpet, giving the interior the humid, chemical ambience of a dry-cleaner's; the outside temperature gauge prophesied a catastrophic acceleration of global warming and every hour or so there was a scary and mysterious stone-on-glass crack from somewhere behind the steering wheel.

None of these, of course, was especially important (although that noise – or more accurately the fearsome anticipation of it – did eventually give me a slight stammer). But interestingly, the more dramatic flaws were those connected to the marque in general, and as such led me to conclude that far from being the world's finest motor car, Rolls-Royces were actually a bit crap. On a straight road the steering was approximate; to negotiate a corner of even moderate radius was to transform the car into a lopsided centrifuge. The steering-column gearshift was positioned in such a way that it was impossible to perform the multiple wheel rotations required in parking without accidentally knocking it into reverse. Main beam was toggled on and off by an Army-lorry foot switch. Finally, and most damningly, it is some time since I have owned a car where the flash rate of the indicators corresponded directly to the speed of the engine.

But the enduring figurative use of the term 'Rolls-Royce' to denote arrogant opulence ensured that these failings and JPM 455V's actual value – less than that of a half-decent second-hand Fiesta – were an irrelevance to pedestrians and fellow road users. On that first drive back from Merton to my home in Chiswick, I'd found myself almost hypnotised by the bonnet-end silhouette of those little front fins and the rising prow of the mascot-topped grille. Together these formed the outline of a huge 'W'; the flamboyantly wristy schoolboy gestures that greeted me from every bus stop gave some idea as to what this might stand for. The sight of that silver lady nosing out tentatively at a junction brought out the white-van man in every motorist; if I dared to reciprocate by not predicting and accommodating the intentions of each and every vehicle in the vicinity a furious volley of audio-visual reproach blazed around me. It was appallingly stressful.

Nor did the fretting stop when I parked outside my house. I'd hardly closed the front door before it was rapped upon insistently; on the threshold stood my neighbour Walter, Chiswick's very own Uncle Monty. In a voice destabilised by impassioned concern, he urged me to remove the Rolls's mascot before nightfall. 'Please don't think I'm interfering, but I lost one from a Bentley up in Maida Vale. People can be so beastly.' I was now responsible for a 17-foot, 2¼-ton lump of metal; metal that attracted beastly people round the clock, a beast magnet even as I slept. If it was bad in London, how would I cope in the suburbs of Turin? It was all terribly wearing. Inadequately rested on the morning of my departure, I woke up and peered blearily out of the bedroom window. No one had nicked the hubcaps. And unfortunately, no one had nicked the whole bloody car either.

TWO

France

The vehicle that began flashing and hooting me on the M25 down to Dover was not the first, and, unlike most, its driver had sound non-sociological justification for his actions. I had interrupted my attempts at positioning the Rolls's massive girth in the middle of the slow lane to fiddle with the cruise control (broken) and the twin-unit radio cassette (astonishingly loud), and even at 55 miles per hour (the recommended maximum speed for those reluctant to experience single-digit miles per gallon) the resultant meanderings were extravagant. However, I had suffered enough that morning – particularly at the petrol station, where after a fifteen-minute search for the remote switch that opened the fuel filler cap (a dashboard button marked 'REFUEL' – clearly an order to be barked out of a briefly opened electric window rather than a seemly self-service activity) I had treated the cashier to my Oliver Twist face when handing over £82 for a tankful.

So, having satisfied myself via the rear-view mirror that anyone driving a Ford Ka would be unlikely to initiate violence, I slowed to allow the driver to overtake, having first posted a well-known abusive hand signal in the window for his perusal. The Ka driver drew alongside, held his speed and began to apply the horn in earnest. After about ten seconds of this, during which I began memorising the registration plates of possible witnesses, I stole a furtive glance to my right. There, waving furiously and with concern and doubt clouding what had once been a cheery beam, was Christopher Hunter, a friend I don't see often enough, and may now see less of. I instantly supplemented my two raised fingers with the rest and effected a feeble facsimile of a royal wave. Then, for the first and only time, I floored my right foot and, at an outlay of about £13, covered the next four miles in fewer minutes.

The Wilton under my feet was still hot from this mechanical recklessness when I lumbered on to foreign soil three hours later. I thought it would be nice to go into the first foreign building that Coryate did, but as I took my place in the traditional British vehicular conga around Calais's raw concrete outskirts I remembered that the whole town had been comprehensively flattened in the war. You'd think that Coryate's debut experience of foreigners would merit some sort of excitement, but there was no hint of such an emotion in his words on taking those portentous first steps on foreign soil: 'The principall Governors name (whom we saw not) was Monsieur de Vic, who hath one wooden leg.'

I suppose he was already acting out his new role as a seen-it-all-before man of the world – though perhaps, as the town had been British territory for the 200 years up to 1558, it wasn't at the time all that French. But for my part, even though I've been to Calais more often than to Birmingham, there's still a ludicrous thrill at the sudden foreignness of it all. Later tourists brought back souvenir words with them, and as Coryate went all blasé, I was now the faux-naif. Those boys fishing off the jetty, those students cutting me up in their mum's Renault Megane, those old men on bikes with berets and stripy T-shirts and burning sheep round their necks – *they're all French*. For the first day it always seems impossible, and there's the lingering suspicion that they all go home at the end of the day, wearily slam the front door behind them and sigh, 'This speaking-French bollocks is doing my head in.'

It was certainly doing mine in. My linguistic proficiency had degenerated to Jean-et-Colette standard: it took me an hour to remember what 'Friday' was (admittedly while pointlessly pondering that TGI Friday's would do a lot less business as MDC Vendredi's), and the nearest I got to decoding a mysterious advertising slogan that haunted me from billboards throughout France was 'the good pipe which reheats you' (fair enough, though – I'll take a couple).

Use of the phrase 'it was ever thus' is always likely to earn one a big smack, but even if Coryate feigned nonchalance, the sudden foreignness of Calais was a feature of the Grand Tours that invariably kicked off there. 'The difference of dress, dialect, manners and persons struck us exceedingly,' wrote one eighteenth-century tourist; the young MP John Mitford, stepping off his boat in 1776, proclaimed that 'to a traveller leaving his country for the first time, every object is new'.

If the Grand Tour was about experiencing these differences and learning from them – Italy had been home to the cultural Renaissance, France to the philosophical Enlightenment – what could I expect to learn today? It was encouraging at least to be reminded of the enormous differences that persisted despite the homogenising pressures of globalisation in general and the EU in particular, continuing to make a mockery of the mere 20 miles of water that separated France and Britain. United by a certain messy dreariness, Dover and Calais were otherwise chalk and cheese, white cliffs and

Camembert. Calais had ornamental flower beds, a huge surfeit of public buildings and an almost Third World sense of traffic anarchy. The astonishing displays in delicatessen windows and the astonishing amount of foundation worn by the women behind the counters reminded me that France's cultural reputation was founded on food and fashion, just as the enormous hill of Cockney flesh shovelling P&O potato waffles down her gaping, hair-lipped maw in the Motorists' Lounge had reminded me that Britain's was not. Would my palate – plebeian enough to be persistently enchanted by a wristy splash of Tabasco – be sophisticated by prolonged contact with *haute cuisine*? And how long before the forces of *haute couture* assessed my velvet suit and mid-length hair with damning reference to Sacha Distel's unfortunate pomp?

All I could hope was to sustain this spirit of enquiry for longer than most of the Grand Tourists, who found it difficult to entertain even the most bogus profundity for long. John Mitford immediately blotted his copybook by embarking on a rather unenlightened discourse upon the comparative visual merits of the women: 'The fair sex at Dover are not the beauties of England, but the women of Calais are not entitled to the appellation of fair: they are browner and uglier than the men.' This, at heart, was the inherent problem faced by the Grand Tourists: you boldly went where no Englishman had gone before, but when you got there, it was full of bloody foreigners.

After a day in Calais, Coryate had headed off on foot to Boulogne – with a minimal budget and a keen sense of economy inspired by years of relative poverty, he generally chose the cheapest available travel and accommodation options. It was getting dark, and though I'd vowed to follow his exact route, it suddenly seemed stupid not to go on the motorway. I pulled in at the first service station, receiving an idiotic mock bow from a refuelling lorry driver as I did so. The polar gale that had almost cost me my breakfast mid-Channel was now at its icy peak, and my attempts at fixing the Continental head-lamp deflectors were as painful as they were ineffective. Having realigned my dipped beam to somewhere around Orion's Belt, I rushed into the café.

In the previous forty-eight hours, I had noted that the deep mental unease of life as a Rolls-Royce owner-driver was begin-ning to express itself physically. Alongside the nascent stammer and a sort of shrinkage of the scalp I came to associate with urban parking and width-restriction bollards, the most interesting symptom was production of an improbable volume of supernaturally irides-cent topaz urine – the pee of fear. I wouldn't have mentioned this regrettable and unsavoury side-effect were it not for the fact that exiting the café I noted an even more impressive quantity of an identically tinted fluid cascading from the underside of the Rolls's chromed-tombstone grille.

The sight of an Englishman in distress is enough to gladden the heart of any French service-industry operative; add a purple suit and a leaking Rolls-Royce to the mix and you're talking punched air and high cinqs all round. The white-capped fellow who had sold me the coffee quickly rounded up three of his similarly attired colleagues from the kitchen, and as I stood by the huge opened bonnet holding a very big screwdriver as a shy schoolgirl might bear the Olympic torch, I could see a barbershop quartet of eager, impish grins pressed up against the glass. Equipped with an appropriate form guide, even a cautious bookmaker would have offered generous odds against my remedying this situation without mechanical assistance and probably a skin graft, so no one was more surprised than me – except perhaps the crestfallen Frenchmen – when I diagnosed a detached radiator hose, rectified it, refilled the coolant and drove off, all in the space of ten minutes. I was so delighted that I treated myself to bypassing Boulogne and leading a queue of impatient heavy goods vehicles down the N1 to the hilltop town of Montreuil, where Coryate had spent his second night.

Despite its empty, windblasted streets, Montreuil cheered me. It was French in the right kind of way, the Thomas Coryate kind of way. There were city walls and medieval alleys you could imagine knaves lurking in, and in a little square dominated by a church Coryate had visited, I found a cosy attic room above a bar that was closing at 8 p.m. Then, of course, during my chilled wanderings in search of any sort of food – after half an hour, I stuck my *haute cuisine* quest to simmer on the back burner – I found the main square, infinitely grander and better proportioned, or so it looked from the window of the first restaurant I rushed into to escape the wind.

The Grand Tourists may not have wanted to admit to it any more than I do, but there's no getting away from the fact that the average French town is considerably more appealing than its British equivalent. In Britain, Montreuil would be somewhere like Ashford, and if you were French and spent your first night there you would either laugh or cry. But by French standards Montreuil is no great shakes, meriting only a couple of paragraphs in the Michelin guide. It has the air of somewhere that had been a big noise back in the days when being on top of an easily defended hill was important, and was now being left alone to make a smaller but probably happier noise, perhaps similar to those I emitted while walking home after a cheap and vast pizza served with matching carafe of wine. Stamping off the cold as I climbed the dark stairs to my room, I paused at a landing window to look out at the Rolls, conspicuously grand and vulnerable alone in the middle of the market square below. My jauntiness drained away as quickly as coolant from a detached radiator hose. Unlike Coryate, who would have had far more justification, I suddenly felt completely overawed by the prospect of completing the journey I had just begun.

'*Amstel . . . non, Heineken. Non, Amstel.*' There are some conversations you really don't want to overhear at 8.45 a.m. on a Tuesday, particularly while trying to tackle a sweaty microwaved breakfast, particularly when your plate is a bald wooden ping-pong bat and you've just bitten into the croissant and found out where all its dimpled rubber has melted off. We've all read those surveys that unfavourably compare the average Briton's messy and childish lust for booze with his Continental cousin's sophisticated alcoholic awareness, but as I watched the three binmen on the next table draining their beers – and, in one case, a double pastis chaser – I finally understood that such surveys are the result of systematic dishonesty on an impressive scale. Though of course it's not always easy to translate the questions verbatim. You probably didn't know, for instance, that what the French understand as 'How much do you drink (after 7 p.m., and not including wine with meals, because that would just be stupid)?' is interpreted in England as 'Are you a sad alco, or what?'

After laboriously reaffixing the mascot (the Rolls was now surrounded by irritated stallholders, who treated me to 'who the fuck do you think you/we are?' looks that invariably accompanied this morning routine in the weeks ahead), I went into Coryate's church, St Saulve. This was our first shared Continental building, but it was difficult to feel much affinity. Not because its gloomy, incense-blackened Gothic interior had changed much – it patently hadn't – but because his assessment of all such establishments was coloured by a scarily rabid anti-Catholicism.

Visiting a church in Calais, he rants about the 'mutilated Sacrament' in which the priest 'defrauded' his congregation of the wine; three days later he is outraged when a nun – the first he had ever seen – refuses to let him nose about her Carmelite retreat. I suppose it wasn't surprising that only three years after the Gunpowder Plot feelings would be running high. What is surprising is that Coryate lost no opportunity to express his opinions, aware that to do so was to risk rebuke at best. In 1592 and 1595 the Pope had felt the need to protest about the number of heretical Englishmen in Paris, and the mutilated corpses of Huguenot French Protestants were strung up by their feet in the streets throughout the civil wars that plagued the country for most of the late sixteenth century. Foreign visitors were by no means exempt: in the same year as Coryate's journey, an English Protestant, John Mole, was jailed by the Inquisition for his faith; he died in a Roman prison thirty years later. Unsurprisingly, those ex-pat Protestants who escaped the massacres and persecution fled to England or lived as quietly as they could.

After our own Charles I married the King of France's sister Henrietta in 1625, the Inquisition more or less left English travellers alone, but you can't keep a good war down, and religious conflicts were largely to blame for the 500 revolts that racked France during the middle of the seventeenth century, and the Thirty Years' War which put Germany out of bounds to all but the stupidest tourists from 1618–48. Coryate was lucky to return through the Netherlands during a quiet period in a war of independence against the Spanish that ran for over sixty years, and when the Dutch had won it, they took on the English: thirteen sea battles from 1652–73. Then, near the end of the seventeenth century, Louis XIV lost his rag, and before it was found he'd started on Spain, England, the Dutch, Sweden, Austria and various German states.

Even after a war ended it could be years before law and order were restored. Though generally Continental roads were safer than those in England (where highwaymen were 'as common as crows'), during the anarchic aftermath of battle travel could be foolhardy. After the Thirty Years' War, one tourist riding into Hamburg counted memorials to thirty-four murdered travellers in a single day. For once, and despite his own impressive efforts to spark off a religious war, history was on Coryate's side. Stick a pin in a list of dates from 1600–1715 and you'd be lucky to spear a year in which a Grand Tour would have been feasible.

Not that he'd have minded the gore. Just outside Montreuil I tried to find the site of a set of gallows, the first of many whose form and function are described by Coryate with unashamed relish: 'two goodly faire pillars of freestone, where there is no cross beame as upon our English gallowes, but that cross beame is erected when they are hanged, and taken down againe immediately after the execution'. They were gone, of course, or at least lost in a ground-hugging morning mist so thick that the tractors busy ploughing up great piles of root vegetables still had their headlights on at lunchtime.

I'd realised when plotting out my route on a floorful of Michelin maps that I could shadow Coryate through France by taking just three roads, the N1, N7 and N6. That these highways passed through exactly the same towns as he had emphasised the extent to which rural France has remained unchanged for centuries. Coryate's route to Italy was followed almost precisely by most Grand Tourists: by 1750, the road from Calais was littered with inns situated expressly to fleece the Brits hurrying through on the three-day trip to Paris.

Coryate describes the Veronne Forest as ridden with knaves and deer, and sure enough as the road entered its dense, dark heart there was a big red triangle enclosing a prancing stag, with knave rampant. The farming was all fairly lo-tech, and the towns − strung out along either side of the wide main road − had a timelessly flyblown look about them, with every other building a roofless barn decorated with faded inter-war advertising murals for washing crystals or some horrid-sounding aperitif (usually Noilly Prat).

And in between the towns, the roads were straight and flat and tree-lined, reminding me of the joke: Why are there trees along all French roads? Because the Germans like to march in the shade. (Actually, that's slightly unfair − most were planted by Napoleon so his own armies could march in the shade.) The other thing about the roadside trees is that they're really good at killing motorists − I always think of Albert Camus, adding the 'non' to existentialism as he slid off carriageway and into poplar in 1960. These were France's main arteries before the autoroutes were built, but they were still familiar to me as a veteran of childhood touring holidays planned almost exclusively around the avoidance of motorway tolls. A sign reading 'Péage' has the same effect on my father as a garlic-marinaded crucifix on Christopher Lee.

And it wasn't just the trees. Many of these roads were three-lane chicken-run free-for-alls, with the middle lane shared by both directions for overtaking. In case of conflict, priority is given to the driver with the most powerful main beam. Those responsible for this traffic-planning initiative went on to achieve even greater fame as patentors of 'powerslam', a variant of bungee jumping in which the elasticated rope is foregone in favour of an electrified anvil.

But rumbling along the vergeside, I was merely an obstacle, albeit a considerable one, in this regional round of the national reckless overtaking championships. It was quite refreshing, as well as practical

– at these speeds I was able to multi-task, laying a map across the enormous steering wheel, glancing at *Coryats Crudities* open on one of the green leather armrests and assembling quite complicated baguette sandwiches on the other.

I had forgotten that the Somme was a river, but noticing from the map that I was about to cross it made me realise why towns like Abbeville, which Coryate had described as 'a goodly faire citie of Picardie', nowadays resembled an uglie olde dumpe of Easte Germanie. It had been flattened – probably twice – and rebuilt on the cheap. I supposed the First World War at least would have slotted neatly into the volatile Europe of Coryate's day. The idea of countries changing hands every few decades seems absurdly quaint, but these parts of France, I reflected, had been occupied by foreign invaders for a sizeable fraction of the twentieth century.

And culturally, that fraction is well over a half. Hallowe'en was almost unknown here until the Nineties, when someone noted the lucrative possibilities of spicing up a slack month in the high street with an imported consumer-led festival. This, however, doesn't quite explain why, as I drove down a lovely sun-dappled minor road along the Somme, even the tiniest hamlet was a riot of orange and black. On 17 October.

Anyone can declare a spurious celebration of commercialised vulgarity, but it takes a special sort of national psyche not just to fall for it but to embrace the concept with open wallet and empty head. I stopped for coffee in a grubby establishment in Picquigny, a small village just north of Amiens where Coryate had talked Latin with a 'certaine Friare, attired in white habites', and got my hair tangled up in a mesh of zombie paperchains slung above the door to an authentically gruesome lavatory. I mean, will that really improve business?

'I'm not drinking in Gerard's any more, Serge. Only a couple of animatronic vampires on top of the optics and a token witch hiding under the pinball table – it's almost as if he actually *wants* us to be eaten by the returning souls of the dead.'

'Too right, Claude. I had my doubts about Gerard when I went in during National Cat Food Week and he thought he could get away with dressing up as a saucer of milk and training half a dozen ginger toms to flick MiaouMix pellets off the bar.'

Later, in Paris, I saw a whole shop devoted to Hallowe'en-themed toiletries and bath linen, and in McDonald's (or 'McDo', as it is rather foolishly known to regulars), they changed the colour of Orangina – an untouchable soft-drink institution – to blood red. The verdict of a folk musician who later explained this recent history to me: *'Les Français sont stupides.'* (Regrettably, I had left France before the 31st, but it was almost as bad in Italy. At a Chinese restaurant in Milan, an electronic skeleton scared my pork balls off by blurting 'Hooo! Scared you there!' in a camp, C3-PO trill as I walked past the cash desk. And in fairness to both countries, I later watched a report on CNN which revealed that in the US, Hallowe'en is the 'second-most spendingest' vacation, accounting for an idiotic $5 billion of consumer expenditure.)

Amiens was the first town Coryate enthused about; the first place, in fact, where he said anything interesting. I was already heartily sick of the expressions 'goodly', 'faire' and 'marvellous rich', and the way that he began his account of each city with 'Observations of [insert city name]' and ended with: 'Thus much of [insert city name].' And he was so long-winded: describing some murals in Amiens Cathedral, he writes 'they were the full proportionable length of a tall man's body', meaning 'life-sized'. There had been no details about where he stayed, what he ate or whom he met – nothing, in short, to give any ambience to the description of his journey. In a rare charitable moment, I pondered that during these early stages he was still unsure of his style, not yet having invented travel writing. But then he hadn't even commented on the weather, which surely must have been an important concern to someone intending to travel 2,000 miles on foot and horseback.

It certainly was to me. My experience of Amiens was soured by a frosted variant of the dispiriting quest for urination possibilities that is a feature of motoring holidays. The pee of fear was already heavy in my bladder as I paid and displayed; having left the Rolls I stumbled frigidly among locals similarly caught off guard by the cold snap. Two crimson-cheeked men were carrying an electric radiator home on their shoulders; an over-made-up housewife cowered in every shop doorway. What I wanted was somewhere I could void myself without charge or prior interpersonal communication. The eventual answer was a McDonald's: warm, anonymous and no purchase necessary. It really is very decent of them to offer this service across the globe – except in bloody Switzerland, of course, where you have to buy some of their ridiculous food in order to get a loo token.

It was the cathedral at Amiens – a Gothic masterpiece with an impressive collection of holy-relic body parts – that really got Coryate going, and one can't deny it's a cracker: 'The Queene of al the Churches in France, and the fairest [sigh] that ever I saw till then.' The façade was undergoing its 700-year service beneath polythened scaffolding, but inside, the towering 150-foot vaulted ceilings are almost as humbling now as they must have been in his day. To think (or rather read) that it was finished in 1305 emphasises just what a cultural backwater England was at the time, and – although he stubbornly refused to admit it – how belittled Coryate must have felt as a result. What was the finest building in Britain in 1305? Possibly Salisbury Cathedral, but you'd have had to wait fifty-five years for the spire. And here they had all this and John the Baptist's forehead too.

I slipped out past the authentic consumptive beggar at the doors, and had a quick dash about the little square in front. It was appealing enough – French town planners have a cocky panache that somehow lets them get away with wedging glass-and-steel office cubes between wooden medieval townhouses – but it was also getting colder. I retired to the Rolls, where I sat on the back seat eating a tub of supermarket salad off a honey-coloured Wilton footrest detached from the floor and placed on my knee. I decided that things really could have been a lot worse. Warm and absurdly comfortable, the passenger compartment made a fine restaurant, and I cannot pretend not to have enjoyed attracting the attention of one of the squads of heavily armed riot police that bring such a vibrant splash of brutal authoritarianism to most public places in France.

Like the Grand Tourists who followed in his wake, Coryate was clearly in a hurry to get to Paris: after Amiens he starts dismissing towns as 'meane & ignoble' and waving aside dozens of miles of countryside as featuring 'no memorable thing'. Following a deeply dissatisfying fifteen minutes spent reaffixing my headlamp deflectors in a sudden cloudburst, I urgently reciprocated and got on the first (non-*péage*) autoroute I came across. But something bad happened, one of those preordained holiday awfulnesses that requires all visitors to a major foreign metropolis to get repeatedly and comprehensively lost in some farflung and frightening suburb.

I thought Saint-Denis might be a nice place, featuring as it does a famous basilica that hosts a record haul of dead saint bits. But it really wasn't. Hotels leaking drugged-up tarts; buzzing and broken neon; a smell of pee and kebabs that penetrated even the Rolls's armoured exterior – it was like King's Cross, only with more lost tourists being strung up by their bollocks from lampposts. During one of my half-dozen laps of a dark and lonely warehouse car park (don't ask), a rheumy-eyed man with rusty teeth leapt out from behind an abandoned container and somehow contrived, in a single cathartic gesture, his intention to relieve my comprehensively abused corpse of its clearly considerable reserves of hidden valuables. While waiting at traffic lights, a young gentleman on a moped rapped my window with such ferocity that I almost looked at him. St Denis, be-doo, I'm not in love with you.

The rush hour had started, peaked and tailed off before I finally made it to the barely less unappealing northern suburb of Le Blanc-Mesnil (The White-Mesnil), near the old airport at Le Bourget (The Bourget). But despite the fact that the hotel I found was located in a pallet-riddled *zone industrielle*, with two railway lines and eight lanes of motorway traffic where the cocktail terrace should have been, I wouldn't for one minute want you to think that I was depressed. In fact, having squeezed the Rolls into the only space broad enough – the one with the wheelchair painted in the middle – I strode up to the reception with a spring in my step. I was, at last, overnighting in a hotel that embodied everything I held dear to my heart as both traveller and man. Soulless, bland, spartan and cheap as China – welcome to Formule 1.

Ever since reading a newspaper story about the success of the Formule 1 phenomenon I had wanted to stay in one. The chain owns 300 hotels in Europe, an empire built on the simple promise advertised outside each on a large illuminated hoarding, a promise that up to three people can share a tiny, plastic room for almost no money. At Le Blanc-Mesnil, I would be paying 129F, or £13. If I'd had two like-minded associates (um . . . my father, and, I don't know, Steptoe), it would have been less than a fiver a head.

I'd noticed the young receptionist eyeing me incredulously as I clambered out of the Rolls, removed the mascot and approached his little sentry box with a velveteen flounce.

'You stay in Formule 1 before zis night?' he said with polite scepticism.

'No. *Non.*'

'You know is barce-room and toilette outside ze room?'

'Yes. *Oui.*'

'You know is no restaurant?'

Shrug.

'You know room is like Sweden young offenders institut, wiss TV remote controlle welded to bunk bed and camion-driver wee-wee stain in sink?'

The Grand Tourists had stayed at five-room, three-guinea suites in the centre; as I inputted my homely six-digit entry code in the keypad outside my door I wondered how the Earl of Huntingdon would have coped at a Formule 1. But then I realised that Coryate wouldn't have cared less, and in any case – *beep beep beep beep beep beep buzz-click* – it was fine, if you thought of the room as a cabin, and the ceaseless Doppler whoosh of the autoroute as . . . naval warfare.

I sat on the double bed, painfully ingesting some of the vicious brown alcohol I had bought in a vaguely brandy-shaped bottle in Abbeville, and trying to understand the television news. But everything about the room was intended to deter the lingerer. The lighting was harsh and fluorescent, the plastic fixtures blindingly primary-coloured, and the tiny TV dangled from the ceiling at an angle designed to impact vertebrae after five minutes' viewing. Despite this, the set was plastered with anti-theft stickers, and when I ventured outside in search of food there were further indications that the clientele differed somewhat from my imagined F1 stereotypes: penny-wise polyester reps and young couples on a budget break with their first child. Through an open door I saw three vested men training hard for the coveted yellowed moustache worn by EuroSmoker finalists. The one on the bunk above the double bed blew his nose in the sheets as I passed; the thought of his two friends below cuddling up together for the night was not one that repaid contemplation. Further down the corridor, a trio of floor-starers lurked conspiratorially beneath a sign requesting those patrons who wished to smoke in the shower not to leave their butts in the soap dish. Cheap it might have been; cheerful it most certainly was not.

Who were these horrid, scary people? What were they doing here? But as I walked among the abandoned HGV trailers and half-burnt packing cases that littered the route to the only feasible dining option, a prefab Pizza del Arte chain restaurant, it occurred to me that their presence was in fact wholly appropriate. This was the kind of place where gangs changed getaway cars in *Crimewatch* reconstructions, and the shower-smoking vest-wearers were convincing extras. On the way back, I laboriously and noisily removed the Rolls's hub caps and stuck them in the boot. Then, seeing two pairs of eyes peering at me from the cab of a rental van in a darkened corner of the car park, I went back and disconnected the battery.

After showering in a pube-strewn Portakabin half the size of an aircraft lavatory – pausing only to take up cigar-smoking and brim the soap dish with smouldering panatellas – I set off into the velvet-flapping morning wind to see Paris. Not taking the Rolls was in some ways a cop-out, but one justified by the infuriating excellence of Parisian public transport. The nearest RER station was ten minutes' walk; a train arrived almost immediately, and twenty-two minutes later I was standing in front of Notre Dame. This from a suburb as far from the centre of Paris as Hyde Park is from either end of the Northern Line, and on a train so smooth it was possible to write postcards without embedding my Biro in the nostril of any space-invading adjacent fatty. Accidentally, anyway.

Coryate spent six days in Paris, though he never confesses to occupying himself with the vices that detained most of the countrymen who followed him there in the years ahead. Yes, yes, they were supposed to be improving their minds, but as their tutor loomed over them with a copy of *An Essay to Direct and Extend the Inquiries of Patriotic Travellers* (sample questions to ask the locals: 'Which are the favourite herbs of the sheep of this country? What is the currency value of whales of different sizes?'), it wasn't hard to imagine a young lordling's attention wandering.

In Paris, a Grand Tourist could do everything he was supposed to do, and everything he wasn't. It was this that made it so popular with Britain's gilded youth, who hoodwinked mama and papa into thinking they were honing their minds and palates in the world's best-stocked libraries, galleries and kitchens. 'It is certain that men of large fortunes can in no city in the world indulge their passions in every respect more amply than in Paris,' wrote Philip Thicknesse in 1766, no doubt explaining why twenty years later one newspaper estimated that British tourists in Paris spent over £1 million a year. Gambling was an obsession in eighteenth-century France, and many of the young Brits who arrived succumbed. Sir John Bland committed suicide in 1755 after running up card debts, and Charles James Fox was so infected during his time in Paris that by the time his Grand Tour took him into Italy he was making bets with his travelling companions on how many sheets of paper they had on them (and winning).

Heavy drinking was the norm in England, but cheaper on the Continents. Then, of course, there were the women. In 1752, John Mackay wrote to a friend from Paris that 'There is a mother and a daughter that embarrass me greatly . . . I am somewhat conscientious, and would not choose to try both, though that seems to be the only chance I have for succeeding.' One London newspaper asserted that Paris was 'a city the most noted for intrigues of any in Europe' and claimed that 'a Frenchman will almost suffer you to court his wife before his face, and is even angry if you do not admire her person'. This is what they had come for. And failing the women of good repute, there were plenty of others. In 1751, Edward Digby, priding himself on having found 'a very good pimp' in Paris, wrote that one of his companions had not been so fortunate: 'Steavens . . . goes to all the bawdy houses he can find and fucks the first whore he meets . . . [he] reckons himself very happy if he can find one who tells him she is only clapped.' But the British were quick learners – twenty years later, Louis XV was ordering his condoms from London.

One tradition Coryate did inaugurate was gleeful British declamations of the filth of the French capital. 'Many of the streetes are the durtiest, and so consequently the most stinking of all that ever I saw in any citie,' he rants almost immediately. But what we want are details of this squalor, and for that we have to wait for the testimony of an anonymous eighteenth-century Grand Tourist: 'The side of the stone steps near the Cathedral is a perfect lavatory . . . As I descended the hill, a full-dressed avocat, his tie-wig nicely powdered, his hat under his arm, was squatting with his bare backside completely exposed to view . . . Two women walked by while he very composedly pulled up his breeches.' Coryate had noted, passing through the plush and distant northern suburb of St Brixe, that it was home to most of Paris's lawyers. It was as true then as it is now – you don't shit on your own doorstep.

Sadly, in an odd way, it's all changed now, and in an astonishingly short space of time. I was in Paris for two months in the early Eighties, and well remember the petrifying mouth-of-hell footprint bogs and consequent enthusiasm for public urination. But as I stood in front of Notre Dame trying to detach the towers-and-round-window façade from tourist cliché, the square around me was abuzz with men on green motorbikes vacuuming up dog crap (there's a job to impress the girls), and I didn't have to squat on those vitreous-enamel size 14s until I got to Italy. All that remained was a universal fondness for flamboyant expectoration, and the bizarre aromatic combination of popcorn and farts that continues to haunt the Métro system.

Even the pigeons are moving on. Notre Dame had been recently steam-cleaned, and a banner proudly informed visitors that the façade was now wired with low-voltage electricity to discourage birds. I spent more time than I wish to confess to watching for an active demonstration of this deterrent, before joining the bored and cold multinational queue to get in. Coryate was unimpressed with Notre Dame, preferring Amiens, and as I shuffled funereally along the atmosphere-soiling 'tour route', crowded despite the many disincentives of a windy October morning, it was hard not to agree. The only bright spot was the English translation on one of those desperate, have-some-respect religious-slogan placards that are a feature of churches overrun with foreign heretics: 'I Was Thirty And You Gave Me Water'. (Restaurant menus are, of course, the prime resource for those who, like me, procure cheap and prodigiously hypocritical amusement from such linguistic failings. 'The Six Edible Snails From Bourgogne' tops my own list.)

It was much better out by the river. Parisians have always had an unmatched appreciation of the visual appeal of moving bodies of water in an urban setting, and looking at the gorgeous, golden-stoned houses lined up along both sides of the Seine it was impossible not to agree with the eighteenth-century Englishman who said, 'it is in their [housing] which they principally excel us; the magnificence of their apartments, the lighting of them and the furniture is what you don't see in England'.

Yet few of the cities I visited in the weeks ahead had houses built along their rivers; a surprising number even seemed embarrassed of them, siting themselves half a mile away. I suppose the Seine's islands help, making the river narrower, easier to bridge and less of a social barrier than in other cities. 'Sundry faire buildings of goodly white free-stone – the neatest shew of all the houses in Paris' was Coryate's description of the banks of the Ile de la Cité, and, despite the adjectival awfulness, I concurred – even though most of those I saw had been built long after his visit.

But, as I discovered during the next couple of windy hours, a surprising number of buildings had escaped the twin ravages of sans-culottes mobs and urban developers. Coryate describes witnessing the finishing touches being put to an as-yet unnamed bridge of GWFS (goodly white free-stone); I can still feel the smug glow that momentarily banished the cold after I calculated that this was the Pont Neuf, which, as I beheld striding up to its golden approaches, had recently been buffed and bleached back to its Coryate-era virginity.

The Conciergerie, with its conical Sleeping Beauty turrets, was equally easy to identify from Coryate's description. It had originally been a palace, and was some sort of law-courty merchanty place in his day, but by the eighteenth century its main role was as a prison. Most of it was scaffolded for restoration (of course), though the French Revolution cells were open to view. Through some curricular oversight, I seem to have spent most of my childhood studying the French Revolution, but it was still startling to see it laid out in all its oddness. Changing the calendar so that November was Foggy-One and so on, the sinister Stalinist contradiction of the Committee of Public Safety, and of course the fact that Robespierre was known as 'The Sea-Green Incorruptible' – something I've never understood, but often wanted to write in an 'occupation' box. On one cell wall was a list of the 2,780 Parisians guillotined by their fellow citizens in the half a dozen years after 1789, along with their professions. You'd think those responsible for the massacre would have taken this opportunity to insinuate guilt ('Jacques LeBlanc – pederast, royalist running dog and Anglophile'; 'Gaston Mesnil – cake-eater'), but as far as I could see most of the victims were watchmakers, glaziers and even a '*limonadier*' who must have served someone important a glass with too many pips in.

But there's nothing like a volatile social structure for stimulating urban regeneration – having seen what a fired-up mob was capable of during another bout of crowd trouble in 1848, Napoleon III's Baron Haussman had all the major streets widened into boulevards to make it more difficult to erect barricades and easier to mow down troublemakers. This bold scheme ensured that the next time Parisians went on the rampage, during the Commune revolt of 1871, they only burnt down half the city. Astonishing to think that within fourteen years they'd kissed and made up and were building the Eiffel Tower.

Did you know that the volume of air that surrounds the Eiffel weighs more than the tower itself? And that the pressure it exerts on the ground is that of a man sitting on a chair? And that I sat in a café spinning one cappuccino out for an hour while reading guide-books and hoping it might get a bit warmer outside? (Actually I stood. Visitors to the Continent will be familiar with the multiple tariffs concerning whether you sit outside or at a table or stand at the bar. I'm never quite sure how widely this rule applies, and so spend a lot of my time abroad trying to kneel in taxis and going into cinemas on all fours.)

The royal palace at the Louvre was being extended and reno-vated during Coryate's visit, and I walked up to it through the off-season Renoir painting that was the Tuileries gardens. (Where do they get that nice white boules-playing gravel from, and why can't we have some?) Surveying the grand vista up to the Louvre, I could see how for poorer or lazier travellers a few weeks in Paris was a Grand Tour in microcosm, a crash course in Continental culture. And I suppose it still has that reputation, a city where a civilised man might complete his education. I was eighteen when I spent those two months here; if it had been Berlin or Naples or anywhere else my parents would have assumed I was preparing for a career as a drugged-up crustie, but because it was Paris, they just went, 'Ah . . . Paris,' and imagined their youngest son reading Baudelaire in a brasserie, making insightful contributions to impromptu student debates on the steps of Montmartre and generally indulging in all other forms of accordion-fuelled academic earnestness.

To atone for the fact that my time there was largely spent eating tinned-pea sandwiches on park benches and running away from ticket inspectors, I joined the queue outside the Louvre and belat-edly prepared to kickstart my cultural coming of age. But then I remembered that I had in fact been in before, bunking in amid a party of German sixth-formers, and noticed just how long the queue was, and that the cold wind was probably starting to give me chilblains, whatever they might be.

So instead I went into the shopping arcade beneath that famous glass pyramid in front of the Louvre. I know it's not a perfect comparison, what with the French having stuck the last incumbent's head on a pole a couple of hundred years back, but can you imagine that in the courtyard of Buckingham Palace? And it was designed by an American. But I noticed it gets two stars in the Michelin guide, which doesn't give three to much, and rightly so. The French aren't scared of things looking silly next year, or even this year. This is how cities develop, after all, and probably helps explain why Paris seems significantly more vibrant and dynamic than London. Who cares if the Pompidou Centre now looks totally flared? It's still more interesting than the utterly dull Edwardian office buildings everyone seems so desperate to preserve in London. No wonder there's no real English translation for *joie de vivre* and *éclat* – just as there's no real French translation for 'It's a fair cop' or 'Sorry, I'm married'.

In London we talk about style over substance, but in Paris style *is* substance, an end in itself. And always has been – when, in 1756, the Earl of Cork pleaded with future Grand Tourists 'not to see fashions but states, not to taste wines but different governments, not to compare laces and velvets but laws and politics' he must have known he was pissing in the Parisian wind. In the arcade – which wasn't in fact remotely radical or interesting architecturally, but there you go – I found a shop selling nothing but chromed domestic accessories. And not bathroom mirrors or whatever else might possibly qualify as a run-of-the-mill chromed domestic accessory, but the most mindless fripperies imaginable, stuff like chrome-handled brushes to clean behind radiators and screw-to-the-wall chrome dispensers for make-up removal pads.

The peculiar inconsistency is that most French people, however well turned-out, actually look rather boring. Paris had attracted the dandier Grand Tourists as the home of elite *haute couture*; this it remained, but in failing to go mass market it had failed to cover the spread of fashion from court to street. Yes, the middle-aged women were all 'chic', but only in an Identikit, orange-foundation department-store-cosmetic-lady kind of way, and their husbands all had the receding Jacques Chirac hair and paunchy cardigan of a tiresome golfing uncle. And the youth – most of the kids shrugging about the arcade were still in the cords and Kickers their parents had worn during my French exchange visit in 1978. I even saw a few pairs of ironed jeans. It's as if they have no individual sense of style, preferring to leave all that to the government. 'I'm personally rather unremarkable, but look – there's a turquoise tower block with a big triangular hole in the middle!' While pondering all this I caught sight of my reflection in a pumpkin-strewn shop window. The sagging, soiled lilac suit; the hair Bonnie-Tylered by the gale. I decided to start pondering something else.

It was still too cold to walk about for any length of time, so I set about getting the full worth out of my one-day Métro pass. It didn't take long to finish the Coryate tour – last stop was the church at St Germain des Pres, where he 'saw a gray Friar shrift a faire Gentlewoman', an incident which sounded fun, but of course wasn't at all and actually meant 'taking confession from'. Now central, St Germain was a leafy suburb in 1608, and it was here that Coryate stayed during his Parisian visit, in the house of Monsieur de la Roy, one of the few eminent Protestants living openly and who proudly displayed the scars he had picked up fighting the Papists.

Then it was time for my tour: up to the Pont d'Alma to check out the Di and Dodi shrine ('Dodi & Henri Paul – Victimes of racisme'; 'Why Queen Elisabeth did you do this?'; 'You was personification of human feelings'; 'I killed Lady Di!'); across to St Paul for a beer in the café in which I spent the balance of those two months in 1982 playing (or anyway watching) pinball; and finally up to the Rue Montmartre, utterly exhausted and almost hallucinating with hunger, for a nostalgic meal at Chartier.

With its apron-wearing career waiters and expanses of *fin-de-siècle* mahogany, mirrors and brass, Chartier should in theory be a hallowed gourmet oasis, an appropriate place to begin the education of my pizza-polluted palate. Actually, though, it is a feed-up-and-fuck-off establishment where the starters cost less than a quid, and as such has a special place in my heart (though not my wife's, who refers to it as 'that soup kitchen you made me go to'). Having wordlessly established my solitary presence, a waiter with the moustache and bearing of a wartime cabinet minister dragged me off to a distant table, where I was pushed into a chair opposite another solo irrelevance, a local in a threadbare Lacoste with forested forearms and a single, forehead-spanning eyebrow. He looked about as pleased as me with this arrangement – on a proverbial wet Wednesday in October, there were dozens of empty tables – and then noticeably less pleased upon hearing the waiter take down my order for '*un grand carafe de vin*'.

They print a new menu every day, but I don't know why as I recognised every dish from seventeen years ago. The salad that was thrown at me the moment I ordered it was a tribute to the possibilities presented by a knife and a tomato; a tiny *steak au poivre* followed cold on its heels. With much complicated cutlery action and some very deliberate chewing I managed to eke this out for fifteen minutes, but it wasn't nearly enough. I realised I had come to the worst possible place in terms of fulfilling either of my requirements that evening: a huge amount of food, and a huge amount of time to eat it in. It was 7.15; the prospect of such an early return to LeGhastly-Awful was deeply saddening. I couldn't face another Métro journey just yet – in the morning I'd witnessed a poster of Sporty Spice promoting her solo album being pasted up at Châtelet, and had subsequently passed it enough times to see her getting first chewing-gum eyes and, by late afternoon, fully Hitlered up. I had learnt that RER trains now have names – like Pépé and Eric – and, worse, I was beginning to know them all. Also, the wine had gone straight to my feet. I didn't want to go anywhere.

When Forearms paid and left, a pair of waiters began to chivvy and pester me like wasps at a picnic, making pen-writing-on-pad signals to indicate that it was now my turn. Every superfluous item of tableware was ostentatiously removed, leaving me with just a huge, half-empty carafe of rosé and a glass.

It could have gone either way, but a carafe-draining draught of wine decided the issue. As one white-cuffed hand darted to whisk away the empty receptacle and the other, ballpoint whirling, began to scribble down my bill on the paper tablecloth, I slowly raised a traffic-stopping palm and stifled a painfully vast belch. Then, in an alien rasp that scared even me, I said: '*Vin*.'

Of course, this meant war. The waiter who arrived with the second pink flask was followed by another eagerly frogmarching a pair of filthy loons. The younger was wearing a green fake leopard-skin shirt buttoned up to the neck and an expression that suggested he not only knew the names of all the RER trains but considered some of them friends. His mother, as I suppose she was, had side-burns and smelt of vinegar. As they flumped and squeaked down next to me their mouths opened wide in extravagant but mercifully silent greeting to reveal a joint complement of teeth comfortably exceeded by the number of dirty plastic bags dropping from their grasp around my ankles. A supplementary chair skidded across from out of shot, and my table – which, I should point out, was perhaps the size of an opened tabloid newspaper – was suddenly strewn with the plentiful detritus of smelly mad people. The waiter beamed and winked, and I suddenly understood that this pair were not customers at all, but kept in the wine cellar and let out only for strategic use against uppity tourists.

I know it's unfair to be too hard on smelly mad people, but when they start eating raw eggs straight from the shell – didn't see them on the menu – I think charity takes a back seat. Perhaps I should have invited them back to my Formule 1 – there were two beds free in the room, and they'd certainly not have been out of place – but instead I gulped down my wine at drinking-contest speed, and tried to pay and leave before it took effect.

I almost made it. Halfway to the door, disturbed by the suddenly sinister-sounding swirls of echoing conversation, I felt an irresistible surge of blurred bravado and bodychecked a speeding waiter. Actually I completely missed, but he stopped anyway, and after sort of dusting his arm a bit, I spoke. 'You – you have your smelly mad people. But I,' and here I prodded my own chest far too many times, 'I have a Rolls-Royce.' As I tried to open the door, I realised I had been talking English, and to right this wrong turned to address the staff and diners with open arms and fruitily rolling Rs. '*J'ai un Rolls-Royce!*'

In the eye of that second wind – a ragged hurricane of public humming and the consumption of unwrapped confectionery found on adjacent Métro seats – I accepted I would be falling asleep on the train and waking up in the middle of nowhere. Which was fine, because that was exactly where I was going.

The rule of thumb in a Formule 1 is that when you start remembering your six-digit code by heart, it's time to move on. Coryate didn't tarry: six days was more than enough for even the most enthusiastic bigot to tire of the detailed mockery of profane and superstitious Papist ceremonies. So far, he'd travelled mostly on foot, with small sections of the journey in carts and coaches. But from Paris until his arrival in Venice, he was usually on horseback, riding in small groups with a guide.

On that first day in the saddle, his mount tires just outside Fontainebleau. Coryate eagerly exercises the full range of pain-inflicting inducements, lacerating the horse's flanks with his spurs and 'taking great paines to lash him'. But the beast continues to lag, and eventually a travelling companion, identified only as 'Master I. H.' approaches, his features no doubt a study in leave-this-to-Muscles condescension. His answer – a more systematic beating – is no more successful, and having been made to look a little foolish he rather surprisingly elects to stab the horse in the arse: 'He drew out his Rapier and ranne him into his buttocke near to his fundament, about a foote deep very neare.'

This isn't an ideal situation, and the pair desperately attempt to conceal the rather obvious injury from the horse-owning guide by rinsing the animal's ravaged hindquarters in a pool with their bare hands. Of course the guide notices, becomes 'extreame cholericke' and persuades 'I. H.' to part with six French crowns (about 36 shillings, or perhaps £400 in today's money) 'to stop his mouth'.

I mention this blackly slapstick incident because by the time I'd spent an expletive-laden morning driving right through the middle of Paris I had a keen desire to re-enact it, with any number of fellow motorists (and the odd too-cool-to-break-stride jaywalker) playing the horse and my Olympic screwdriver resplendent in the role of the rapier. 'I. H.', I couldn't help thinking, shared with me all the behavioural characteristics of a man with a bad hangover – the sudden loss of temper, subsequent extravagant remorse and the fact that Coryate notices him gorging on chicken nuggets and Coke.

Well, hold the remorse. I'm sorry, but what is it with this 'priority to the right' rule? I mean, it would be fine if it always applied (actually, no – it would be unutterably ludicrous, but at least consistently so). Instead the French prefer a more flexible approach, with some roundabouts operating in the globally accepted way, but others structured in a less tediously predictable fashion. Here, motorists approaching the roundabout are granted the choice of stopping to await a gap in the circling traffic, slowing vaguely to establish a climate of doubt and fear, or – the generally preferred option – slewing wildly into the melee with hands and feet depressing all available pedals and such controls relevant to the vehicle's output of *son et lumière*. The genius of these parallel schemes is that whereas common sense might demand some sort of large and prominent warning as to which is in operation ('Normal Safe Roundabout Ahead'; '*Mort ou Gloire*'), the only indication of priority is the little yellow rhombus, with or without a black line through it, that you drove past three hours ago and thought was a school-bus stop.

As a result, I had little control over my route. It was one thing to join the mechanical stampede around the Arc de Triomphe; quite another to leave it. It was like being a ball in the lottery machine – occasionally you got lucky, and were flung out of the scrum down a random exit. One minute I was heading south past the Eiffel Tower, cut off at its knees by an oppressive, dirty mist; the next I was

somehow driving back up the Champs Elysées. Did I say 'minute'?
How frightfully quaint. It was two and a half hours before I was
passing through the heavy industrial black belt that encircles Paris.

My hangover was proving to be one of those dispiriting all-dayers,
like having to nibble away from dawn till dusk at a huge bowl of
some hated foodstuff you've been ordered to finish. A skull that
someone had spent all night measuring with a Mole wrench slightly
too small for the job; a heart that feebly pumped thick red paste
through barnacled arteries – I actually felt disabled, suffering from
a blighting condition that surely merited free parking on double
yellows and concessionary entrance fees.

With my pulse down to that of a bored whale's, I drove wearily
up to Fontainebleau, still surrounded by the dense hunting forest
that first encouraged the French kings to build a palace there, and
recalled dully that I'd been here before. This was, however, during
my adolescent car-park period, when opting to play with the handbrake for half an afternoon was preferable to accompanying my
parents and siblings around any site of historic or natural signifi-
cance. And I have to confess, as I parked up in front of the geomet-
rically sculpted greenery that is a feature of any noteworthy French
establishment and settled back in leather and Wilton to consume the
wonderful 20F chip-stuffed kebab I had just purchased, the desire
for a nostalgic return to this stage of my development was almost
overpowering. I'd probably still be there now if it hadn't been for
the party of French schoolchildren whose dense and disturbingly
silent vigil at my windows blotted out the daylight and triggered
claustrophobia.

Coryate's front never failed to astonish me. He had marched up
to the gates of this enormous and regal place – surely more splendid
than anything Britain had to offer at the time – and demanded the

right to come in and poke about. That he was let in rather than being casually garrotted may have been because the fellows at the door were the French king's elite Scots Guards, impressed by Coryate's connections with the Stuarts back home. (The Guards retained Caledonian names and Gaelic passwords until the nineteenth century. There's an interesting story attached to this historical oddity. No doubt.)

Compared to the warehouse scale of Versailles, the rooms behind Fontainebleau's sombre façade were grand yet somehow homely – haughty but nice. Walking about with only the guards for company, though, it was difficult to feel much of a privileged thrill. The trouble with France is it just has too many palaces and châteaux, the legacy of a huge agricultural land littered with country estates. At a newsagent in Paris I'd leafed through a 400-page monthly magazine called *Propriétés de France*, which consisted entirely of for-sale ads for stately piles you'd expect to have to pay an entrance fee to visit – and for tantalisingly reasonable sums. Knowing that for the price of a claustrophobic London flat I could have my own moat and turrets makes it difficult to sustain an appropriate sense of awe walking round one of the only slightly grander showpiece palaces.

Large bits of the palace were unchanged – I was particularly struck by the François I gallery, a sixteenth-century prototype of the Versailles Hall of Mirrors. It was lined with huge panels engraved with 'FRANCO REX'; I was very pleased to discover one which read 'RRANCO', a little snapshot of the almost universal illiteracy of the time. In the ballroom, the ceilings were fulsomely decorated with Henri II's initials intertwined with those of his wife (Catherine de Medici) in such a way as to form a sneaky double D – the monogram of his mistress, David Dimbleby (or possibly Diane de Poitiers). But Coryate, not normally one to miss a chance to get on his high horse, doesn't mention this. The more robust line taken in these matters by his own Henry VIII, not yet dead sixty years, stabbed that particular high horse in the arse.

Out in the immaculate gardens it was just me, the mist and a man with a leaf blower doing the work of forty serfs. There were advantages doing this off-season, I supposed, but the looming threat of nightfall wasn't one of them. If only I could get up earlier, which meant a drastic reappraisal of my wine policy, then I wouldn't have to spend the rest of the day scurrying about trying to see stuff before it got dark. And so I succumbed to one of those hungover panic attacks, running back to the Rolls to do battle with an imaginary spider resident behind the sun visor before throbbing away down the N7.

The forest ended and I was driving through the bread basket of France, or at least whatever crumbs are left in October. Coryate, touchingly proud of Odcombe's agricultural heritage, was forever unfavourably comparing the relative fertility of the areas he passed through with that of Somerset, but the further south he went the more difficult this became. Walnut groves, 'massy fields of rye', 'faire and beautifull Vineyards', even 'great store of hemp' (for rope, not dope) – the best he could do by way of complaint was to point out the lack of 'one speciall commodity, wherwith (God be thanked) England is so abundantly furnished, being indeed a thing exceeding necessary for the sustenation of mans life, viz. sheepe'. But he was so invigorated by the pastoral bounty that he left the horse party and set off on foot, covering an incredible 36 miles in one short day.

Up on top of a gently pitched plateau littered with house-high heaps of harvested root crops the sun came out, and I was presented with an opportunity to cultivate a parallel interest in agriculture.

What were these things, I wondered, possessed at last by a keen Grand Tourist's spirit of enquiry, and why were there so many? The road was empty, and I parked up alongside the most accessible pile and got out, feeling like my tutor had just asked me the question after 'What is the currency value of whales of different sizes?'

I booted one around a bit to knock off the worst of the mud, then picked it up. It was a bit like a big turnip, but I couldn't believe there was a demand for such an industrial quantity of this medieval foodstuff. Perhaps, then, something like chard, scallion or curly kale, on the grounds that I had no idea what they looked like. I had just decided on a toss-up between an EU-subsidised chicory mountain and some sort of Hallowe'en fanaticism for stunted albino pump-kins when a thunderous mechanical roar abruptly burst into life behind me. My first thought was that the Rolls was being stolen – a growing hole in some pipe somewhere had given the exhaust note an earthy *Mad Max* touch – but turning, I saw a tractor bouncing towards me over the churned mud with its headlights on. Escape from such a famously lethargic vehicle should not have been too demanding, but in my fascination I had walked right to the far end of the barn-long mound. I might make it back to the Rolls, but it wouldn't look good if I ran. It would look – and feel – consider-ably worse if I ran and didn't make it. And in any case, starved of human contact by hours in a car and days in an impersonal city, I thought I could do with a bit of a chat. Why, look at this nice man getting out of his tractor with his . . . dark glower and his . . . purposeful stride and his . . . big loud dog.

Ignoring my silly-sounding '*Bonjour!*', lost in any case amid the frenzied display of dog stuff, farmer and friend slapped through the mud and stopped very close to me. He muttered something to the dog, who reluctantly sloped off back to the tractor. Then he raised his eyebrows, placed his filthy hands on the hips of a Grant Mitchell puffa jacket and gave me a brisk little upward nod, an any-last-requests nod. I smiled feebly at him, then we both looked down at the root crop in my hand. The only sound was the whispered roar of a high jet, and I suddenly remembered that it was about here that an outbreak of cholera was linked to Air India planes flushing out their water tanks as they began their descent to Heathrow. There was a short pause while I waited for him to contract this disease and die. Finally I spoke French.

'Um . . . What this is, please? I am a tourist with an interest!'

Gratifyingly, but also slightly scarily, his considerable nose wrinkled up and he began laughing extremely loudly, chuckling something between roars I couldn't remotely understand, appended by something I could, '*pour le sucre*'. Of course – sugar beets. Behind his shaking shoulders I could see the lights of a distant farmhouse shining out in the late afternoon gloom, and I suddenly had an image of his daughter looking out at me and shrieking, 'Oh, Papa, there is a man in a silly suit climbing about on the beet pile!' and Papa rushing out with the conviction that I was some Brussels busybody come to close him down for harbouring mad beet disease.

That should have been that, but it wasn't quite, because I was now to be treated to a long lecture, possibly but not certainly connected with the ways of beetlore. Then, as we walked jovially round to the front of the mound, there stood the Rolls. The farmer's last chortle faded, dying away into a little hateful snort. '*Tracteur*,' he said, looking ill with sudden anger, cocking his head back at his machine before snapping it forwards at mine, '*Bent-lay*.'

'Rolls-Royce,' I unwisely corrected. 'But cost not is so expense – justly 50,000 francs, as an old Peugeot perhaps!' His features were hardening as I watched. I had to think of an alternative conversational gambit, one with a sunnier aspect, and so I heard myself say: 'Your beets are very beautiful. Can this one I have like souvenir?' It was an error. A 300-year family history of punishing aristocrats was condensed into a single disgusted glare; I suddenly felt like some Grand Tourist caught up in a peasants' revolt. For a brief moment he seemed poised to boot the beet out of my velvet-cuffed hand with a great, cloddy punt from his steel-capped Wellingtons. Then he flared his enormous nostrils, flicked me a curt backhanded wave that said, 'Oh, just keep it, keep the fucking beet if it makes you so bloody happy,' and squelched bitterly away.

Back in the Rolls, I shakily dumped my souvenir in the footwell and consulted the map for my route beyond the next town, Montargis. Then, regrettably, I consulted Coryate: 'A little on this side of Montargis I saw a very dolefull spectacle: the bones and ragged fragments of clothes of a man remayning on a wheele, where many are executed: the bones were miserably broken asunder, and dispersed abroad upon the wheele in divers places.'

At Briare I drove down to the Loire. The farmer incident had added an edge of paranoia to the evening-after depression, and my hopes for a soothing vista were fulfilled. A gorgeous sunset was melting on rippled sandbanks white as tropical beaches; men in waders were fishing in the lazy, fat waters between. I'd promised myself (and, more crucially, my children, who reminded me every time I phoned home) that in a feeble half-nod to authenticity I would sleep in the open as often as Coryate – he'd already done a walking-through-the-night stint (before Paris), and to make it 1–1 I should camp as soon as it stopped being . . . uncomfortable.

The evening was warm and dry; I had no excuse. And astonishingly, just outside Châtillon, I almost instantly located one of the finest campsites in France: right on the river, daftly cheap and –

unsurprisingly perhaps in the week before it closed for the winter – totally empty. There was a slightly rundown but still magnificent three-storey classical villa of a lock-keeper's cottage alongside, and out of this emerged the middle-aged proprietors. '*Oh – belle voiture!*' exclaimed the fat and jolly wife, while her matching husband made slightly inappropriate Benny Hill groping gestures to signal his appreciation. '*Le moteur?*' he enquired at length, motioning me to restart the engine and so savour the sleeping-lion purr of a Rolls-Royce at idle. I was to become accustomed to the confused and slightly repelled wince that the ensuing building-site racket elicited. It was like owning a prize-winning dog that farted when anyone patted it.

The husband watched me put up my tent, which was nice of him, and then watched me change out of my suit and remove the mascot. '*Bonne idée,*' he said as I shoved the silver lady headfirst into the pocket of my jeans, noticing for the first time as I did so that she was essentially topless. '*C'est une voiture capitaliste. J'ai un 2CV.*' There was none of the farmer's malice about this, but his comment cemented my decision to deflect the attentions of France's many vindictive communists. I was dressing down and, as I heard myself beginning to do as I tried to tell him the car belonged to my father's boss, telling stupid lies about the Rolls's provenance. How much worse would it all have been had my search for a 'My Other Car's A Porsche' sticker borne fruit.

This far west the Loire was barely touristed, especially in late October, and on foot it took an age to find a restaurant. I crossed the river – Coryate had said it was a mile wide, and it certainly seemed so as I cowered behind pillars on the pavementless old suspension bridge to escape speeding, beet-laden HGV trailers. I wandered alone about Châtillon's steep and narrow streets – twice almost being brained by ground-floor shutters swung shut by unseen hands – and only found two establishments, the first a near-deserted bar with Pat Butcher standing in the doorway. '*Andouillettes*' was displayed outside as the speciality, and though I might have forgotten the French for 'want', 'then' and 'dictatorship of the proletariat', I had a strong suspicion that this was something deeply horrid. (Post-return dictionary action confirmed this with the troubling definition 'small sausages made of chitterlings'.) So – for the third time in four days – it was pizza, served in a converted riverside barge and with a consequent nautical theme. I ordered the Titanic, a sad flan of a thing soggy with crème fraîche, which tasted like it had gone down in 1912, and very nearly came back up again in 1999.

But cheered by a post-prandial flick through the many astonishing bargains advertised in a property magazine I'd picked up in Fontainebleau – always a sign that I'm starting to acclimatise – the walk back was a happy one. It was oddly warm, and a huge moon picked out the ruined rowing boats at the side of the black and silent Loire. As I stood beneath the bridge's central span, the preposterous grille of the Rolls grinned at me from the far bank, absurd beside the dark, sagging outline of my Millets tent. This was a good place.

Camping is the little girl with the little curl of the accommodation world. As I retired the night before – no inquisitive fauna, a clear sky – she had been very, very good. But some time before dawn I awoke to the erratic staccato of rain on plastic, and understood I would be experiencing the full spectrum of her character. Is it really beyond the ingenuity of man to manufacture a tent that doesn't leak? It's certainly beyond mine to erect one. Maybe it helps if you spend more than £24.99.

The patron came out to watch me as, wild of hair and damp of arse, I bundled armfuls of wet polyester into the back of the Rolls while his dog peed on my hubcaps. He saw me off with a hilarious up-the-workers clenched-fist salute and a dirty-old-man gurn that conveyed his merry scepticism about the prospect of such a clearly hopeless oaf getting much further in this dying behemoth of a car.

Hurrying to Italy, Coryate's route from Paris to Lyon was direct and reasonably well paved. Later Grand Tourists generally followed him down what is now the N7, unwilling to experience the considerable excitements of the alternative river route, down the Saône from Chalon. Those who went for this option found their carriages, stripped of wheels, being hoisted on to decks as cabins, before setting off into the glacial torrents aboard craft so ramshackle that 'they were always sold for plank and firewood on their arrival'.

I drove for half a wet day in Coryateland, over single-track stone bridges, past the occasional grand château, through humble villages crowned with hilltop churches that would have been ancient in his day, as old to him as he was to me, or something. The more rural things became, the closer I felt to Coryate – I was now beginning to think of him as 'TC', as in 'close friends get to call him TC' (what was the next line of the *Top Cat* song? I've no idea, though I'm indebted to my friend Paul Rose for suggesting 'Crow-fighting is special to see'). After all, there was only one Queen Elizabeth between us.

Coryate's description of the cathedral town of Nevers had sounded promising: crowds of long-haired 'Ruffians and Swashbucklers' dancing in the streets to 'vaine lascivious songs'. But the flat-nosed wino who came up to beg as I was parking (today's lie: 'This not my car. My work is with a mechanist, and I shall returning the car to the man who has the car') didn't quite fit the

bill, and nor, yet, did the growing Hallowe'en hysteria. I found a
stall selling football-style pumpkin scarves, and imagined street-
roaming mobs filling the night of the 31st with lengthy chants that
began: 'Give us an H . . .'

I woke up hating Coryate. He didn't speak a word of French but
somehow got by; instead of improving, I was now reduced to entering
restaurants with a finger raised to indicate my desire for a table for
one. He wore shoes made out of single strips of leather and walked
on rutted dirt tracks, yet never once complained of fatigue or pain;
I awoke with every muscle and ligament taut and tender, despite
the fact that I'd spent most of my time in a car. Even my buttock
muscles hurt, and I wasn't aware of using them at all (despite a slight
grey area in the two hours following my meal at Chartier). And now
I felt sick. Why didn't all the rank garbage he must have stuck away
make him ill?

As I'd now more or less given up on him ever mentioning what
he ate, I lay in bed and queasily read the Food and Drink chapter
in one of the Grand Tour books I'd brought along, Jeremy Black's
The British Abroad. And actually, he would have done rather better
here than in England. In the absence of refrigeration, there was a
rather heavy reliance on eggs, which at least had some shelf life, but
otherwise he'd probably have had better bread and wine (no change
there, then), decent mutton pies, vegetables such as broccoli, which
he'd never have seen before and, along the Loire, plenty of good
fish.

Many Grand Tourists, raised in a land whose lack of agricultural
variety implied meals with an emphasis on quantity rather than
quality, ideally an enormous slab of the Roast Beef of Old England,
were suspicious at first of French cuisine with its endless parade of

poncy garnishes and complex sauces. But, if only because they had no choice but to eat frogs' legs or starve, and assisted by the resilient truth that dining out in France was generally far cheaper, they eventually came to appreciate the subtleties. Variety was the spice of life, and the Grand Tour was all about bombarding the senses with new stimuli.

Of course, that wasn't the whole story. Plenty of well-off travellers took their own cooks, preserved meats and even pots and pans, having been scared off by the lurid accounts of apocalyptic rancidity detailed in books such as the peerlessly titled *A Gentleman's Guide in his Tour through France by an Officer who lately travelled on a principle which he most sincerely recommends to his countrymen, viz., not to spend more money in the country of our natural enemy than is required to support with decency the character of an Englishman.*

Had my own quest for gastronomic sophistication been diverted by a variant of this attitude? Had I eaten pizza almost every night just because it was neither expensive nor French? It was depressingly possible, though I felt better recalling my growing fondness for the alcoholic-gobstopper kick of pastis, which at less than a quid a shot relocated the focus of blame from xenophobia to economy. Like the Grand Tourists I had arrived in France with a philistine palate, but unlike them – or at least those who couldn't afford to bring their own cooks – I had the option of leaving the country with my epicurean horizons unbroadened. Variety had failed to depose Tabasco as the spice of my life.

It was reassuring, however, to recall that even my conservative diet was still authentically affected by what was in season, if only because the more I biliously pondered last night's inevitable pizza, the more it seemed probable that raw beet had been involved at some stage in its preparation. As a half-hearted nod to culinary adventurousness, I'd rashly decided on a 'Tarantella', whose ingredients, promised the multilingual menu, were selected 'according to the humour of the chef'. After the tiny child who took my order departed, I realised this was a mistake. Of course, there would be days when the chef would be in a good humour, and on such days your Tarantella pizza might contain capers or anchovies. But turning to follow the boy waiter's path to the open-plan kitchen, I beheld the chef, a bare-skulled no-neck viciously Jackson Pollocking flour bases, and understood that this was not one of those days. That night the chef's humour would dictate a choice of less traditional ingredients, and two that suggested themselves during my short-lived relationship with his creation were sweat and wire.

As it worked its way south, the N7 was becoming ever more rural. Through a thinning veil of quease I saw muddy Charolais cattle grazing beneath thunderstruck oaks in lumpy, thistled fields; I saw, and in fact almost flattened, my first beret-wearing cyclist, an old man with splayed knees wobbling about at sub-walking pace. I drove through villages with inbred compound names: Pouzy-Mésangy, Saincaize-Meauce and Lurcy-Lévis, where I exchanged humiliating mimes with a lady in a hardware shop in a fruitless quest for antifreeze and had coffee in a bar where loud farmers huddled round a solid-fuel stove drinking small, dark aperitifs from grubby conical glasses. Here the Rolls earnt me a rare thumbs-up, though this merely offset the raspberry-accompanied hand-in-bent-forearm that had welcomed me to Saint-Pierre-le-Moutier.

Anyone strange enough to be following this on a map will have noticed that I had at various points veered off the N7, Coryate's road. This wasn't, unusually, due to some combination of navigational incompetence and comedy signposting, but because I had an appointment. I was going to meet a seventeenth-century folk musician.

I arrived at Maxou's house late and hungry. He lived at the edge of the Forêt de Tronçais, the largest oak forest in Europe, and as I drove through its dense, dark heart I kept expecting Obelix to cross the road in front of me, pigtails aflutter and a boar across his shoulders. I'd have eaten it if he had; it was Saturday afternoon, which apparently required every tiny shop in every tiny village around the forest to pull down the shutters. In the end I excavated deep into the debris of wet tent, wet sleeping bag and partially folded maps that had filled the Rolls to chest level, and found a sad, forgotten block of Emmental the temperature and consistency of living flesh. I ate a very small part of this while parked by a farmyard strewn with half-buried horse-drawn farming implements, trying to understand the latest radio update about the arrest of Maurice Papon, a Vichy regime official accused of sending Jews to Auschwitz.

The French are more uncomfortable than anyone, including the Germans, about discussing their wartime indiscretions. War criminals like Papon and Klaus Barbie have only recently been tracked down, and organised tours of Vichy refused to mention the town's unfortunate history until 1987. Even the new Michelin guide to the area glosses over the issue: in the historical timeline at the front, sufficiently encyclopedic to include such details as '1832: Barbier and Daubrée open a factory in Clermont and begin working with rubber', '1889: Phylloxera damages the vineyards in the Limagne' and 'Late 19C: Metalworking in Lyon enjoys a period of expansion', blandly asserts: '1939–45: Second World War. Vichy becomes the capital of France'. And well may they hang their heads – I'm sorry, but why is it that half the Métro stations in Paris are called stuff like Eisenhower West and Roosevelt East and Uncle Sam How Can We Ever Repay You Circus, while Churchill and Monty don't even get a bus stop? Okay, we did run away at Dunkirk, and sink the entire

81

French fleet at Toulon, and never spent more money in the country of our natural enemy than was required to support with decency the character of an Englishman. But even so.

Maxou was, and hopefully still is, a maths professor whose spare time was consumed with playing the hurdy-gurdy and completing a thesis about seventeenth-century musicians in Moulins, a town just to the south. These passions had so filled his brain that the unannounced arrival in his small courtyard of an enormous crap-laden Rolls-Royce failed to unsettle him.

After nonchalantly welcoming me into the trim, churchside cottage where he lived with his wife and two boisterous children, he listened patiently as I falteringly explained my connection: I had been given his address by my elder brother Simon, whose own dark obsession with rosin-wheeled instruments had twice led him to Maxou's door. '*Ah, Simon le gros,*' breathed Maxou reverentially, inspiring me to stand very slightly on tiptoes. '*Oh, Simon, Simon!*' exclaimed his suddenly animated wife, clapping her hands to her cheeks as she wheeled round from the coffee percolator. '*Simon!*' chorused their daughter with a joyous squeak, before the three settled into a glazed reverie upon my brother's boundless splendour.

If I had chosen this moment to leave, no one would have noticed. Presently, though, the family emerged from their reflections with a collective sigh, and Maxou refocused on me with slight embarrassment. I was like Simon, he said, with a sympathetic inclination of the head that meant, 'in a shorter, less interesting and generally slightly more crap kind of way'.

There's no doubting that my brother is a fine fellow, with none of the tight-arsed misanthropy that blemishes my character. But what exactly had he done here to inspire such a slavish personality cult? Led away a plague of rats with his hypnotic hurdy-gurdy playing?

Taken the village to an unlikely victory in the regional Tall Tourist trophy? Spent more money in the country of his natural enemy than was required to support with decency the character of an Englishman? I still don't know.

Eager to atone for his family's unsightly Simonist outburst, Maxou covered the kitchen table with maps and books and began to talk about seventeenth-century life in this part of France. Unfortunately, though, I didn't understand very much of this, mostly due to it being in French, but not insignificantly because of Maxou's distractingly eerie similarity to Jack Straw. The slightly tinted granny specs, the ever-threatening five o'clock shadow, the nascent lisp – there he was, probably trying to tell me about the design of river boats being influenced by the Vikings who sailed up the Loire in the ninth century, and I kept wanting to ask him about prison overcrowding or if, when his children were infants, he'd ever taken a photograph of an artist sketching them and entitled it 'Drawing the Short Straws'.

When he asked what Coryate had found, I was deeply embarrassed on my man's behalf. The stuff about the Ruffians of Nevers was prefaced by an ugly rant on the town's 'roguish Egyptians' (probably dark-skinned Romanies): 'their faces looked so blacke, as if they were raked out of hel, and sent into the world by great Beelzebub, to terrifie and astonish mortall men'. And he wasn't much better on Moulins: 'I saw nothing but one very ruefull and tragicall object: ten men hanging in their clothes upon a goodly gallows made of freestone, whose bodies were consumed to nothing, onely their bones and the ragged fitters of their clothes remained'.

After this one-sided academic forum, I followed Maxou's Citroën estate to a remote clutch of farmhouses at Le Veurdre, near the River Allier. Here he and a few dozen likeminded souls gathered most weekends to dress in period-style clothing, play period-style instruments and generally make their own period-style fun. With the sandy-banked Allier sliding past in the distance and few signs of the twentieth century blotting the horizon it was a wonderful place, and at last gave me some insight into how Coryate would have passed his evenings.

Indeed, standing there watching two young boys Tarzaning on a rope across what could well have been a seventeenth-century cesspit, I realised Coryate actually got a far better overall picture of the countries he visited than the tens of thousands of Grand Tourists who followed him. Yes, he went to Fontainebleau; but then he also went to places like this. His limited resources, coupled with an aspirational obsession with the nobility, meant he got to experience the full social spectrum. 'There are but two methods of travelling,' wrote a Grand Tourist in 1772, 'one being admitted everywhere as a gentleman and spending a great deal, the other of living at coffee-houses and spending little.' And yet somehow Coryate managed a bit of both.

Take music: though he clearly wasn't a huge fan – here was a man whose favourite tune was the sound of his own voice – he did at least get to hear both the vaine lascivious ruffians of Nevers and the courtly orchestras. And he knew his stuff: in Venice, he describes a three-hour 'feast of Musicke' as featuring 'ten Sagbuts, foure Cornets, two Violdegambaes of extraordinary greatness . . . three treble viols and a Theorbist', going on to praise a forty-year-old who sang like a eunuch, 'but he was not, therefore it was much the more admirable'. ('Hey, Meester Tomaso – dis man, he sing like a bird, and look: he still have his knackers, innit!')

You'd think the Grand Tourists would have had more incentive to experience the full majesty of the musical arts as part of their aesthetic awakening, but no – all they cared about was opera, and even that was more to do with passing saucy messages to the widow in the next box. In 1772, Philip Francis wrote, 'Much to my surprise, I hear little or no music; there is ten times more in London than in any city in Italy.'

The Grand Tourists might have scorned folk music, but I was always amazed by the extent to which it still influences Continental popular culture. Not so much in France, perhaps, but later in Italy, Switzerland and Germany I rarely managed an FM sweep on the car radio without blundering across some combination of accordion, barrel organ and yodels. It was like turning on Radio 1 and getting Steeleye Span all day.

Leaving the boys to play chicken with the chicken shit, I walked back inside. One of the cottages had been kept as authentic as possible, with stunted eighteenth-century beds and mossy barrels in the wine cellar. In its kitchen, heated to discomfort by blazing, log-fuelled ovens, two headscarfed women toiled over huge shanks of meat and crosshatched Queen-of-Hearts pies; men with long beards hid their cars behind the purpose-built dance barn and emerged with armfuls of felt hats and sackcloth. Everyone was scurrying about, but one or two slowed after Maxou muttered the mantra '*frère de Simon*', pausing to look me up and down with a disappointed scepticism that must have been familiar to Keith Guevara and Derek Shakespeare.

It transpired that a large party – 100 people, I gathered – was taking place tonight, in honour of a fellow troupe of musical nostalgics from Nevers. To stay, though, would have meant imposing myself, talking French and prancing around a huge effigy of my brother while dressed up like an arse. In any case, I'd been worried to learn from Maxou that Coryate's pass over the Alps, Mont Cenis, was invariably closed by November; it was now 23 October, and I was only two-thirds of the way through France. As the Rolls bounced and slid laboriously out of the field, in audio-visual homage to the German armoured advance stalling outside Stalingrad, I passed a forthright, dour-looking man in a buckled Guy Fawkes hat and immediately thought of the lynch mob frogmarching those ten men to their goodly freestone gallows.

Panicked by thoughts of snow-bound Rollers, I made it all the way to Lyon that night. Dusk came early, and by the light of a low, pink moon I followed the N7 south-east towards the Monts de la Madeleine.

It was a little scary. With my three-watt headlights feebly illuminating the treetops I led a long train of excitable motorists up the hairpins, peering uncertainly through the filthy windscreen while grazing from a vast sack of crisps open in my lap. Even at speeds well below those recommended by typically cautious road signs the body roll was nautical, my snack-oiled hands sliding about the huge wheel. On the descent my followers lost patience, each succumbing like moths to the glare of approaching lights and surging past at the very stupidest moments. By the time the road flattened – oh look, at a place called Bully – I'd been using the brakes so much that when I got out at the next petrol station the hubcaps were too hot to touch. But I licked the bastards on the roundabouts (I'm not talking about the hubcaps any more), barrelling through on the inside in an apex-clipping straight line while they were fretting over who had priority.

On the outskirts of Lyon I again helplessly followed the flow, passing under the city's old clifftop centre through a vast and terrifying Gates-of-Hell motorway tunnel entrance. After two circuits of the slot-car ring road I somehow wound up in the centre, wedging the Rolls up tiny, vertical alleys in an increasingly unfocused search for accommodation. It was 10.30 on a Saturday night, and the streets were crowded with an eclectic blend of merrymakers – Hilfigered dope-smoking North Africans alongside blokes like that wryly smiling tuxedoed git from the old this-is-the-man-who-put-it-all-on-red-and-it-came-up-black VW Golf casino ad.

I, however, wasn't really in the party mood. The petrol light had been on for half an hour – an eternity in the realm of Rolls-Royce fuel consumption – and I'd had to watch in growing horror from the front of a long jam while two firemen sawed the roof off a steaming, deformed Peugeot 205 and removed the floodlit blonde corpse at the wheel. The night before I'd been reading of the tedious regularity with which Grand Tourists' coaches overturned – at eighteenth-century rates of progress, though, serious injuries were rare. Watching the ambulance ease slowly away, lights on but no siren, I recalled those early Victorians who spoke out against the railways, fearful that the human body could not cope with such speed, and realised how right they were.

My nerves shot, I gave up. I would find a petrol station and ask directions to the nearest swimming pool, where I'd be able to sleep in the car in relative security and have access to bathing facilities the next morning.

Of course, the loudly theatrical BP cashier would have none of it. My attempts to explain the swimming-pool gambit confused and appalled him, and he immediately set about Sellotaping together three petrol receipts to make a map upon which he indicated the nearest hotel, as well as other points of local interest such as his brother's house and a good place to go for dog-weighing (possible crossed wire here). I'm sure his recommended hotel was splendid, but just past his brother's house I looked into the sky and beheld the sacred yellow glow of a Formule 1 sign, and drove sleepily into its razor-wired car park.

I didn't realise in what a state I'd been until I got up to my red plastic cell, shed a random selection of clothes and discovered what I'd bought myself for supper at the BP shop: six bottles of Kronenbourg, two Snickers bars and a packet of Tuc biscuits. I hate Tuc biscuits. And I haven't had a Snickers bar since it was called Marathon, or indeed since Marathon was called Brown Peanuty Glue. In other news, I didn't have a bottle opener, though this didn't stop me from liberating a Kronenbourg by the rather foolhardy use of my ignition key.

For the Grand Tourists, Lyon was the first real city since Paris, and being a lot cheaper – a meal was 'half what it would have cost' in the capital – they loved it. 'The pleasantest city in France,' said one; 'wonderfully romantick' said another. Sir Thomas Nugent probably thought he was being nice when he wrote that the local women 'could be very attractive were it not for their losing their hair and teeth so soon'.

It was different for TC and me. Coryate walked into Lyon 'drooping wet to the very skinne', the first time he mentions the weather or any personal discomfort it may have caused him, and as I waited the next morning for the F1 receptionist to progress from the silent astonishment elicited by my request for a further night's stay, it suddenly got very dark and slanting hail began to clatter the windows.

I had not slept well. Constant traffic whoosh and the barking of a persistently stupid dog had been standard features of the F1 hotels I'd stayed in – the Do Not Disturb sign they'd given me to hang on the door should really have been stuck outside the window, particularly as I hadn't yet been troubled by any service staff, except the one who knocked to ask why I hadn't cleaned my ears out on the curtains yet. I was still scraping Snicker residue from the inside of my cheeks when, just after midnight, a shriek of brakes sent me to the window: in the car park below, a van driver had almost knocked over a young lady who, by neglecting to button up her long leather coat, revealed a preference for yellow lingerie over apparel more appropriate to the season. I suppose 149F is what other hotels might charge for an hour. Peripheral to this scene, though shortly to become the focus of my lonely window-side vigil, was a boiler-suited man with a yellowing Billy Connolly beard, persistently scanning the tarmac around the Rolls with a view to supplementing his dog-end collection. He was still there, sheltering in the car's considerable lee and stuffing damp, recycled tobacco into a pipe, when the hail abated and I walked out into an unpromising Sunday.

Vaulx-en-Velin – which you might as well pronounce 'vol-au-vent', because no one will understand you anyway – quickly revealed the desolate nastiness that in my experience invariably attracts Formule 1 developers. Hard-bastard tenements skirted by burnt-out lock-up garages, a high school where even the top-floor windows were hidden behind steel security shutters – I could see old Lyon, perched on its steep hill miles away under horrid grey clouds, but had no idea how to get there.

It all worked out quite well in the end, though, because after blindly trailing a growing crowd in an ambulatory version of my vehicular herd-following I ended up in the largest, most squalid flea market it has ever been my pleasure to root grubbily about in. Single hubcaps, a haul of stolen Barbies, mounds of slightly soggy fruit – nothing gladdens my simple heart like a really big load of cheap crap. I happily sucked in a great lungful of WD40, merguez sausage and fake aftershave and lost myself in a tight, loud mass of North Africans, most carrying dented bumpers and great spiky fronds of some possibly narcotic shrub. The enthusiasm was astonishing – one man was doing a roaring trade in old airline lifejackets; an unsightly stampede broke out when a neighbouring stallholder triumphantly whisked a dusty carpet off a cage full of dying pigeons.

Vicariously invigorated by my fellow man's shared lust for an improbable bargain, I didn't even need to buy anything to come away with a smile, squeezing on to a bus already as full as an Indian train behind two students carrying a fridge-freezer and a headscarfed old crone with a stack of ninety-six eggs – make that ninety-five – in her outstretched arms.

Take one teeming bazaar, one rainy afternoon and stir in several miles of famished tramping and you have the makings of a seventeenth-century day out. After the authentically filthy babel of the market and a Coryate-style drizzly hike I ended up in the old quarter, the most evocative place I'd yet visited. The narrow streets around the cathedral were lined with battered, bring-out-your-dead wooden doors, one with 1619 carved above it, another with 1611. If you looked about 10 feet up, above the falafel-shop signs and piggyback racing students, you were back in Reformation Europe. It was tantalising. Here Coryate had booked himself into the Three Kings, 'the fayrest Inne in the whole citie, and frequented by great persons', and still the preferred accommodation for Grand Tourists 150 years later.

This utterly uncharacteristic extravagance was down to a rumour that the Earl of Essex – whom Coryate claimed as a fourth cousin – would be in residence. It was typical of him to blow what was probably a whole week's budget on the off chance of getting in some social climbing, and even more typical of his sod's-law life that Essex had left the night before.

Poor old Tom. Donald Grey had been right back in Odcombe.

A surprising number of those ancient wooden doors were opened, and as I stepped carefully over the pungent rivulets of mammalian urine into the double courtyards behind I kept thinking of Coryate. On a warm evening in June 1608 he had stood in a courtyard like this, maybe this actual one, desperately wanting to join the 'gallant, lustie' Euronobles who'd come outside for a post-prandial prance, but knowing, deep down, that here as in London he was an impoverished irrelevance.

But the other thing I was learning about Coryate was that you can never pity him for long. I went into the cathedral to escape the rain, and while the Tannoyed mass echoed nasally about the granite and marble ('The Roman Catholic Church regrets to inform customers of the postponement of the Day of Judgement') I read on. And, of course, having failed to ingratiate himself with the French ambassador to Rome, another guest at the Three Kings, he winds up in the company of a lowly member of the ambassador's entourage, a Turk, and takes it all out on him in the usual fashion. 'I asked him whether he were ever baptized, he tolde me no, and said he never would be . . . At last I fell into some vehement argumentations with him in defence of Christ, whereupon being unwilling to answer me, he suddenly flung out of my company.' I walked back into the rain as the Tannoy wound up ('Ladies and gentlemen, Jesus Christ has left the building'), suddenly very glad he wasn't here.

Coryate got through more ambulatory sightseeing in a day than most Grand Tourists managed in a week, and despite the inappropriateness of the weather conditions I decided to take him on at his own game. Reflecting that the Romans had ruled Lyon for a lot longer than the 400-odd years that separated me from Coryate, and mindful of the importance of Classical architecture to the ruin-sketching Grand Tourists, I started off at the old Roman centre on Fourvière.

As later became apparent, anything worthwhile in Lyon is located on top of a small mountain, and my ascent of Fourvière's inundated south face involved 410 stairs (Coryate had said 180 – thanks for that) and an exciting Indiana Jones sequence involving a runaway wheelie bin. There was a splendid view from the top, but the climb had left very little oxygen available for my brain. Having dimly registered some vaguely mountainous outlines lined up in a Rolls-defying way on the horizon, I stumbled robotically into the Gallo-Roman museum. Here I laboriously concluded that everyone likes a good mosaic, and that it must have been tough to persuade your average Visigoth to carry on smashing a town up once all the fun knocking-the-noses-off-statues stuff had been done.

Then I walked all the way back down again, sliding down steep, drizzle-smeared cobbles and contemplating the life-blighting fears of the ancients, obliged to perch their towns on top of attack-resistant cliffs even though it would have meant breaking both ankles every time they went down to crap in the river. And what of Coryate, forever at the mercy of murderous robbers of the type he'd seen rotting on a dozen gallows? By comparison, I had no excuse. But that still didn't stop me wondering how Yellowbeard was getting on with my hubcaps, nor indeed from dreaming, as I had in Paris, that Elvis Costello was outside letting down my tyres.

Fatigue, inclement weather and Sunday are not ideal partners to a quest for authentic self-improvement. I walked along the empty banks of the brown Saône, full to the brim with rain and bits of melted and powdered Alp, rushing off in one direction while low, heavy-metal clouds flew past in the other. Why couldn't nature mellow out? The wind began to push me along the towpath, sending squadrons of fallen leaves hurtling past and ballooning carrier bags over church roofs. I walked a mile and only saw two groups of people – a pair of teenagers snogging on a bench, their black hair windswept into a single, flapping tress, and a dozen disabled scouts unhappily watching their troop leaders playing energetic head tennis on a muddy strip of riverside grass. The Saône rose almost while I watched, acquiring the pregnant billows of a body of water about to lose it. Only the most reckless ducks braved the torrents, exchanging frightened-but-excited 'Sorry! I'm completely out of control!' looks as they tumbled past each other.

By the time I got to Perrache Station, the gale had flayed the streets clean of leaves, litter and any fag-ends Yellowbeard might have missed, and ball-bearing raindrops were starting to work on the dog crap. Paris might have its poo-bikes, but down here it was a faecal free-for-all, seven shades of shit. How can anyone not find this disgusting? We're all familiar with the buckets of toby flung out of bedroom windows in Coryate's day, and to my mind this isn't much better. In thirty years' time, the memory of dog poo in the streets – alongside boxing, Third World starvation and Jonathan King – will be one of those things I hope people look back on with disbelief, appalled and ashamed that they were ever tolerated.

I think I went to the station for a chance to look at the TGVs – officially Europe's flashest trains – but if so, I never made it. Approaching Perrache from the side, I was besieged by unsavoury, leering men clicking their teeth and beckoning me with oily nods and yellowed fingers, offering a variety of sexual and pharmaceutical experiences with unhappy endings. I turned into the wind and headed back down to the riverside, where I was immediately soaked to the knees by a phalanx of motorcycle outriders speeding through one of those leaf-blocked-drain lakes. There was a moment of static reflection – long enough to think that it could have been worse, but just too brief to recall that the purpose of motorcycle outriders is to clear a path for larger vehicles – before the Olympique Lyonnais team coach barrelled through, sending up a curtain of water so mighty that some of it arced straight over my head. Most of it, however, did not.

It was quite cathartic in a way. I remember feeling a kind of mid-level slapstick resignation, the type experienced when you lie back in a nice bath to read the Sunday papers, then open up a supplement and four dozen advertising inserts slide out into the water. I was soaked as a Coryate, and at least I no longer had to worry about the rain. After a brief drip-dry in the scarecrow position, I sluiced off up the main drag to see who else had had their Sunday outing ruined.

Ronald McDonald certainly had. Despite the bouncer on the door, the showcase three-floor McDonald's on the Place Bellecour was being systematically sacked by bored French teenagers. I went in for a comfort stop, of course, but the relevant facilities were taped off, shards of vitreous enamel being desultorily swept up. On the way out, I saw a bespectacled thirteen-year-old carefully remove a frosted-glass globe covering the light beside his table before passing it to one of his similarly unassuming friends, who gently rolled it, crown-green-bowls style, across the floor.

It's as if the French hate themselves for loving McDonald's so much – after anti-globalisation activists comprehensively destroyed a newly opened branch of McDonald's in the southern town of Millau, 45,000 supporters thronged the streets. Even the Prime Minister, Lionel Jospin, spoke out in their favour. Can you imagine that happening anywhere else on earth?

And in a land with a long tradition of civic destruction, Lyon boasts one of the proudest records. Grand Tourists were often appalled at the autocratic oppression in eighteenth-century France (despite concluding that the natives were 'too wicked and insolent to be trusted with liberty'), but would have been far more disturbed by the regular outbreaks of mob rule that flared up around the country for almost a century after the French Revolution. In 1848, the huge bronze statue of Louis XIV on his horse that still stands just outside McDonald's was saved from a threatening crowd only after someone persuaded them it would be an even more effective insult merely to replace the royal inscription with one in praise of the sculptor, a local boy.

No one seems to know who brokered this unlikely feat of diplomacy – only in France could a baying mob be prevailed upon to throw down their pitchforks in favour of irony – but his descendants weren't in McDonald's that afternoon. The festive sound of the glass globe smashing came just as I walked out past the beleaguered bouncer, who tried very hard to pretend he hadn't heard it. Or maybe he was too busy wondering why he hadn't noticed the Swamp Thing going into his restaurant.

The rain was clearing the streets, sending the many youthful gropers into pumpkin-plastered shop doorways and dispersing cinema queues ('*Austin Powers 2* – C'est d'un Bombe, Baby!'). I don't think I have ever experienced such a consistently heavy downpour, certainly not from the wrong side of the double-speed wipers. But as I was sloshing across the square in front of the opera house – another of those oddly admirable hybrids: a glass-and-steel dome topping a venerable columned façade, like a spaceship landing on the Parthenon – two young people came up to me and something really Continental happened.

'*Je vous présente ma soeur!*' exclaimed a dark-haired young man with an actorly flourish, flicking rain off a floppy fringe before pointing the flat of his hand at the young Sophia Loren adjacent.

By coincidence, I had just been pondering (with what I hope my wife will understand as low-level biological pining) the arresting number of full-lipped, raven-haired lovelies resident in the Lyon area – many of them, for Sir Thomas Nugent's information, with their hair and teeth intact. '*Elle est belle, non?*' The young Sophia Loren shot her brother a mock-shock 'Oooh, you are *awful*' look, followed it with a slightly more convincing 'Oooh, you *are* awful' one for me and splashed off across the square. After showcasing a charmingly helpless shrug and muttering something about finding her a man, the brother winked at me and set off in giggling pursuit. It was like being in a 1970s perfume advert.

Better anyway than my subsequent ascent of Hovis-advert hills in Pirelli-advert weather, or the fidgeting, skeletal loon I sat next to on the Métro who asked everyone the time and urgently muttered, '*C'est bon, c'est bon*,' whenever he got a reply, only he never asked me, and when I rose to get off my fellow passengers warily peeled away and I realised they all thought we were together.

A Formule 1 isn't really what you want after a day like this. Yellowbeard was still there, as were the greasy fingerprints where he'd tried the Rolls's boot catch, but I didn't care. I walked in past the rows of red doors, knowing that behind each was a sad, fat man dressed only in a vest and a petrol-station digital watch, staring bleakly at the archery on Eurosport while making the beast with one back. Without going to my room, I went straight into the shower. I probably haven't mentioned that you don't even get a towel; there's just an industrial-sized version of a hand dryer mounted on the cubicle wall. As I stood there being blasted with diesel-scented air and the previous occupant's scabs and fag-ash, it was not difficult to decide that I would never, ever stay in a Formule 1 hotel again.

✦   ✦   ✦

Lyon was being nice to me the next morning, but I was in no mood to forgive. In fact I'd rather have done without the blue sky, an unwanted conciliatory gesture from someone you'd just got into hating, like a cheery good-morning wave from a tramp who'd been trying to break into your car the night before. 'There is a bad man in the parking,' I told the receptionist as we settled up. 'I watch him much often. You are seeing the man?' She was. Yellowbeard grinned Fagin-like through the glass. 'He is happy today, but while former evenings he had touching my car.' The receptionist looked at the Rolls, at Yellowbeard, at me. '*Il est concierge*,' she said, clearly sad that my life should be blighted by such malignant paranoia.

Painfully returning Yellowbeard's horrid smile, I set about festooning the Rolls with undergarments washed in the sink the night before – beer bottle as plug, shampoo as soap powder; the perfect end to a perfect day. My stupid desert boots were salt-stained and crusty, and I realised I was beginning to smell like the Rolls – damp, old leather and a generally neglected, oily must. Maybe it was worse than that. Maybe I was actually *becoming* the Rolls: the Eighties heyday, the pompous xenophobia, the slightly shabby bodywork and suspect mechanical reliability – only a gaping disparity in running costs distinguished us. It was just me and my Shadow, glowering haughtily at the foreigners, making enemies of potential friends with our deluded arrogance, trading on past glories while the rest of the world moved on.

The N6 didn't help. Like all of Coryate's roads – trade routes since Roman times, abruptly abandoned by long-distance traffic in the Sixties after the opening of some parallel motorway – it had a mournfully resentful 'I could have been a contender' air. A few clapped-out hotels and restaurants still half-heartedly plied for passing trade that had long since passed – the sign reading 'Stop! Beer

Advised!' was an arresting reminder of drink-driving's Golden Age. But most had gone, replaced by a never-ending hinterland of bed showrooms and the regional headquarters of American computer firms.

I'd just passed a breaker's yard full of cars people had died in when my journey properly began. Up to now, I realised, there wouldn't have been much to astound Coryate – everything was just a variation on themes he would have been familiar with from England: a bigger cathedral, a more fertile field. But then I followed him off the N7 and into Savoy, and there, suddenly, were the Alps, savagely serrated, gigantically granite-flanked.

Coryate had never seen a mountain before, let alone crossed a whole range of them. For him and future Grand Tourists the Alps were an appalling prospect: 'an awful and tremendous amphitheatre,' wrote one eighteenth-century traveller; 'I could not behold them without terror,' wrote another, perhaps one of the many who insisted on a blindfold before being ferried over. And as well as being physically intimidating, the Alps were a cultural barrier: just ten years before Coryate's journey, Lord Burghley had written: 'Suffer not thy sonnes to pass the Alps, for they shal learn nothing there but pride, blasphemy and atheism.'

Coryate was now in a small party of travellers being led by a guide from Lyon to Turin, and as rugged porters bearing sedan chairs came up to the group at the foot of Mount Aiguebelle, he must have realised odd things were about to happen. With the Rolls now shaking at idle speed like a Ukrainian tractor and the ice warning light briefly flickering on for the first time, it was clear that for me, too, novelty lay ahead. Or more particularly above.

In lending its name to an expensive London hotel, permed cabbages and a confectionery truffle celebrated in song on the Beatles'

White Album, Savoy's impact on my life to date had been minimal. I was pleased, then, to note almost immediately that the region was exceptionally lovely. As the road rose and twisted up to Aiguebelle, everything went all *Sound of Music* – steep-roofed wooden chalets, doe-eyed cattle with bells round their necks, brown paper packages tied up with string. Everyone was growing neat little rows of sunflowers and vegetables in their gardens, and when I lowered the window a muted, Indian summer symphony of distant bleats and birdsong wafted in. It was the sheepdog's bollocks.

'I observed an exceeding great standing poole a little on this side the Mountaine on the left hand thereof,' wrote Coryate, and deciphering this typically blathering passage as a description of Lac d'Aiguebelette, I stopped there for an early brunch. Sitting on a quiet lakeside bench in my T-shirt with half a supermarket delicatessen on my lap, I was astonished at how much better things had suddenly become. A single fisherman dangled a rod from a rowing boat drifting timelessly on the lake's glassy flatness, as if paid an annual retainer to do so by the tourist board. Around the banks were campsites and hotels, studies in endearing close-season melancholy with lichen-streaked, flat-tyred caravans and drifts of leaves edging netless tennis courts. Brooks gurgled; ripe elderberries hung above me, dappling the sun on my back. Even the distant motorway was a picture, one of those sexily daring tunnel-and-bridge spectaculars they always used to put on the covers of European road atlases.

It seemed an unlikely war zone, but Savoy has been invaded and occupied more frequently than almost any other place in Europe, and for centuries reluctantly played the 'Oh, all right, I'll throw in my Get Out of Jail Free card as well' understudy role in peace-treaty horse trading. As gateway to the Alps, and hence the buffer zone between Italy and France, it was endlessly overrun by both these countries, or their forerunners, as well as Spain. By 1860 the poor Alpine shepherds had had enough, and in a plebiscite voted for union with France by 130,533 to 235, which can't have done much for the all-night election special's viewing figures. But out of habit they still enamel their regional flag on every road sign, a familiar white-on-red cross that says, 'Sorry, love to be invaded by you, but the thing is, you're actually in Switzerland.'

All this I learnt later. Sitting on the bench, however, my sole source was the 1947 Michelin guide to the area. (This is the kind of thing that happens when you ask your father, or anyway my father, for any helpful travel literature and don't bother to check inside the big box he gives you until you arrive in Calais and find yourself leafing through Weimar Republic trolley-bus timetables and blotting-paper pamphlets entitled 'Motoring in the Ottoman Empire'.) As well as featuring line drawings of Albert Camus negotiating a hairpin on the Grand St Bernard, this publication was in French, which meant that I learnt facts such as 'In the nineteenth century, 30,000 Savoyards furnished themselves in Paris: decrusters, commissionaries and other men of pain. There were also entertainers: players at barbarian orgies, dressers of bears, rats and marmots. There were also, finally and above all, rubbers.'

The motorway had sucked away the traffic from the little Napoleonic road that most closely followed Coryate's route over the mountain. It was the first time he lost his nerve, and as I slalomed creakily up a helter-skelter of tight hairpins, engaging low gear for the first time and staying in it for twenty minutes, it wasn't hard to see why.

Keen to save the cost of paying the porters to carry him over in one of their sedan chairs – and to be honest, I can think of fewer more disturbing methods for scaling what is essentially an enormous cliff face – he attempts to follow them up on foot. Their response to this is to speed off ahead with the rest of Coryate's party swaying on their shoulders. 'Finding that faintnesse in my selfe that I was not able to follow them any longer, though I would even break my heart with striving, I compounded with them for a cardakew, which is eighteene pence English, to be carried to the toppe of the Mountaine, which was half a mile.' Eighteen pence was a day's budget, yet Coryate says, 'I would not have done the like for five hundred.'

Memorable words from one with such a finely honed sense of economy. I had found a physical weakness.

Excited to find himself for the first time in his life 'above the clowdes', Coryate briefly surveyed the city of Chambéry below before being whisked down by the mad porters. A thin mist was arranged in watercolour rainbow layers as the Rolls gratefully breasted the summit of the Col de l'Epine, long gossamer threads shimmering from the silver lady's waist. The road narrowed sufficiently to entertain fears that it had become somebody's front drive, coiling past barns incorporating live trees in their construction and woodsmoke-wreathed orchards perched above vertical eternities. Little roadside waterfalls were blocked with large bits of tree, the legacy of yesterday's sustained rainfall; a walnut-faced peasant woman reluctantly waddled off the road at my approach, leaving me to negotiate a flock of geese and an Alsatian eating its own sick. Then it was down into a mammoth and circuitous descent in which my right foot was a stranger to the loud pedal, or anyway the louder pedal, two and a half tons of steel, walnut and wet pants on the hoof.

Down in Chambéry, parked in front of the castle with a gypsy woman rapping my window ('My grandfather wins this car with a ticket in a contest, and I selling it for he in Zürich'), I looked up at the great fists of rock, girdled with brown autumnal cuffs, which hemmed the town in. Despite the motorway, these first Alps remained formidable barriers – on the Aiguebelette side, every number plate had borne a 38 regional prefix; here, they were all 73s. The idea of men carrying people up and down such obstacles was frankly monstrous, as was the thought of Napoleonic navvies building roads over them. I supposed that the latter were descendants of the former, and suddenly understood the great nineteenth-century exodus, the rush to go off to Paris and dress marmots or rub.

Chambéry had been blandly pleasant – the first graffiti-less town I'd visited, sharp air, even a bit of history in Coryate's revelation that it was once home to the Turin shroud. But back up in the Alps, everything except the road went downhill. The evergreens, black amid the pale yellows, gave the mountainsides a scabby, burnt look, one complemented by an unexpected concentration of distinctly unAlpine heavy industry. Lured here by hydroelectric power, enormous blast furnaces glowed in the dusk, flanked by assorted quarries and chemical plants and a succession of dirty old towns.

And through it all, claustrophobically hemmed in by filthy Alps, ran a criss-crossing plait of transport history: railway, motorway, the canalised River Arc, the N6 and the old village-linking Coryate route. I alternated between the latter two, constantly swooping under the autoroute or over the river.

The signs were all for Torino and Milano, and most of my travelling companions were toll-avoiding Italians heading home in a hurry. They hooted and flashed; I hoisted V-signs out the window; together we hurtled through hideous, semi-abandoned villages with rust-holed road signs and boarded-up boulangeries slowly collapsing on to high streets strewn with weeds. A lorry-load of youthful conscripts took particular exception to my sloth and imprudent gesturing, and after carving past on a blind corner pulled back their transport's canvas flaps to rain purple-faced epithets upon me. Responding to this with a hefty blast of main beam right in their unshaven faces was an action I had cause to regret over the following twenty minutes, uncomfortably reminiscent as they were of the films *Duel* and *Apocalypse Now*. At Modane, they mercifully buggered off with everyone else towards the Fréjus Tunnel and suddenly, after a pathetically defiant farewell toot, I was alone. It was 6.30 p.m., and I set off in search of accommodation.

It isn't wise to expect too much of a place with a suburb called Furnaces, but a hotel of any sort would have been nice. In the end, happy to have found a street where people weren't smelting anything, I parked up beside a church in a little car park offering facilities to motorhomes and prepared to bed down. Of course, there were no motorhomes, or indeed facilities, but my rue-rage confrontation with the military had exhausted me beyond caring. At least until two eleven-year-old boys sidled up out of nowhere, pretended to play football for a bit and then flobbed fulsomely all over the Rolls's offside rear flank.

I am not proud of what happened next, and if it had come to court the local press coverage would have been extensive and unfavourable. '"He was a nutter," said brave Jean-Claude, 11, after his ordeal at the hands of Monsieur Morre, the self-styled King of Britain in his la-de-dah limousine and handmade wet-look panties.

"He come at us with all his lights on, hooting and shouting, and chases us into the paint-factory car park. Then he traps us in between two lorry trailers and runs out of his big car, screaming some stuff we couldn't understand, something about us spotting on his car, and something else about Modane being a stupid town with naughty armies." The trial of Morre, who is both guilty and evil, continues.'

I am genuinely sorry. One of them actually started crying.

Appalled and contrite, I sped through Modane's smut-streaked outskirts and turned right up the first road out of town. Fifteen minutes later I was parked in the middle of a ghost-town coach park behind a ghost-town chalet in a ghost-town ski resort. This was good. Exile from society was all I deserved. I would spend the night here; it would give me time to clear my brain of bad thoughts.

Stuck at the top of a cul-de-sac mountain road, La Norma was a literal dead end. It seemed less like an off-season resort than a suburb of Chernobyl, with rows and rows of black-windowed chalets lining soundless, weed-cracked streets. Before I'd even switched off the engine I was already failing to pretend the prospect of sleeping here in the Rolls didn't scare me witless.

The only light in the whole town was provided by an illuminated phone box at the far corner of my car park, which should have been comforting but instead looked the sort of place an imminently doomed teen in a horror film would set off towards with the words, 'Screw this, guys: I say there is no escaped whacko, and I reckon the cops are gonna agree with me.' In the last squints of twilight I could just make out huge claws of rock scratching the sky high above my head; from far below came the ceaseless slapping slosh of a considerable waterfall.

At 7 p.m. I was strolling round the car park in a T-shirt knocking back the first of the Lyon-leftover beers that were to be my sedative and sleeping draught. At 7.15 breath was visible; at 7.30 the windows started frosting. Having hugged the remaining warmth from the radiator, I got back into the car, bundled the crisp packets and maps and beets from front passenger seat to rear and laboriously zipped myself into a sleeping bag, not at that stage noting the rogue pair of damp pants that sneaked in with me. For supper, I had this: no supper. The beers came and went; some sort of generator rumbled distantly into life; after pondering which of its diminutive sharp accessories would be least likely to inspire an assailant's laughter, I opened my penknife's saw blade and laid it open on the dashboard.

There are two calls of nature, and I had exited my vehicle to heed the more logistically awkward of the pair beside a car-park-backing pine tree when a sweep of headlights rounded the corner by the phone box. With a gravel-showering handbrake turn my sole occupancy of La Norma ended. Dress adjustments desperately effected, I emerged from the fir cones with as much nonchalance as I could muster, though the open saw blade and handful of McDonald's napkins told their own story, which was at best a curious one.

The car, an old white Golf, disgorged four teenagers – one of them female – beside a stack of railway sleepers next to the phone box, perhaps 30 yards away. I acknowledged their sullen stares with an imbecile wave and got back into the car, arousing renewed attention when the cast-iron clunk of the coal-fired central locking echoed accusingly around the valley.

What on earth were they doing out there, up here? For an hour I watched them display the classic symptoms of dangerous boredom, playing desultory football with a small bean bag or just sitting in silence on the sleepers, folded arms shoved up in the pits of their inadequate baseball jackets, heads bowed, breath steaming furiously in the fluorescent light. Beginning to accept that it was only a matter of time before they killed for kicks, I started up the engine, filling the night with ugly noise and hydrocarbons. Literally and figuratively chilled, I'd remembered my sister-in-law's father telling me how he used to keep warm when sleeping in his Skoda during walking holidays in the Lake District: 'Drive around for a bit to get the engine hot, then quickly stick the fan on full for five minutes.'

And so the aimless Alpine youth warily beheld me lap the car park with mad, slow circles, waiting for the Rolls's enormous engine block to build up a sweat. It took fifteen minutes, which was at least thirteen more than I had anticipated and allowed plenty of time to consider that when my body was finally discovered by the season's first skiers, earlier events in Modane would lead to these young murderers being fêted as heroic vigilantes. I suddenly understood that I would have to gain their confidence, and abruptly pulled up alongside before buzzing my window down. 'Happy night!' I shouted above the fan, expensively acquired heat rushing out with my words. The girl nodded slightly; the rest did not. 'I am here waited for my father.' The girl spoke. 'English?' she said, her features instantly cringing in an oh-shit-why-did-I-say-that kind of way.

I turned off the fan. 'Yes!' I replied in my native tongue with lunatic, show-no-fear gaiety. 'Well . . . he should be here pretty soon, any time now possibly, or maybe in the morning.' Four flat faces. 'No time, you see, for any . . . anyone . . . for anything stupid to happen. To me. Or indeed to you.' One of the boys nudged his neighbour with a knee; heads dropped and bobbed with ineffectively restrained laughter. 'My car,' I continued, 'is not my car. No. No, actually I rented it from a special company as a present − *un cadeau*, a-ha ha − for my father, who is a, er . . . poor carpenter, you know, making toys with wood. We are going to an exhibition together. The Vienna Wood Show.'

The merriment had passed, and all four were now contemplating the tarmac with sad resignation. Banishing with difficulty the memory of Ted and Ralph's exchanges on *The Fast Show*, I continued. 'Are you interested in wood? Only I notice the pile there under your . . . bottoms, I suppose. Trousers for you three, and . . . oh, trousers for you too, *mademoiselle*. My mother cleans tables in a restaurant, so the upshot of all this is that I don't have any money or items of value, really, in fact I haven't even eaten for twelve hours and I have to say I do feel a little . . . Good night!' I whooshed the window closed, sparked up eight cylinders and roared back to the other side of the car park, arriving just in time to see the laden Golf's taillights disappearing at speed down the mountain towards civilisation.

Relief was short-lived. Within minutes improbable new fears engulfed me, and I was soon missing the teenagers desperately. After a sudden conviction that an avalanche would send the surrounding pine trees crashing on to my roof, I drove into the middle of the sloping car park, even though doing so meant parking at a sleep-discouragingly oblique angle. I turned on the radio, but up here couldn't get anything except ethereal jamming signals and elusive snatches of short-wave Slavic and stilted English. Cowering in the Rolls's dimly lit 1950s interior amid the dead houses, this sound-track made me feel like an unmasked double agent trying to send a desperate last message as the men with silencers closed in.

I awoke at least twice every hour until 6.30 a.m., when I finally gave up trying to persuade the sleeping bag's nylon to get it together with the seat's age-smoothed leather. Unfed and filthily unrested, I drove back down the snow-veined mountainside beneath stars fading into a pale blue sky, the Golf's registration number streaming endlessly through my mind. (Slightly disturbingly, it's still there, lurking about behind the Magic Bus bouzouki. 975 BW 73, if someone with spare brain space wants to pick up the baton.)

Lanslebourg was Coryate's last stop before his party ascended the fearsome Mont Cenis Pass and crossed into Italy. I stopped there for a lovely custard-filled croissant, and another, and a vast slab of chocolate, and another, carpeting the car with pastry flakes and foil. It was a funny time of year to visit the Alps, this ugly, brown inter-lude that bridged James Bond winters and Julie Andrews summers. Idle ski lifts joined Lanslebourg's bare hotels to Mont Cenis's bald slopes, and I thought, not for the first time, how strange it was that anyone over the age of seven should find sliding repeatedly down a hill the sound basis for a long holiday. (I've only been skiing once, and that was with my father, which meant salopettes crafted from bin-liners, bottles-in-the-bedroom après-ski and slapstick on the slopes. He once contrived to ski over his own thumb, which caused much hilarity in the watching ski-lift queue, at least until I emerged at speed behind them, bin-linered bottom first, and achieved a memorable 'human nine-pin' effect.)

The road up to Mont Cenis was open – other passes, I'd noted from roadside information, were already snowed shut – but it was still bleak, cold and a little scary. On the map its hairpins were as tightly packed as a diagram of the alimentary canal, and again it was no surprise to read of Coryate's distress. Consulting his touchingly parochial frame of reference, he quavers that the slopes of Mont Cenis are littered with fallen rocks 'foure or five times greater than the great stone of Hamdon hill', site of the quarry behind Odcombe. Disturbed by these, and more particularly by the sheer pathside drops 'five times as deepe in some places as Saint Paules tower in London is high', he again decides to follow on foot, this time as the rest of his party proceeds on horseback. And all the time the party's guide is at the front, bellowing, 'Have no fear, gentlemen – the devil is dead!'

Coryate really hated mountains, and who can blame him. In those hand-to-mouth days, the beauty of a landscape was a function of its productivity. Fertile, life-giving plains were his ideal; barren, life-taking mountains were right at the other end of the spectrum. Even those who lived among the mountains could hardly bear to talk about them – when early geographers asked how they should refer to the range of summits, they were told 'alpes', in fact a reference to the high pastures. The locals had no word for the peaks themselves.

Generally unsettled, Coryate even whines about 'needing a ladder' to get into Savoy's high beds (thereby allowing me, in the light of last night's accommodation, a rare triumph in the what-are-you-moaning-about stakes) and that the locals were all hideously deformed by great goitres on the throats, 'almost as great as an ordinary foote-ball'. This he confidently attributed to 'the drinking of snow water', though of course we now know that it was actually due to the drinking of footballs (or possibly iodine deficiency). Here was a man who could not wait to get to Italy.

In crossing Mont Cenis, Coryate set a trend for subsequent Grand Tour Brits. By the eighteenth century a whole industry had sprung up, dismantling coaches in Lanslebourg and carrying the bits over on mules, with sedan chairs for the aristos of the type Coryate used at Aiguebelette. Even so, it could be awful – Horace Walpole's crossing took six frostbitten days, during which he enjoyed a shoulder-high view of his beloved spaniel being killed and eaten by a wolf.

I stopped at the unspectacular summit of Mont Cenis – 2,081 metres, a third higher than Ben Nevis but perhaps a shade less than the 'fourteene miles' that was Coryate's estimate – and looked down Napoleon's road towards Italy. Everything was dead – grey granite, brown bracken – and waiting to be buried by snow. A big, square fortress jutted out distantly over the mountaintop lake, and I thought of the descriptions of wartime heroics in my 1947 Michelin guide. The finest referred to the defence of the St Bernard Pass, first attacked by Mussolini on 21 June 1940, but staunchly held 'right until the armistice'. And when might that have been? I had to look in the index for the answer: 25 June. The poor French. It was a far cry from the Napoleonic excitements of 1800, when 60,000 troops built four roads across the Alps, poured over them and drove the Austrians out of northern Italy. In crossing Mont Cenis, Napoleon had emulated Hannibal. And so, as the Rolls steamed through the abandoned customs post on the Italian side, had I. I had crossed the Alps in a white elephant.

THREE

Turin, Milan, Cremona and Padua

Italy was what the Grand Tour was about. It was in Richard Lassels's 1670 publication *Voyage of Italy* that the term 'Grand Tour' first appeared, and for 100 years afterwards most serious tourists aimed straight for the country the other side of the Alps. British culture had been dominated by the Classics for centuries – Coryate hero-worshipped Livy and Virgil – and as the home of the Renaissance, Italy scored double culture points. No less importantly, by being reasonably far away from Britain and composed of unthreatening republics there was no practical reason to despise the locals on principle.

Not much has changed. The lingering obsession of a certain class of Englishman with the country is the one real legacy of the Grand Tour. Even in next-door France, few cities have bespoke British names; in Italy, there are few that don't. Venice/Venezia, Naples/Napoli, Turin/Torino, Rome/Roma, Padua/Padova – and then there's the slightly ridiculous media creation of Chiantishire.

I suppose a lot of our fascination with Italy is down to the British love of heroic failures, and squandering European domination twice in a millennium is about as heroic a failure as you can get (there's also added empathy from the fact that we had our turn later). This aside, though, slightly pretentious Brits have always appreciated Italy as offering the perfect cover for notably unpretentious British behaviour involving hot weather and cheap booze. The Grand Tourist could lurch and letch about Venice in a way he'd never dream of doing at home, just as John Thaw rolling out the barrel in *The Sweeney* is a very different proposition to John Thaw rolling out the Barolo on a Tuscan veranda. When in Rome . . .

Personally, however, I have to confess that Italy daunts me a little. Going there on holiday is like hanging around with boys from the year above: it's exciting to be seen in the company of such cool people, but you're so eager to have some of that coolness rub off on you that you don't quite notice in time that they only invited you along to nick your new trainers or get their sassy girlfriends to take the piss out of your haircut.

In fairness, it has to be said that my opinion of Italians is coloured by two incidents, which together have convinced me of a healthy national appetite for criminal conspiracy.

It is the summer of 1977. As Elvis Presley's considerable buttocks gradually cool on the porcelain, a family holidaying on Italy's Amalfi coast sets off in its Rover for a daytrip to Vesuvius. The road up to the crater is long and lonely, but the prospect of being able to throw stuff into a great caldera brimming with unstable lava cheers the heart of at least one member of the group, a lavishly locked thirteen-year-old boy who has said little in the two months since the judges at a Silver Jubilee fancy-dress parade asked him to go and stand with the other little girls. Leaving the vehicle in the car park just below the crater, the group walks through the sulphurous air up to the rim, peers over at a hole with all the febrile volatility of a slightly smelly opencast mine and returns, beginning to understand why the mother opted to stay by the hotel pool reading *The Magus*.

But all is not well with the Rover. The front passenger window is askew and off its hinges; the interior comprehensively ransacked. The father grimly tightens his forearm around a much-derided Italian gentleman's handbag, home to all cash and cards – a rough-and-ready inventory suggests that all that is missing are the tourist petrol coupons (a week later an additional, and more intriguing absence becomes apparent: a cassette of George Harrison's *Living in the Material World*).

As his three children grapple with torn maps and chase hotel bills across the windy car park, the father notices a neighbouring family of locals having an uncomfortable picnic in a Fiat 127. A post-war childhood spent in Rome has bequeathed him an impressive degree of fluency in the language – along with a fondness for poncy gentleman's accessories – and he approaches the family. Had they seen anything? Why yes, says the mother cheerfully. In an eager performance forcefully illustrated by her two young children's back-seat mime work, she describes two men jemmying down the window, pillaging the interior, and stabbing the offside front tyre with a small screwdriver before departing in a black BMW. Why the tyre? She leans out of the little Fiat's window with the practised, wide-eyed thrill of someone preparing to reveal the punch-line to a favourite ghost story. They find no money in the car; they make a small, slow puncture which only becomes apparent halfway down the lonely hairpins; they've been waiting round the corner and are now following behind, and when the victim stops to change the tyre, they leap out and employ a little old-fashioned armed persuasion to procure any valuables kept about his person.

The English children can understand the family's reluctance to tackle the thieves, but not the crackling walkie-talkie the husband keeps trying to hide under his seat. The troubling presence of this object may explain why instead of changing the tyre there and then, the father takes a decision that is to have a profound effect on a thirteen-year-old boy and his attitude to the Italian race. The English family makes a run for it. Barrelling drunkenly round the hairpins, smoke billowing off the deflating tyre, they are soon joined and closely tailed by the BMW and the featureless silhouettes of its driver and passenger. Peering over the back seat below bulbous 1977 fringes, the boy and his elder brother and sister watch through a shower of wheel-rim sparks as the pursuit continues right into the suburbs of Naples. Only when the father grates to a halt outside a police station does the BMW overtake, and then with snail-paced intimidation.

Now let us go forward fourteen years. We are on a rural railway platform at dawn, somewhere in the north of Italy. The overnight express from Nice makes its final stop before Venice, and before it has quite come to a halt two figures emerge and make rapid but wayward progress across the chilled, empty concrete towards the exit stairs. Figure A, to the rear, is an Englishman, recently awoken from an early hours reverie that his childhood terrors on the road from Vesuvius were merely an unfortunate one-off. Figure B, the instigator of his untimely reveille, is a youth disturbed in the process of ransacking A's sleeper compartment. A briefly closes on B, but is not in a position to apprehend him, nor indeed to attract attention from the appropriate authorities. This is partly because the train is preparing to leave, and partly because of B's superior stamina, but it is mainly because A is dressed in one sock, a jacket and a pair of underpants.

These just weren't the sort of things that happened in Ealing, at least not then. I calculated that since 1976 I had spent thirty-eight days in Italy, meaning that I'd woken up each morning looking forward to a 5.3 per cent chance of falling victim to robbery with menaces. And here I was, driving through the place in a bloody Rolls-Royce.

At least my fears were authentic. Grand Tourists felt safer in France, where the policing was better than they were used to in Britain, but in the eighteenth century, Italy was more anarchic. The main concern of the law-enforcement officials employed by the jumble of independent states, duchies and republics that made the country up was making sure that no tourist entered their territory without handing over the right bribes. In 1751, four English gentlemen were found murdered on the road between Milan and Turin; Italian robbers invariably employed violence, and the crime-deterrent corpses Coryate had seen so many of strung up along the roads of France were regular features in rural Italy during the Grand Tour's eighteenth-century heyday.

The sensible tourists dressed down and kept quiet, but there weren't many prepared to forgo their new red velvet shoes and blue wigs, and their answer was to tool up. Travelling through a notorious hill pass near Lugano in 1791, Lord Bruce and Thomas Brand claimed to feel 'very little apprehension, knowing the antipathy of your Italian to a pistol'. A decade later, sailing into Livorno, Matthew Todd felt compelled to deal with the captain's rudeness by threatening him with 'a brace of pistols which he did not much like the appearance of'.

The lack of a sense of anyone being in charge is and was the problem: Italy somehow seems a bit of a shambles, in a vaguely Third World way. The first town, Susa, was dusty and chaotic in a way unthinkable on the other side of the mountains that stared the place out: very old men on very old Vespas; three-legged cats; laundry strung across the street; cars hooting at girls, girls winking cockily back. A couple of weedy police officers propped up a wall, both smoking, both mirror-shaded, both seedily bribable. Lock up your daughters, I thought – oh, and your valuables.

There was also a dramatically enhanced interest in the Rolls, up to the point where I can state with confidence that for every ten pedestrians who saw the car, five would stare after it, one would wave and two would run alongside for half a mile kissing their fingertips. (The other two asked not to be included in the survey in case the taxman used it to get their addresses.) Yes, Italians love their cars – but not quite as much as they love your cars, which was why the silver lady lay in rear-footwell hibernation under four hubcaps and a Wilton over-rug.

Even the gardens were different: a couple of fruit trees, maybe a scraggly row of maize, a ragged hotchpotch of self-sufficiency that was as exactly as Coryate describes. And the vines were still grown in the distinctive way he'd noted, 'upon high poles or railes, a great deal higher from the ground than in France'. Just outside Susa, the twin castles of San Giorio stood precisely as he described them, only presiding now over the motorway to Turin. In France, these would have been immaculately restored by a wealthy weekender or the government. Here they were, respectively, a hen house and a tractor graveyard.

The only time I've seen Turin before was in *The Italian Job*, and inching the Rolls through the fake football shirts and last-harvest grapes of a heaving market place – now there's a smart route for the main road into town – I dearly wished for a Mini Cooper and a crash helmet. But for the very first time in my life, following the campsite signs actually led me directly to a campsite, and by lunchtime I was nailing sheets of sour-smelling nylon to the mud in front of an enormous, dilapidated nineteenth-century villa.

At the top of a hill just to the east of the River Po, rain-swollen now to a Tinky-Winky, the Villa Rey stared majestically down at the city's boulevards and piazzas, or would have done if a fat mist hadn't squatted over everything. The campsite was an incarnation of all things Italian – the mysterious, faded grandeur of the setting; the combination shower/loos; the dodgy old bastards eyeing up the Rolls from the leaf-covered canopies of moss-smeared caravans that were clearly their permanent homes.

It was melancholy and depressing, but I wasn't going to succumb. After a wary shower and a matching peek through the Villa Rey's knackered shutters – a huge, brick-dusted entrance hall with a flat-tyred Fiat 131 parked at the foot of a sweeping double staircase – I set off through the lions-and-ivy gates and went down the hill to be Italian.

The Grand Tourists arrived in Turin in a sense of some excitement: their first Italian city. And it didn't matter that most found the place itself rather uninspired – the court was 'old and dull' and the streets and piazzas, though occasionally handsome, were, in the words of Lord Stanhope, 'mournfull'. No, they had come to meet the people, or more particularly the women, and on this basis they were not disappointed.

James Boswell, eighteenth-century lawyer, biographer and dirty old goat, wasted no time in trying it on with a fifty-year-old Torinese countess who had a reputation for welcoming young Englishmen with open legs. Lord Charles Spencer, Sir Brooke Boothby and the Duke of Hamilton had all recommended her, and Boswell soon found himself 'quite in the Italian mode' and enjoying her 'animal spirits'. Soon after, at a ball, he admires another 'oldish lady', being told, 'Sir, you can have her. It would not be difficult.' But following a swift 'imprudence' in her box at the opera, he quickly moves on for his hat trick with another middle-aged noblewoman, only being put off when she got changed in front of all her guests, 'changing even her shirt'. 'We indeed saw no harm,' wrote Boswell, 'but this scene entirely cured my passion for her.'

'Elisa, please read this note from Paolo. I can't live without you. I beg you, don't leave me. I love you and will love you above all others.' Sprayed on a wall near the bottom of the hill with the strident urgency of a political diatribe, this cheered me no end. Partly by reasserting a less tawdrily Boswellian snapshot of Italian romanticism, but mainly because I could read it. My prowess in Italian, messily assembled during a one-year, hour-a-week university course that I only did to be a ponce, has never been impressive. The lowest of many low points came during a brief exchange with a curator in the Archaeological Museum in Naples, wherein I somehow ended up describing my father as '*Il Duce*', the title applied to Mussolini by his Fascist adherents.

I read after I got back that only 11 per cent of Italians speak English – and that was the most popular foreign language. It's down to 7 per cent for French, 3.5 for German and only 1.5 for Spanish – particularly daft, because as we all know that's just Italian with a lisp. A grasp of the language is consequently vital, and my affinity with Paolo's words suggested critic-confounding linguistic glories lay ahead. Of course things weren't perfect – a huge queue of lorries had built up behind me at a tollbooth that morning while the interested but uncomprehending operator appraised my attempts to mime 'money', and I've glossed over Paolo's last sentence, which apparently beseeched Elisa to indulge his compartment. But I strolled along the Po's misty, traffic-crazed banks a happy man, smiling benevolently at the Paolos inspecting themselves in any reflective surface and feeling at one – or '*uno*', as we Italians say in Italian, here in Italy – with my surroundings.

I may as well confess now to an element of *schadenfreude*. In expressing his personal Alpine rigours, Coryate seems to have been jolted into a more open account of his journey. 'My observations of Turin', which should on past form have begun with a description of the goodly citie walls, instead kicks off: 'I am sory I can speake so little of so flourishing and beautifull a Citie. For during that little time I was there, I found so great a distemperature in my body, by drinking the sweete wines of Piemont, that caused a grievous inflammation in my face and hands; so that I had but a smal desire to walke much abroad in the streets.'

Well, well, Tommy boy! Little under the weather today? Come on, son, out with it – you stuck it away in the tavern last night and now you've got a great, big hangover. 'Sweete wines of Piemont'? Bit of a bad-pint/must-have-been-that-kebab excuse, don't you think? (Unless of course he's talking about some fearful precursor of vermouth, native to these parts, in which case he's lucky to get away with a swollen face.)

I lapped all this up. Sleeping in a haunted car park while Coryate climbed into his warm bunk? Walking abroad in the Citie while he slept it off? If I listened very carefully, I could hear the sound of tables being turned.

In thickening fog I crossed the river and walked into the agoraphobically enormous Piazza Vittorio Veneto, a colonnaded oblong built to the epic proportions of Turin's eighteenth-century makeover. At the time of Coryate's visit Turin was just becoming wealthy; its baroque heyday lay a century away when the city was home to the various Victors and Charleses who ruled first the northern states and, after 1861, the whole of the newly unified Italy. (I was interested to read, as I just know you're going to be, that after its birth Italy went through three capitals – Turin, Florence and Rome – in just ten years.)

It wasn't hard to find a mahogany and brass café bubbling with espresso and animated conversation, full of strangers talking like friends and pearl-toothed urbanites in long coats laughing into mobile phones in a way I didn't think happened outside television commercials. It was slightly harder, though, to explain to the waitress that I'd forgotten to take out any Italian money, and would she accept plastic for a coffee, no, didn't think so, what about if I have a couple of sandwiches and a mineral water as well, no, I see, well, I'll have to leave my passport here as security and go off to a bank, and then come back when the bank wants to see my passport.

Of all its Third World features, Italy's financial system is the most hopelessly tin-pot – the plethora of zeros, the how-much-of-this-Mickey-Mouse-money-do-you-want 30p banknotes, the way that you queue up at a cashpoint for half an hour and then it spits out some stupid, useless Eurocheque at you, which you'll find screwed up in your tent two years later the day after it expired.

My financial embarrassments painfully concluded, I walked up to the royal palace. I could see why Italians liked the Rolls, with its thin veneer of classic style not quite concealing years of neglect and decay. Even right in the centre you'd turn into a heartbreakingly lovely street, all courtyards and crests above doorways, and then notice it looked like it had been recently reclaimed by man after a long nuclear winter: dumped cars, dead rats, piles of rubble. By the same token, although the covered colonnades were graffitied and filthy, the shop windows within were a constant delight, as were, in up to 50 per cent of cases, the crisply immaculate people looking in them. I spent ten minutes entranced by a display of boiled sweets arranged with the minute care of a Victorian butterfly collection – one box was a yard long and contained fifty-four separate compartments filled with carefully colour-coordinated confectionery. And it was only £30. Or £3,000, or possibly 3p.

At about 4 p.m., the sun finally burnt through the mist, heralding other good things. I found a 10,000-lire note in the palace gardens, spent a quarter of it on the best ice cream of the previous decade, and after a search for the Turin shroud church somehow ended up in the university, drinking subsidised coffee and perusing the psychology exam results on a noticeboard. (As usual, the girls all got 100/100 with the boys 60 marks back. This is why half of all Italian men are called Nicola or Andrea.)

And then I went to look at the Mole Antonellioni, possibly the strangest building on the planet before the start of the twentieth century, a 300-foot random compilation of architecture's greatest hits with a ground floor like the Bank of England and a pagoda roof. Even better, it was being restored (in the rather laissez-faire way the Italians do these things), so I didn't feel compelled to go up it, and instead wandered down towards the station amid church bells, the flappity-slap of car tyres on cobbles and a great shrieking clank of trams.

Is it okay to say that trams are a bit rubbish? I know that public transport enthusiasts melt into an unsightly nostalgic mess at the mention of trams, and that people in Britain somehow have the idea that their reintroduction in any city is guaranteed to banish traffic congestion, street crime, poverty and impotence. But actually, they're a total bloody liability whose main role is to scare the piss out of pedestrians and motorists, or in fact anyone not actually aboard. Imagine you're driving down the road and a pram rolls out in front of you. Now imagine that you can't steer, or slow down in any meaningful way (not a huge mental leap for an Italian), and that your wheels aren't soft and rubbery but great iron discs like industrial versions of the rotary cutting blades in can openers. And that's without mentioning those city-spanning lattices of high-voltage wiring that take away your freedom to walk the streets on stilts wearing a tall metal hat.

I walked through Holy Mother of God Square, straight down Christ on a Bike Avenue and wound up in front of the station. The Piazza Carlo Felice was peopled by madmen, winos and dozens of groups of smart old gents in hats and blazers playing games with cards that looked like Tarot rejects and generally shooting the breeze. At first I thought: How communal, how timeless, how totally unBritish. But then I saw a bloke who looked like the creepy granddad in the Werther's Original ad smarming all over a passing pair of females, and imagined his black-clad wife at home hand-crafting his tagliatelle, and I thought: Go home, you lazy, selfish bastards, go home and do some bloody washing up or something.

And then I thought: *Tagliatelle*, and realised I'd eaten nothing since the Savoy croissants, and ran straight into the first restaurant I found, which in a hilarious twist of fate turned out to be the canteen of an old people's home. But I had better luck in the more conventional establishment next door, where I had my first starter since Paris, my first actual bottle of wine since London, and my 3,412th pizza since the day before yesterday. And then my 3,413th, which made the hour-long uphill walk back through Turin's noisy and mobile Friday night rather an ordeal, causing me to pause, bloated and envious, while gorgeous, laughing couples traipsed carelessly across my path into bijou little courtyards and up to the bijou little bedrooms whose ceilings danced with candlelight.

The tent was awarded an honorary title that night, known henceforth as 'the bastard-arsed' tent. It had leaked rain from above and earth from below, leaving the inner seams of my sleeping bag, and so also my body, covered in muddy Rorschach-pattern motifs. I didn't use it again, though it continued to play an important role in my life as the major backseat prop in my 'the owner of this car is not rich but actually quite mad and a bit smelly' crime-prevention campaign.

As I drove out, curiosity triumphed over linguistic ineptitude and I asked the terribly grumpy campsite owner what had happened to the villa. Though clearly distracted by the Rolls's disfiguring streaks of wind-dried juvenile phlegm, he reluctantly answered. I didn't get it all, but I got enough. A Count, then the war, then the Nazis. Of course. Italy fought on both sides in the war, swiftly shifting allegiance in 1943 after the Allies invaded Sicily and Mussolini was ousted. The Nazis quickly moved into the north and you could just see them up here, jackboots on the balcony rail, staring down over Turin and cursing Benito for messing it all up. And after the war? '*Niente*.' Nothing. What a waste, I thought, but then as I drove around the neighbouring hills trying to get out of town I noted dozens of similarly abandoned mansions.

It's a clear case of heritage overload. I remembered visiting Pompeii a few years back and being astonished to find that over a third of the city hadn't yet been excavated. Here was a nation who'd had it all, not once but twice, masters of the ancient world for twelve centuries, and the cradle of the Renaissance for another three. Was it sad that they couldn't now either afford or be bothered to preserve these unique legacies? Or was their attitude healthily forward-looking, a refusal to dwell on past glories as Britain does? They had taught the world how to fight, and then how to paint, and now it was time for a fresh challenge. Just time for a quick coffee first. And maybe a bite of lunch. Actually, Rafaella's doing us veal tonight, and of course the next day is booked for swishing about town looking at ourselves in shop windows . . . shall we say day after tomorrow?

I had begun to notice that Italian roads, or at least the ones Coryate had chosen for me, were a bit on the small side. It was difficult to keep the daft bulk of the Rolls on one side of the white line, if there was one; once I parked at the head of a row of Fiats and it looked like a line of ducklings being led home by an ostrich. The driving habits didn't help, of course. I'd never driven in a country where they don't even let police cars out at junctions. I was tailgated with a diligence that discouraged both hesitation and deviation, helplessly bustled at speed past inviting town-centre cafés and other places of interest. In the end I just stuck the indicator on as a kind of advance booking of my intention to turn off at some point in the near future, even if – as at Vercelli – that meant having coffee in a bowling alley.

Bowling is both rather foolish and monumentally uncool, and it was typical of the Italians to transform it into a performing art. The only previous time I've been bowling it was like watching a humour-stripped episode of *The Simpsons*: fat, bald men with yellow skin and missing fingers. Vercelli's Saturday-morning line-up, however, was a study in graceful athleticism and handcrafted leather accessories. And they were so casually proficient, so negligently graceful, even when they weren't bowling. I drank my tiny espresso next to one of those amusement machines in which a handful of coins and two handles procures brief and fitful control over a chromed claw dangling above three feet of soft toys and cheap watches. I don't believe I have ever seen anyone successfully coax anything from such a machine, yet as I watched, a silver-haired cigarillo smoker flamboyantly extracted three Tweety Pies and a fag lighter for two eagerly demonstrative grandchildren in matching velvet coats.

It was all improbably sophisticated, and I remembered the introductory passage to my Michelin guide: 'In this land abounding in every type of beauty, the Italian lives and moves with perfect ease. Dark-haired, black-eyed, gesticulating, nimble and passionate, he is all movement, romance and fantasy.' Reading this hopeless bollocks in the café in Turin had caused the messy expulsion of half a mouthful of cappuccino froth, but now I saw that it was true, even in the unhelpful surroundings of an out-of-town bowling alley. Only then I went into the loo, where broken-hinged doors swung lopsidedly in front of a rank of unspeakably soiled porcelain footprints.

Nothing had changed. It was at Vercelli that Coryate describes his epoch-making encounters with the fork, explaining both how locals of all classes used this novel tool, and why: 'because the Italian cannot by any means indure to have his dish touched with fingers, seing all mens fingers are not alike cleane'. (Typically keen to attract attention, Coryate explains his intention to practise this fancy habit upon his return. He did so at every opportunity, and so earnt the nickname that Donald Grey had tried to remember in Odcombe: 'Furcifer' — a funny-at-the-time double meaning of fork-user and rascal. It was still 100 years, though, before forks were a common sight on English tables.) But then, seamlessly continuing from this account of Italian fastidiousness, he describes public defecation by women and children 'wearing breeches so made that all the hinder parts of their bodies are naked'.

Yesterday's fog was back, and I cannot pretend the drive along the ancient, dead straight, dead flat road that ferried me to Novara and thence the outskirts of Milan was anything other than authentically rural. The great fertile plain that stretched across most of northern Italy, from Piedmont to Lombardy, was Coryate's idea of heaven on earth: 'beautified with such abundance of goodly rivers, pleasant meadowes, fruitful vineyardes, fat pastures, delectable gardens, orchards, woodes and what not, that the first view thereof did even refocillate my spirits, and tickle my senses with inward joy'. Steady on, TC. Any more of this and he'd be leaping over the fence to get off with a cabbage. But it was all still there, somewhere out in the mist. Italy makes more wine than any other country, and is the world's top producer of oranges and lemons. I even drove across a load of paddy fields.

And in fairness, it wasn't just him. All the later Grand Tourists had been appalled and terrified by the mountains (Mont Blanc wasn't scaled until the end of the eighteenth century), just as they raved about the flat but fertile plain of Lombardy. 'Not a tree without a vine training upon it'; 'gardens of fig trees and pomegranates hanging over the walls' – in the pre-industrial age, unless a landscape was good enough to eat you quickly spat it out.

Milan is the second largest city in Italy and its commercial capital, facts that alerted me to the probability of starring in a more harrowing than usual episode of *Urban Traffic Hell Hotel Quest*. And a feature-length special it was, too: a quarter of a tank of petrol and the entire length of a radio-broadcast football game. Confounded once more by the dearth of city-centre hotels with car parks, I patrolled some arrestingly awful suburbs. The Rolls tailed a speeding funeral cortège down an endless avenue of Bronx tenements flanked by burnt-out cars; stopping at a red light in a lonely stand against the forces of anarchy, I watched a grinning urchin prop his scooter against my front wing, thumb the hearse as it jumped the next set of lights, then draw his finger across his throat with a wink. After this incident, and the acceptance that as the driver of a filthy Rolls-Royce I was poorly equipped to resist the advances of Squeegee merchants, I executed a tremendous *Dukes of Hazzard* U-turn, squealing over the tram tracks and not slowing down until I hit greenery.

Not being a man of the world, I didn't think there was anything odd about a sudden rash of motels in the middle of nowhere. Those two girls in short coats and long boots outside the first were probably just hitchhikers. That old feller who stopped and let one of them in was probably her uncle, and no doubt when they drove into the car park and her head disappeared from view it was because she'd dropped something in the footwell, although it can't have been very important because the longer it took her to find it the happier he . . . urgh. Well, I'm sorry. You really don't expect that sort of thing at 4.30 p.m. on a Saturday afternoon. Suddenly there were tarts everywhere, jiggling their hot-panted bottoms from bus shelters and pouting clumsily through the mist on every garage forecourt. It was horrible and depressing. Most of the girls had a stout, East-European look, each no doubt led to this foggy fate by a tragic trail of deception and exploitation. But it was the kerb crawlers – for once I was doing the impatient tailgating – who really got me. Smug men in big Alfas and BMWs, all like the bowling-alley crowd in immaculate weekend casualwear; politicians dressed for a populist wife-and-kids photo-shoot. You could just imagine the scenario: 'Just off to watch the football at Carlo's, *cara mia*,' and stopping off on the way home for a knee-trembler with some smack-raddled Albanian. It was like the bowling-alley loos, the filthy secret behind the veneer of sophistication.

It was almost dark before I found a tartless hotel, a Sixties low-rise that smelt of gravy and hamsters and overlooked six lanes of city-bound traffic. The grey-suited proprietor and his sidekick were elderly, straight-backed whisperers, attributes which in conjunction with their nationality made it impossible not to imagine two life-times spent honing a mastery of cold violence. They were a great double act. When I asked if the round-the-back parking space was safe, the boss took off his half-moon specs (gangland nickname: Il Professore) and delivered a minute, mirthless smile that said, 'Well, we haven't had any torchings.' Then his slightly taller number two, briefly controlling a theatrical cheek-twitch (Il Loco), raised an eyebrow: '. . . Yet.' Waiting for the lift, I idly opened the top drawer in a huge, neglected Scottish-castle sideboard. Inside it were several dozen pairs of talcum-powdered surgical gloves. I don't think I've drunk brandy at 5.30 before.

Beyond the opera, Milan didn't hold any great attraction for eighteenth-century Grand Tourists. 'Blackguard boys' blowing their noses in ladies' dresses, £25 to buy a carriage, three bob for a night on a bag of straw – all there seemed to be in the literature was a list of typical holiday grumbles. On this basis, I thought: a bit of a lie-in, then straight off down the SS9 towards Cremona. But I messed up bad.

The deciding Grand Prix of the season was being broadcast live from Japan, and during a homely but stilted discussion of Anglo-Italian sporting themes with a neighbouring couple at my Chinese restaurant the night before I had been advised to set my alarm for 4.45 a.m. As I was doing so, the TV screen had been filled with a big clock face, the sector between two and three shaded red. Of course – end of October, the clocks . . . change. How do they change, please? It's stupid, but I always forget. The TV clock beamed stupidly at me, flaunting its ambivalence. And the patronisingly deliberate voiceover was an unhelpful jumble of sounds I couldn't begin to make sense of, littered randomly with numerals that I just about could: 'De de de flada da da *two*; di di fladi de da *three*. Fla didida? *Two*, di da *three*.' In the end, on the basis that when you really want an extra hour's sleep you lose one, I put my clock forward. Consequences: long dawn hours spent watching women in bikinis bouncing on a trampoline while trying to catch fruit thrown at them by a hairy man in shorts; falling asleep, when the race had finally begun, between laps 10 and 42; rushing down, still clueless as to the hour, for a bleary, intimidating breakfast; emerging into a throat-filling fog at 10 a.m., but in fact 8 a.m. On a Sunday.

I'd been intending to head out of Milan, but the weather had taken me prisoner. The fog was the worst it had been, and while eating my shrink-wrapped croissant in the oppressively empty dining room under Il Professore's quietly repulsed gaze I'd noted through the window that the preferred motoring tactic for dealing with the conditions was raw speed. I suppose the justification is that accidents only happen when someone wimps out and slams on the brakes, but seeing this initiative embraced to the extent of shooting across the serried ranks of red lights at the junction opposite convinced me that I would let the side down. Instead I bought a bus ticket into town from a man selling pornographic comic books at a roadside booth.

The bus stop was in a fascinatingly awful backstreet parallel to the main road, a semi-industrial, semi-derelict assortment of failed and failing business ventures. It was the kind of place you only ever end up in when someone asks you to do something unusually manual, like having the office fire extinguishers recharged or dumping asbestos. For fifteen minutes it was just me, the cartoon-flat corpse of a rat and nervous, skeletal cats who covered open ground as if the area was overlooked by snipers. Then a squat housewife waddled out of the fog, looked in vain for a timetable on the bus stop, fixed me with an accusatory stare and waddled back from whence she came. After twenty minutes of aerosol-can football and mournful urban birdsong, I was joined by a sixteen-year-old with curdled skin and a hooded sweatshirt. He shivered unhappily, smoked as if he hated it and generally had the air of someone returning from a party at which he had been bullied by gatecrashers.

Half an hour later the bus rounded the corner, and as we rubbed our hands in anticipation of warmth I heard a baby crying. Jamming the wrong end of my ticket into the validating machine, I looked up at the abandoned low-rise offices opposite – boarded-up reception doors, a rotting sofa upside down in the car park – and saw a face peer down fleetingly from a glassless third-floor window.

In contrast to the scepticism of the later Grand Tour visitors, Coryate found Milan fascinating, writing more about it than any other city he'd visited yet. And it was all good stuff: I was delighted to learn that the city's name is a contraction of Mediolanum, 'half-woollen', after its early Roman founder chanced upon a sow, 'halfe her body covered with bristly haire as other Pigges are, and the other halfe with very soft white wooll'. (Interestingly, he interpreted this as a lucky omen; in today's less sentimental climate we'd be cordoning off the area and sending in the blokes with Geiger counters.)

I trusted Coryate's judgement on cathedrals, and having read that he found Milan's 'as faire or fairer than the Cathedral Church of Amiens' I walked up the stairs that connected the metro station to the cathedral square expecting a noble prospect.

What I didn't expect was that my almost dormant quest for cultural self-improvement would be rudely slapped awake by the abrupt and astonishing contrast between the smelly, knackered subway steps and the uniquely glorious structure spearing the heavens before me. I can't remember the last time I just stared at a building, open-mouthed, looking the definitive slack-jawed idiot tourist but being too captivated to care. While others progressed to a considered appreciation of perspective and proportion, my own artistic sensibilities have remained childishly base, with a particular weakness for enormity and lustre. Milan Cathedral's towering triangular façade, a fussy explosion of shiny white marble bristling with statuary, satisfied my tastes more than any other building I am likely to encounter until they commission a four-year-old girl to redecorate Canary Wharf.

But there was more than that, a surfeit of competing stimuli. It was almost too much; for a moment the scale and glory seemed to push me backwards, and I felt it would be easier to shield my bombarded senses by retreating back down into the metro. Almost forcing myself up into the piazza, I wondered if these novel, confusing sensations were the stirrings of a belated artistic awakening. Was this the defining moment that would elevate me to the ranks of those who stood staring at a single painting for hours on end with a sort of narcotic awe? Might the tears that would flow down my cheeks during a drawn-out operatic denouement now be inspired by joy and pathos rather than boredom or inappropriate mirth? Would I henceforth rank theatrical performances by subtlety of stagecraft and allegorical complexity rather than brevity or the number of times the actors tripped over the stage furniture? Had my Grand Tour finally begun?

It isn't every day you get to walk about on the roof of a cathedral, not unless you're a pigeon or the hunchback of Notre Dame. Coryate couldn't wait to climb up for a lusty overview of the goodly and faire plaine of Lombardy, and emerging from my cultural reverie,

I joined the growing Sunday-morning crowds – locals, mainly, at this time of year – trooping towards the tower entrance. In the narrow, damp-smelling spirals I suddenly felt an affinity with Coryate, surrounded by echoing wheezes which expanded my Italian vocabulary to include the phrase 'Fuck – I didn't know it was this tall.' There was plenty of ancient copperplate graffiti carved into the whitewashed walls, and I scanned it all, thinking how wonderful it would be to find a 'TC 1608', though at the same time knowing it wasn't his style. *Coryats Crudities* was to be his 'I woz 'ere' on a grander scale.

At the top, the scents were provided by wafts of incense coming up through the chimneys from the Mass below; the sounds by an unseen party of those flaming Chilean nose flautists playing the *Our Tune* theme down in the square. The sights were compromised by the mist, but it was oddly satisfying to be on a par with the surrounding multi-storeys as I stood on the roof of what was, by literal definition, a bungalow.

I couldn't quite believe that they would allow people free access to roam the marble-slabbed main roof at will, but as our panting, red-faced crocodile passed under another elaborate archway and rounded the corner, an astonishing scene greeted me. Children playing football, dogs fighting, extended families unpacking huge picnics – it was like an aerial stretch of the Copacabana. A number of people were on mobiles, and you could tell from the cheesy smirks that their conversations had begun, 'Hi, I'm on the church.' I was particularly curious about the number of deeply intertwined couples, which seemed a little odd when the people slightly further away from God below us were being asked to cover their bare shoulders and refrain from using flash photography.

It was a busy day. While having a coffee at McDonald's (the swish places in the arcade by the cathedral were all full of benignly confused Japanese tourists wearing '13 trillion lire for a Coke – is that a lot?' faces), I got out the Michelin guide and marked its town-centre map with all the places T.C. had visited. He arrived on horseback at 11 a.m. on 15 June, a Wednesday, and left at 2 p.m. the next day. In this short time, he visited three churches, a library, the palace, the fortress, a hospital and a monastery. And these were no whistle-stop, been-there-done-that flying visits. He would always try to seek out a monk or curator to give him a conducted tour in Latin, and if that failed (as it usually did) he occupied himself by copying down inscriptions or pacing out the buildings' dimensions. It was everything the later Grand Tourists were supposed to do but generally couldn't be arsed with.

In the fortress, he even dabbled in a little light espionage, or maybe just heavy stupidity, striding about with his notebook and making a detailed inventory of the garrison and its weaponry. I walked up the via Dante, repelling the attentions of street vendors offering to paint my name in Chinese or have it ironed on the back of an outrageously blatant fake football shirt. At the end, in a pool of sun, squatted the fortress, its vast, thick walls a study in oppression. What can Coryate have been thinking of? As I was discovering, seventeenth-century Europe was a long and very fluid game of Risk, and in 1608, Milan found itself under Spanish rule. The Milanese hated their overlords with a passion that confined the Spaniards to the citadel, an admittedly huge fortress with its own wells and three years' supply of food. Consequently, most of its big guns were trained on the city to discourage insurrection, and the atmosphere was unbearably tense. Furthermore, Spain was also dealing with a rebellion in the Spanish Netherlands (following a short break when one of the dice rolled off the board), and Coryate, with his grubby doublet and hose and funny North European tones, had a touch of the Dutch about him. So, as he paces about sticking his head down cannon barrels, 'a certain Spaniard, imagining that I had been a Flemming, expressed many tokens of anger towards me, and lastly railed so extremely at me, that if I had not made haste out with my company, I was afeard he would have flung a stone at my head'. And the rest. Honestly.

Inside the citadel's Wembley-sized first courtyard, I sat on a lump of Roman masonry jettisoned randomly on to the grass with the 'there you go, mate' nonchalance of Italian heritage management. Metro trains rumbled under my feet, the sun came out properly and I thumbed through a multilingual guide to the castle someone had dumped in the bin next to me. It was one of those last-updated-in-1959 jobs, with overcoloured photos of Albert Camus and a woman in capri pants parking their Model-T Fiat outside the west tower, but I read it anyway, curious as to how the hated fortress had survived almost unscathed. It was, of course, because the Milanese were, in the final analysis, Italian: 'A raging crowd wished to destroy the castle, but after finding such a destructional undertaking excessive, abandoned this task.'

One of the central halls housed a museum of sculpture, and on the grounds that it was free and boasted Michelangelo's last work, I popped in. Of all the arts, sculpture impresses me the most in the simplistic 'Bloody hell, imagine being able to do that' sense that underpins my critical faculties. Give me a couple of years and I could probably knock out a passable Old Master sketch (on tracing paper). But up on the cathedral roof I'd marvelled at the thousands of beautifully formed marble pinnacles and finials or whatever, knowing that given a chisel, a quarry and twenty lifetimes all I'd produce would be a mountain of bloody shards and a Neanderthal hand axe. Unfortunately, Michelangelo's last work was unfinished, barely started in fact, and I felt the surge of artistic awe that had knocked me flat outside the cathedral ebbing away. Looking at the four-deep crowd gaping at those crude, clay-like limbs, I felt scorn rather than empathy. These were the sort who'd queue up to see a bank statement that Picasso's dad almost doodled on or a flask of Verdi's penultimate expectoration.

It was almost hot now, and the sun revealed that most of Milan was covered in a considerable layer of filth. I read later that the city is one of the last in Western Europe that still pumps raw sewage straight into its rivers. Isn't that disgusting? And it's also the most smog-ridden, in a country where fifteen thousand die every year from pollution-related illnesses. Had I known this, I might have thought twice about helping two girls push-start their Renault Twingo down the via Carducci. In giving assistance I coated both palms in oily soot, which wouldn't have been so awful if I'd noticed this prior to wiping the resultant sweat off my cheeks and forehead.

I was a mess before, and now I was a shambles. Refined during the paranoid aftermath of the tarts, vermin and Il Loco, my campaign to deter criminal curiosity had got out of hand. Even the Monoprix plastic bag had gone, deemed too invitingly Gallic and so vulnerable to Vespa-mounted snatch gangs. Instead, I had transferred books, food and rubbish to the cylindrical holdall the tent had come in. This, I now accepted, was the product of a fear too far. On its purple flanks was emblazoned the slogan 'EUROHIKE BACKPACKER', and try as I might I could think of no two words in polite usage more likely to identify the bearer as a risible irrelevance. And worse, this legend appeared on all four sides, ensuring 360-degree coverage of my unattractive personality: 'Friendless Bore approaching'; 'Pitiful Smelly alongside'.

What made this all the more trying was the languid elegance of the locals. Milan is Italy's wealthiest city, and the dress code was even more oppressively stylish than normal. I suppose it's a state of mind as much as anything. Time and again I was eased into the gutter by families on a Sunday stroll, filling the pavement with proprietorial ease. It was arrogant, but done with such cocksure, sharp-creased panache that you could only stand in the fag-ends and filth and admire. This was their manor, and they were walking the walk and talking the talk. Urban Italians just have a way with them that allows unlikely sartorial combinations to succeed handsomely. Give a pair of British men hairgel, shades and two-wheeled transport and what do you get? Gazza and Chris Evans on a tandem.

The shadows were lengthening; I quickened my stride. The Ambrosian Library – now Italy's oldest public library – was just being finished when Coryate was there, and though it was closed I saw a little plaque commemorating the first book being placed on its shelves on 30 August 1609. I felt like sending Tommy a postcard to let him know. Then it was off to St Ambrose's church, where I joined an eager queue of schoolchildren queuing up to see St Ambrose's 1,600-year-old corpse. Now that I've mentioned his name three times I'm obliged to explain that he was the Bishop of Milan, a man whose gift of persuasive speech apparently worked such wonders that as a symbol of religious eloquence his name was given to a brand of creamed rice.

It was interesting to think that 'Ambro' was already almost 1,300 when Coryate visited the crypt and saw his body 'supported with foure iron chaines'. They're gone now, but he's got a couple of mates, St Gervase and St Protase, lying in the silver- and bronze-medal positions either side of him like the podium at a fancy-dress luge championship. It was slightly odd, staring at these three cassock-robed skeletons amid the squeaks of delighted disgust emitted by a youthful crowd still on a post-Hallowe'en high. I suppose even Coryate, never one to miss a corpse, had been driven here by a similar impulse. I know I had. It was becoming clear that my flirtation with connoisseurship at the cathedral had been a false dawn; here, gloating at stiffs, I was back where I belonged. Sixteen hundred years the old feller had been here – that's a lying-in-state which ran and ran, a particularly fine achievement given that the first few months would have been a pretty tough act to sell.

Coryate would certainly have appreciated the neglected outdoor display I blundered across just round the corner. The Museum of Martyrdom and Torture – there's nothing like setting your stall out – was just a big hole in the ground littered with large bits of old wood. But a series of little plastic notices around the fence above revealed that this was the site of the old civic gallows, and identified the exhibits below as seventeenth-century instruments of execution. I've mentioned Coryate's persistent fascination with faire and goodly scaffoldes and the Continental habit of breaking people upon a wheel, but the author of the notices proved himself an even more gleeful torture buff.

'"The modern image industry portrays the stocks in humorous colours, centred on a grumpy victim being benevolently cajoled by his rough-and-tumble neighbours. The reality was somewhat different. Excrement was often rubbed into . . ." Oh, gross, gross, *gross!*' An American girl was reading aloud to her friend, who stood with a hand-covered mouth as her own wide eyes scanned another notice above the wheel. Soon they both departed, pale, drawn and quartered.

I rushed eagerly to the sign. 'This wheel is from a private collection in Germany . . .' A *what*? I felt better. My interest might be unwholesome, but at least I didn't have a forest of lovingly restored gibbets in the garden. The apparatus itself was unassuming – a cart-wheel mounted flat on a low spindle, as might be a table in a beer garden. I knew from Coryate that the process involved lashing the spread-eagled wrongdoer to the wheel and shattering the limbs with iron bars, which I suppose to some is already Too Much Information. If you don't want to know the result of the Tooled-Up Mob versus Pinioned Victim match, please look away now.

'The effect of the punishments meted out', I read, 'is best described in this seventeenth-century account: "The victim is transformed into a sort of huge, screaming puppet writhing in rivulets of blood, a puppet with four tentacles, like a sea monster of raw, slimy and shapeless flesh mixed up with splinters of smashed bones. The crows then peck out the eyes . . ."'

And remember, this was considered family entertainment until 1750. No Grand Tour was complete without experiencing a Continental execution, 'altogether more impressive', wrote Byron, 'than . . . the English sentence'. In Venice, Fynes Moryson saw two youths having their tongues, hands and finally heads hewn off for singing blasphemous songs; in the same city, William Lithgow watched a monk being burnt alive for 'begetting young Noble nuns with child'. 'I sprang forward through the throng,' he recounts eagerly, 'and came just to the pillar as half of his body and right arm fell in the fire.'

Failing an execution, there were plenty of exotic tortures and punishments. In Paris, John Evelyn watched two buckets of water being funnelled down the gullet of a suspected robber; an eighteenth-century tourist in Rome saw a criminal being tied face down on a trestle and beaten with a bull's penis.

Life was no picnic in those days. Except for the crows, obviously.

The narrower alleys were getting dark, and like a good little tourist I rushed along the dusty pavements back to the cathedral for the recommended sunset view of its façade. On the way I stopped at a supermarket, and down in the food hall had a rather awkward encounter with an inept shoplifter who met my curious gaze as he shoved a packet of Gillette Mach 3 razors ('The Best a Man Can Nick') into his voluminous puffa jacket. I also noted, with historical double-take, the disposable plastic gloves by the fruit and veg display. Everyone wore a pair as they poked the pears or fondled the fennel, and I found myself reminded of Coryate's explanation of fork usage: 'because the Italian cannot by any means indure to have his dish touched with fingers, seing all mens fingers are not alike cleane'. During the ongoing research for my pan-European survey of McDonald's lavatories, I'd found that Italian branches don't have taps but foot-pumps – again, because all mens fingers are not alike cleane. But remembering the bowling-alley loos, and looking at my own Twingo-tarnished digits, that was only half right. In Italy, all mens fingers are not alike cleane, but they are alike filthie.

In the sunset, the cathedral's mad forest of statuary glowed faintly with a Ready Brek inner warmth. The square was astir with promenading locals and Lazio fans, celebrating their last-minute equaliser in yesterday's big match with Inter Milan by cheekily waving their scarves in front of the cathedral like conquering (or anyway last-minute-equalising) heroes. Two or three old blokes were strolling about with caged cockatoos and canaries – not selling them, as I first thought, but just showing off their pets with quiet pride. Everyone else was here *en famille*, and I guessed the old men were widowers, the canaries standing in for their old birds and the children who had flown the nest. It was sad, but it was also touching, and ninety minutes later I greeted Il Professore with a new fondness.

It didn't last. After a series of diagrams – he seemed to take especial satisfaction in crossing out my room number with a deep, bold X – I gathered that I had been moved to a room on the first floor. Was it the air conditioning? A little snort of private amusement. 'No.'

It had not been difficult to conclude from the unbroken ranks of keys behind Il Professore, the clock-ticking silence of the corridors and the well-stocked insect cemetery on my bathroom shelf that I was his establishment's first guest since 1979. There could be no justification for the move – Il Professore clearly just wanted to keep me on my toes. Though, as I was soon to discover, the opportunity of heaving three radiators' worth of humid clothing on to a bed carefully positioned in a flashing triangle of green neon cast by the HOTEL sign outside the window may also have appealed.

The Chinese I'd eaten at the night before was closed, and the only alternative was a takeaway pizza. With a boxed Napoletana smoking in my palms I set off back across the lonely, pedestrian-hostile arterial-road obstacle course, leaping over puddles and road-kill, setting off security lights and getting drizzled on. Presently I noted I had a problem. The exuberant use of anchovies makes the Napoletana one of the more fragrant of the pizza family, and as I shuffled through a particularly deep moraine of urban garbage I almost kicked a rat, head raised, sniffing the air with twitchy antici-pation. I yelped – a schoolgirl squeak – and suddenly the night was full of scuttles and anchovy steam. Something soft yielded pulpily beneath my right foot, and casting the worst possible interpretation on this multi-sensory experience I retched briefly and broke into a messy run.

It was only as I neared the hotel that I grasped the logistical awkwardness of smuggling a hot square the size of a boxed set of LPs past a disapproving psychopath. As the green neon sign flashed above, I unzipped my anorak, pressed the pizza flat to my chest, rezipped and strode in.

My plan had been based on an analysis of previous encounters with Il Professore, cameos of malice that were intense but always brief. I would ask for my key; he would garrotte me with his eyes and slide it slowly across the desk like a suspicious croupier; I would take it with a small appeasing smile before going over to the ancient lift, waiting long seconds while he riddled my back with imaginary small-arms fire.

Maybe he could smell my fear; maybe just the anchovies. Whatever the reason, Il Professore's game plan was to be very different that night. There would be small talk, winks, a little body contact – a veritable festival of false bonhomie.

'*Buona sera*,' he said, brushing off an immaculate grey lapel with little backhand flicks. I reciprocated the greeting, and asked for my key. The pizza had been pleasantly warm outside, but now my chest was feeling uncomfortably humid, and I recoiled slightly from the wafts of hot anchovy emerging from the neckband. He turned as if to take the key from the rack, paused, then turned back. '*Il Gran Premio*,' he said, with a deliberation that signified this as the introduction to a long speech. *Gran Premio*, I knew, meant Grand Prix, but within seconds I was lost in a pile-up of Akkinens, Earvines and Damon Ills. The first rivulet of sweat ran from temple to jaw to chin; my torso throbbed; I swayed slightly on my feet. Now he was asking me questions – 'Ferrari? McLaren?' – which seemed to inquire into my allegiance. Ferrari is worshipped in Italy – during my abortive televisual vigil I had watched coverage of 50,000 fans assembled outside the team's Modena HQ to celebrate an expected victory in the drivers' championship. But it had all gone wrong, McLaren's Mika Hakkinen leading the race from start to finish and so, to my considerable satisfaction, making Michael Schumacher and those assembled 50,000 very unhappy.

'Ferrari,' I said dreamily, glancing down to see a translucent oily line soaking through my anorak from the bottom of the pizza box. He gave a thoughtful little nod, and followed this with a studied appraisal of my flat-fronted silhouette, deciding whether I was wearing cumbersome body armour or had simply forgotten to chew those paving slabs.

'No,' he said, cheerfully, 'no Ferrari.' Battling against heatstroke, I desperately marshalled my muddy thoughts. How should one exhibit protesting disbelief? He smiled as I delivered possibly appropriate gestures and sweat-bathed facial contortions. Then, for the first and only time, he spoke English. 'No Ferrari. I ear you. Dis morning. Schumacher do bad start – and you luff a leedle. Ha . . . Ha. Akkinen win, and *big* luff now, Ha, Ha, Ha.' It was a long time since I'd seen anyone so sour faced suddenly look so pleased with themselves. Had I really been relocated to the first floor to satisfy this bad man's lust for eavesdropping? But there was nothing to say. I held out a feverish hand and pointed wordlessly to my key; with a huge, toothy grin he snatched it from the rack, pressing it into my hand with both of his. Tightening his grip to drunk-uncle level, he pulled me slightly towards the desk, craned his thin neck forward and unleashed a horrible little burst of Hannibal Lecter air-sniffing snuffles. With his wide-eyed face very close to mine – I had a sudden, chilling image of Iggy Pop in twenty years' time – he whispered, '*Buon appetito,*' and abruptly released me with a happy sigh.

At some point in the night someone noiselessly slipped a laminated notice under my door warning against the use of spirit lamps and chafing dishes in the rooms.

✦　✦　✦

I didn't bother with breakfast, and managed to avoid the goodfellas by concluding my business with a portly simpleton in an almost edibly stained lounge suit who had obviously sustained head injuries during a bungled bank job. He smiled beatifically while I piled the desk with banknotes, before handing over a hand-typed bill that looked more like a set of wartime call-up papers. At least there was no charge for damage to the exterior paintwork caused by burning pizza boxes on the balcony, though this may have been because the bill was actually addressed to a man with a French name who had checked out two weeks before.

A tree had shed yellow powder and catkins all over the Rolls, the finishing touches to a picture of neglect. I opened the bonnet to check fluids, staring as ever at the huge pieces of machinery like a first-term veterinary student being asked to operate on a whale, then draped more wet clothes over the seat backs and fired it up. As I rumbled out into the frenzy-filled fog, I suddenly knew that I could not drive this car through another Italian city.

Depressed? Run down? Banish the blues with Two Coffees in a Town With A Funny Name. Pizzeghettone is a small, unassuming place, not even warranting a mention in the Michelin guide, but it was exactly the kind of quiet, timeless town that helped soothe away the road rage with evocative placidity. Coryate rode into Pizzeghettone similarly fraught – arriving late at Lodi the evening before, he found the town gates locked and had been obliged to sleep in the coach he had travelled in.

I parked the Rolls and crossed the excitable River Adda on a bridge crowded with promenading families in their – just a minute – Monday best. Most of the places I'd driven through had been similarly peopled, and as I walked through Pizzeghettone's impressively preserved town walls I beheld a little funfair and an atmosphere of muted celebration. Coryate had been taken in by a local scholar: 'he gave me a cup of very neate wine and used me exceeding kindly' (yes, I was having my suspicions as well).

It was here he made his second contribution to modern British life. The fork business was all well and good, but it is difficult to imagine that without Coryate, we would still be maintaining a lonely – and certainly rather messy – stand against The Third Utensil. The original owner of my Rolls would have seen cutlery profits cut by 33 per cent, and in consequence I'd have arrived in Pizzeghettone at the wheel of his old Ford Granada Ghia. But if Coryate had not reported the number of Pizzeghettonese protecting themselves from the elements with sticks topped by 'something answerable to the forme of a little cannopy, and hooped in the inside with diverse little wooden hoopes', and had not decided to adapt the local term for them, we would not now be walking around under 'umbrellas'. No matter that Coryate's Italians used them as parasols, nor indeed that umbrellas only became widely used in Britain 200 years later; the deed was done. It is my man's word, and sitting in a highly chromed café being served my second double espresso by a man in a blazer, I felt proud on his behalf.

Four men standing by the bar were hunched silently over the pink front page of *La Gazzetto dello Sport*, one of Italy's two sporting dailies. Peering circumspectly at their faces as I placed my empty cup at the other end of the bar, I beheld a scene of shared, yet private grief. All were dumbstruck with pain and sorrow, shaking their heads palely and generally looking as if they were reading their own obituaries in an early edition of tomorrow's paper. One suddenly stood bolt upright, drained a liqueur the exact colour of the pee of fear and banged through the café's polished doors with the robotic determination of a man bent on some act of self-destructive insanity.

As I walked out, I stole a glance at their paper: a picture of Mika Hakkinen holding a trophy aloft and a snatch of a great, stark headline along the lines of 'WE LOST – WE BLOODY FUCKING LOST'. They take bad things badly here. But at the same time they take good things well: I was in Italy during the 1990 World Cup, and every time the home nation got a result – even if it was 1–0 against Austria – the streets were astir with cheering mobs and motorists standing up through their sun roofs waving 12-foot tricolores with their feet jammed on the horn.

Pizzeghettone was a homely place where you could hope to share the good things and the bad things. I saw now that my glee at Ferrari's defeat was a product of big-city alienation, a riposte to the overwhelming unfriendliness of Milan's dirty, wide streets. This cosy little town – less crime, more appropriate ambience, healthier rats – was the kind of place I should have been staying, living among the locals and learning their ways.

And only an hour later I was in Cremona, standing in front of the tallest church tower in Italy, surveying a small piazza of humbling perfection and wondering whether I shouldn't just stay for lunch, but sell the Rolls and move here for good.

Entranced by the wealthy old dears cycling about with dogs in their front baskets, by the shouts of children echoing off the ancient, crest-decorated vaults of the Palazzo Comunale, by the funny-faced marble lions roaring comically at me from the base of the cathedral's columns, I did the unthinkable: I went towards the flashest-looking café in the square, sat down at an outside table and ordered a large beer. Up one road stretched a row of fancy delicatessens with eat-me window displays, up another were stately, ancient colonnades propping up terracotta and ochre townhouses with balconies you wanted to spend whole holidays staring from.

Coryate loved the place too. 'Beautifull . . . stately . . . sumptuous' – he even raved about the deep-fried frogs, 'so curiously dressed, that they did exceedingly delighteth my palat, the head and the forepart being cut off'. Sharing my enthusiasm for size, he recounts how one can see Milan, 'a full fiftie miles off', from the lofty church tower, along with a nice little aside about the governor of Cremona leading Pope John XXII up to the top with the intention of shoving him off, but bottling out at the last minute.

'An from datoppadatower iss possible on clear dace to see Milano.' A passing guide repeated Coryate's claim to a small party of Oriental businessmen, none of whom seemed unhappy at their obvious inability to understand a word of English, nor indeed of what he was saying. On this basis, I saw no problem in beckoning him to the table in my native tongue – which I accept must have seemed intolerably rude – and asking why Monday had become Sunday. As in Pizzeghettone, the townsfolk were strolling about looking in the windows of closed shops, only here they were dolled up to the tens – it was clearly some sort of public vacation, but I knew if I'd attempted to translate that phrase while questioning an Italian, I'd have ended up asking him to go on holiday with me. 'All Saint Day,' he explained with more courtesy than the scenario warranted. 'Everyjuan go to *cimitero*, see dead muttair or fartair, den . . . av good times!'

I'd parked the car down the Corso Garibaldi, and walked back to it past glitzy, marbled shops and two buskers playing an oddly successful flamenco version of 'I Will Survive'. Though Coryate doesn't mention it, in 1608 Cremona was already a centre for musical instrument manufacturing, establishing a tradition that reached its zenith when local boy Stradivarius redefined the art of violin-making in the late seventeenth century. This was a fine place, with fine history and fine people. Milan now seemed huge and filthy and scary, and Pizzeghettone embarrassingly parochial. The car in front of the Rolls was a pampered old Mercedes with a for-sale notice on the dashboard, and with a jolt I recalled being briefly startled by seeing a car similarly advertised in Milan: surely people didn't *buy* cars in Milan, they just walked about, found one they liked the look of and shoved it down their puffa jackets. Feeling a surge of affection for the cultured, prosperous tranquillity around me, I unleashed a quick Knack-inspired chorus of 'M-m-m-m-m-m-m-m-my Cremona'.

My faith in human nature had been restored. An unshaven man of about my age in cords and a tweed jacket was pacing around the Rolls: the day before I'd have thought, Got you, you thieving little pimp, but now I greeted him with a proud smile. Which was just as well, as he was an Englishman who lived in Cremona making violin bows.

Paul Sadka was as glad to meet me as I was to meet him, although being English we didn't actually exchange names until we had ingested two coffees and a huge pizza each (I'm still appalled by his revelation that to an Italian, pizza is just a light starter). He had been in Cremona for five years, and now shared a flat with a local girl and a workshop with a German violin-maker. Before coming here he'd been a photographer and a cellist, giving that up when he accepted he lacked the application to make it to the very top. (I'm still not sure what attracted him to the idea of making bows. I expect he had a dream in which his fingers grew into great long ebony sticks and started scything across his rosined throat tendons.)

Out in the cathedral square, he began explaining how Cremona came to be the cradle of bow-making. Repeated contact with this latter word was now mercifully reducing its comic effect. Aside from a general aura of improbability, it also recalled a label below an obscure little doorbell that had enlivened my journeys to and from the Soho offices of *Esquire* magazine during my period of employment there. 'BOW REHAIRER', that had read, a legend that in conjunction with its location suggested any number of euphemisms. 'Actually, rehairing is a nice little scam,' said Paul as he waved to a fellow craftsman, one of the two hundred-odd bow- or violin-makers resident in the town. 'Twenty minutes' work, sod-all for the materials, and you can get away with charging £45.' Perhaps Soho was just the right place for it. 'See that guy?' Paul indicated a tall Oriental strolling across the road. 'He imports all the horsehair we use. Comes from Mongolia – that's the only place where the mares don't ruin their tail hair by pissing on it or thrashing it against rocks. Three hundred quid a kilo.'

Paul invited me back to his town-centre flat for a beer, and at his request we drove the negligible distance there in the Rolls. 'Well, this is nice,' he said bravely, as I scooped a mountain of post-prandial detritus off the passenger seat. 'A real Cremona car.'

'It is?'

'Richest city in Italy . . . you see that?' As I reversed into a parking space that shared with most of those in Europe the distinction of not being quite large enough for the Rolls, a passing couple rushed up to mouth kind-but-pointless left-hand-downs and bags-of-room-on-my-sides. 'They're just doing that because they respect and admire wealth.'

'But I haven't got any wealth,' I said slightly too quickly, still in the my-old-man's-a-dustman defensive mode.

'Well, it's a Rolls . . . They're obsessed with labels here – Max Mara, Dolce & Gabbana. A friend of mine was actually taken aside and told that unless he smartened himself up a bit he wouldn't be socially accepted.'

It was reassuring to note from Paul's comfortable appearance that he had resisted any such pressure. Indeed, as became obvious as we sipped Peroni in his quiet, courtyarded flat, he had embarked on a counter-offensive. With a wounded bitterness fuelled by five years of expatriation, this mild fellow began to fulminate against the arrogance, shallowness and hypocrisy of Italians in general and the Cremonese in particular. A suspect record on racial tolerance and women's rights; civil servants who work six-hour days and retire at forty-five; the way in which groups of men visit prostitutes as casually as their English counterparts might go out for a drink; a refusal to accept any blame for starting the war or – ta-da! – to credit anyone but the Americans for ending it. 'I don't even bother putting on an Italian accent when I talk any more. I didn't want people thinking I was a local. Apparently I now sound just like the actor who dubbed Stan Laurel into Italian.'

I could vouch for many of his grievances – attempting to dictate a statement to the police at Venice Station after that semi-naked encounter with a train robber, I was repeatedly interrupted by a female sergeant who insisted that the felon be referred to throughout as 'the Arab', despite my protests that the only clear view I'd had was of his rapidly disappearing back. But didn't he have anything good to say about the people? Paul thought, perhaps pondering his romantic attachment to an Italian girl whose property-developer father owned the bricks and mortar currently enclosing us. 'They know how to enjoy life,' he conceded reluctantly.

Then he set off for a fencing class, leaving me four hours to survey Cremona's affluent suburbs, more than long enough to realise that outside the cathedral square it wasn't actually at all exciting. The best you could say of the suburbs were that they were clean – the only animal remains I saw were those of a large rodent later identified by Paul as a coypu. But better that than dogpu. At the end of a long road lined with bland executive homes was an empty, floodlit pitch, and I remembered that the former Chelsea manager Gianluca Vialli had begun his illustrious footballing career here. It was typical of the place that its most famous sporting son should have been born into wealth and privilege – his father was a million-aire businessman – rather than being rescued from the slums in the usual fashion.

So back I wandered to the cathedral, its appealing blend of Romanesque might and Renaissance delicacy flattened against the dark sky by reckless sodium illumination. I sat down at the same outside table – my table – and had another long beer (only two quid, in fact, with free peanuts). And soon they returned, this time in their noisy thousands, the fur-coated, designer-labelled chattering classes, all mouth and trousers.

I saw now that part of my fascination with Milan Cathedral was the almost incredible truth that it had been created by the ances-tors of those slightly dotty old bird-men and raucous scarf-wavers parading incongruously around in front of it. My wife had experi-enced a similar sensation during her own teenage Continental tour, standing before the majestic Duomo in Florence while having her hindquarters manually surveyed by youths whispering unimagina-tive sexual compliments. Here, though, it was different. It was only too easy to imagine the forefathers of Cremona's well-shod, animated masses designing and financing these splendid surroundings.

I had been wondering what the back-home equivalent of Cremona would be – possibly somewhere twee and wealthy in the Home Counties, possibly somewhere naff and wealthy in Cheshire – but now I saw that I was wasting my time. The slightly depressing truth was that such a scene would be totally alien anywhere in

Britain, both in terms of stage and actors. I suppose the embarrassing superiority of Italian city architecture over its British equivalent could be excused in historical terms: Italy, having built its cities during the elegant Renaissance, had subsequently lacked both the wealth and gumption to redevelop the centres; most British cities were of more stolid Victorian design, but even that had since been energetically ruined during the nation's brief resurgence in the Fifties and Sixties.

The sociological rationale behind the differing characteristics of our urban populations was more uncomfortable. Large throngs did indeed invade English town centres after dark, but such gatherings could rarely be described as family occasions and tended to involve arrests. On the face of it, admittedly, trooping around the streets with your kids and great aunts on a cold November night looking in darkened shop windows had little to recommend it, but Paul had been right. An ice cream, a roasted chestnut, a tourist spilling beer on his guidebooks – it didn't take much to make them happy, to get their arms waving about in the cold night with expressive exuberance. This was life, and they knew how to enjoy it.

And they knew how to enjoy death, too. Paul had told me the 387-foot tower was a beacon to Italy's suicidal depressives, who arrived here from all over the country for a glorious farewell. The café nearest the tower had recently had to reposition its concrete plant tubs after a jumper landed neatly into one, showering afternoon drinkers with earth and petals and getting himself so immovably wedged that they had to carry his compressed remains away in it like an ersatz sarcophagus.

I met Paul at his workshop, at the edge of the centre in a dark, haunted road beside an army barracks. The sight of lathes and saws and curly wood shavings was a relief, because during my extended wanderings I had allowed myself to entertain suspicions that everything – his improbable job, his absent girlfriend, his globe-trotting CV – was the wild fantasy of a man bent on dining off choice cuts from my expertly dissected corpse.

Paul welcomed me in, then sat down at a workbench appealingly littered with half-finished bows, tiny little clamps and tools, spirit lamps and other anachronistic paraphernalia that irresistibly smacked of guilds and apprenticeships and all things seventeenth century. Then he talked. 'The bow-maker is not a craftsman; he is a poet, a preacher, an alchemist who turns wood into dreams' might have been the start to the sort of pompously earnest lecture I feared, but bore no relation to the swashbuckling exposé of bribery, theft and fraud that Paul now delivered. Our Englishmen-abroad encounter had been very Grand Tourish, and now I felt I was at last acquiring the sort of knowledge appropriate for a young man sent to the Continent to broaden his horizons.

To make a bow requires one not only to develop expertise working with silver, ebony, ivory and a Brazilian hardwood called pernambuco, but to develop expertise in procuring such valuable, obscure and often fiercely protected materials. The silver is straightforward enough, the ebony slightly less so, but once you get to the ivory and pernambuco you're dealing with smugglers and crime syndicates and it's all ludicrously far removed from whatever concept you might have had of violin bow-making. To get round the ivory problem, Paul now uses mammoth tusk. That's right – big hairy elephant, frozen in Siberian permafrost. Each of the tiny decorative slivers he needs costs him about a fiver, and he calculates that anyone digging up a tusk in the tundra is looking at fifty grand plus. And the pernambuco is no less awkward – that's supposedly a protected Brazilian hardwood tree, but shifty gold-toothed dealers in Rio can sort you out. Apparently they once used the stuff for railway sleepers, and Paul's fantasy is to follow an old Amazonian branch line until he finds one, smuggle it back (bit of work needed on this part of the plan) and be set up for life.

And of course the actual workmanship stuff was wonderfully impressive, a multi-material combination of impossible dexterity that made my admiration for the Milanese roof-sculptors seem one-dimensional. Each bow takes him a week; he sells them for £750 to a dealer; the dealer sells them to the violinists for twice that. But even when they're finished the skulduggery continues – fakes are now coming on to the market, and his German workshop-partner had recently heard that two Albanians had been arrested in Bologna trying to sell a pair of violins stolen from this very studio.

We had a Chinese takeaway – you may or may not be interested to learn that '*flitto misto*' is Italy's entry in the international Flied Lice joke contest – and then went out again, to a pub-like *hostelleria* where we sat at a huge, knackered table and listened to an over-confident pianist batter out rabble-rousing versions of 'You Are The Sunshine Of My Life', 'Moon River' and other terrace anthems. Paul had already asked if I wanted a bed for the night, and after a further beer each back at his flat he unfolded a guest mattress and throttled me with a skipping rope.

I'm sorry. In truth, as the evening drew to its close the trepidation in his eyes was slightly the greater, and I realised that my story was infinitely the more dubious. I still looked and felt daftly out of place in the Rolls; given the choice, more people would vote for 'grubby little thief on the run' than 'traveller following seventeenth-century cheapskate in unsuitably grand manner'. Each morning when I put the key in the driver's door I half expected passers-by to intervene spontaneously and prevent me from continuing.

But we got through the night okay, neither of us doing things the other feared, like making a clumsy pass or pooing in the fridge. His girlfriend was up north and returning today; we watched *Pingu* on a portable telly and went out for a farewell breakfast.

'"Thirty-six die in day of road carnage,"' he read from a neighbouring paper, brushing apricot-filled croissant flakes from his stubble.

'In one day?' I asked, incredulously.

'Public holiday – everyone rushing about to visit their dead relatives,' said Paul, 'and then joining them.'

The fog was thicker than ever – an almost permanent feature of November, apparently – and this wasn't what I wanted to hear. Nor was Paul's account of the local fondness for overtaking you while you were overtaking someone else, or the indulgent attitude to drinkdriving. Did you know it wasn't actually illegal to drive drunk in Italy until 1990? You could have four bottles of Chianti and get in trouble only if you then did something dangerous behind the wheel, like being overtaken or swerving to avoid a coypu. They only changed the law for the World Cup after pressure from abroad, and you can still buy booze at most petrol stations. A few even have bars, so you can get tanked up while you tank up.

In putting self-image above self-preservation, Italians defy the best efforts of road-safety campaigners. Theirs is the only country in Europe where the death rate on the roads is actually rising. For a driver to wear a seatbelt is an effete admission of vulnerability: Paul said he had often been in cars where fellow passengers had prevailed upon the driver to unbuckle. The use of mirrors or brakes while parking is considered hilariously quaint: in a recent survey, four out of five cars in Italian city centres were found to display recent accident damage. And I still can't quite believe that you aren't required to wear a crash helmet on mopeds, scooters and small motorbikes

– no wonder the death rate on Italian roads is three times that of London's. I watched a football game on telly where all the players came on to the pitch wearing crash helmets as a publicity drive to stop Italian teenagers trusting to the impact-absorbing qualities of even quite thick layers of styling mousse. But why don't they just change the bloody law? I bet Italian kids learning to ride pushbikes get their parents to fit destabilisers.

Paying for breakfast was the least I could do, and I did it. We stood outside the café; Paul sniffed the fog. 'I don't know,' he said, with a jaded look at the Renaissance loveliness around us. 'Think I'll try Paris next.' And with that, and an exchange of two thank-yous for a good luck, we parted.

Again the trees were lopped off by the mist, and the windscreen was opaque with catkin smears. The driving was as scary as I'd feared – Paul had described the shameless indulgence of the Cremonese, their inability to resist that second helping or third house, and I supposed that here it was again, screaming past with its main beam on: 'Ooooh, I've just overtaken three lorries, and there's a tractor coming towards me . . . oh, go on then, just one more. You've twisted my arm . . . oh look, and my neck.' There were accidents: two huge arcs of rubber bending into a ditch with an Alfa-Romeo's bottom sticking out of it; a colossal rear-end shunt that had condensed a people-carrier into a person-carrier and a Jeep Cherokee into a papoose.

Thirty-six die in day of road carnage. It was miserable. Every car was a loose cannon, driven by drunks trying to impress their secretaries. I thought how awful it would be if the terrible la-la-la Europop coming out of the radio was the last music I heard, if my last meal were the Milanese cheese slices working up a sweat on the armrest.

'Truely the view of this most sweet Paradise did even so ravish my senses that I said unto my selfe, this is the Citie which of all other places in the world, I would wish to make my habitation in ... were it not for their grosse idolatry and superstitious ceremonies which I detest, and the love of Odcombe in Somersetshire, which is so deare unto me.' Oh, Tommy, you incorrigible old bigot. Still, something about Mantua clearly got into Coryate's soul to move him to unleash this flood of conflicting emotion.

No one else seemed to have found it. In 1784 Thomas Brand and a couple of Sir Jameses all fell asleep in the opera there, and two earlier visitors, having arrived with great expectations, left saying, 'How frequently the traveller and antiquarian are disappointed in their pursuits.' Too right. Especially if they can't find anywhere to stash the motor.

All the way to Padua on the SS10, flashes of Mantua that my eyes had seen but remained unrecorded by a parking-preoccupied brain were belatedly processed. Most were of graffiti encountered during various foiled attempts at inveigling the Rolls into residents-only bays in Mantua's more remote corners: the anti-NATO 'Blair + Clinton = ASSASSIN' round the back of the Palazzo Ducale, with the 'i' of Blair replaced with a swastika (though not, of course, the 'i' in Clinton); the humorous Greek-alphabet pro-Homer slogans on the plinth of a statue of Virgil, Mantua-born Classical poet and a hero of Coryate's. It was all a terrible mess, of course, but it was still immeasurably more impassioned and literate than the British standard.

Everyone makes jokes about Italian governments, but the people of Italy are among the most politically aware on earth. All the newspapers are densely packed with analysis – I remembered buying a copy of *La Stampa* in Turin and finding the first four pages devoted entirely to a study of comparative inflation rates across Europe. And pondering the Homerian graffiti, it occurred to me with a jolt that I had studied Virgil at school. Four years of Latin, and what remained? *'Caecilius mercator est'* and *'polyspaston'* (a crane). Oh, and *'barbam me irritas'*, Latin for 'itchy beard', a derivative of the Jimmy Hill chin-rubbing expression implying disbelief, which is just such a horrible little prep-school awfulness that I'm going to have to go out into the street right now and shout out a prepared apology. Most of the time was spent altering the line drawings in our *Cambridge Latin for Schools* booklets. Grumio the gardener never should have bent over to plant those bulbs, certainly not while Cerberus the guard dog was in such a playful mood. I once had to tear out and eat a heavily amended family dinner scene when Mr Smith asked if I'd come and show him what everyone was laughing at, though on reflection I could just as honestly have indicated his tiny size and ill-advised moustache.

A watery mist bleached the autumnal colours monochrome, and rendered the many roofless villas along the SS10 ugly rather than poignant. It was all rather dull, so dull in fact that I started playing foolish games, like seeing how well I could drive with one eye closed or whether it was possible to negotiate bends using only the knees. I even ran my first red light, a sort of 'trainer' set at a quiet rural junction that would prepare me for jumping the big stuff in town. When I found myself shouting nursery rhymes in Australian, I quickly pulled in for a coffee at an Esso-station 'Tiger Bar', dividing my attention between the incongruous proximity of antifreeze and liqueurs, and the enormous limping rat chewing through the car-vacuum hose on the forecourt.

Coryate, who'd been on foot since Mantua, was so excited by his first sight of a winged lion – signifying he had now entered the

Venetian state – that he didn't even mention Montagnana, a town still wholly enclosed by a pristine set of towering red walls and twenty-four watchtowers. Par for the course in 1608, I suppose, and only preserved by historical accident. But it struck me, as I followed the rush-hour traffic into Padua's crumbling 1960s tenement suburbs, just how badly modern Italian builders compare with their Renaissance forebears. Built from papier-mâché concrete faced with stucco that was already coming unstucco, they looked like they wouldn't last another five years, let alone five centuries. Just after I left the country a residential block collapsed, killing many people – such disasters are an annual occurrence.

I made a mistake in Padua. It took me an hour of medieval claustrophobia to find a parking space, both mirrors scraping ancient alley walls, bulldozing student day-dreamers out of my path; and a further hour to find a hotel. It was only after I had checked in, deposited my hated tent bag in the room and wandered off down a long, dark colonnade that I realised I had forgotten to make a note of the street I'd parked the car in. In it were things I needed: tomorrow's clothes, tonight's wash bag, yesterday's enthusiasm. A couple of turnings later I found myself in a completely unfamiliar piazza and gave up.

Resigned to recycling underwear and cleaning teeth with fingers, I set off back to my hotel, the . . . um, what was it called again? And actually, which street was it in . . .? All my money except – quick pocket inventory – 3,200 lire was in my room. It was dark now, and everything looked different. The narrow vaulted colonnades which covered every pavement in Padua's dense heart were no longer delightfully atmospheric but maddeningly identical. For fifteen minutes I wandered dangerously about in the traffic, looking upwards for a glimpse of a church spire or other helpful landmark, before realising that without a map it was irrelevant. And what could I say to the early evening shoppers, hurrying home before the drizzle got worse? 'Excuse me, have you seen my car? No? Well, that's no good. What about my hotel?'

I started passing things I'd passed before – a fat man walking his fatter dog, a shop selling nothing but scales. An hour went by. As deceptively straightforward tasks go, this was already right up there with stripping the cellophane off a videotape box; soon it would pass flat-pack furniture assembly. I didn't find the fat man comical when I passed him the third time, but hunger and fatigue were doing bad things to my head, and the fourth time I laughed right in his face. Under the colonnades, over canal bridges, past the scales shop – no matter how many times I tried to alter my route, I was just doing laps.

Delirium was setting in. I started looking up at an imaginary rear-view mirror; at one point I found myself at a street corner holding two 1,000-lire notes in the air, oblivious as to how long I might have been doing so. I stumbled into a phone box, shovelled all my coins in it and used the allotted fourteen seconds to scare my wife with a blurry mumble about two kids I'd begun to think were following me.

'I'm sure they're more scared of you than you are of them,' she said with exaggerated pacification.

'So it's a fucking competition now, is it?' I shrieked as the last 200 lire ran out.

In the end, I found an open grocery store, blew my remaining funds on a thin wedge of cheese and ate it, unaware until about halfway through that it was very mature Parmesan, and not caring even then. The calorific reinforcements successfully marshalled my mental reserves, and outside a Banca di Roma I found a little box dispensing promotional leaflets which incorporated a small plan of the city. Though compromised by an absence of information on roads unfortunate enough not to host a branch of the Banca di Roma, this did confirm what I had begun to fear, and what I would have known if I had read Coryate's account of Padua before setting off: 'It is of a round forme like Paris.' Every time I thought I'd been walking in a straight line, I'd been gently steered round in a circle. After criss-crossing the town ticking off Banca di Romas from my map, I eventually found that car and hotel were actually ten minutes apart at either end of the same road.

If the hotel was A and the car Z, I dined at about D, in a pizzeria run by a woman with a big, red Mr Punch face and a tiny, floppy Mr Punch body. With the bones of my legs feeling somehow flared from the knee down I randomly tackled a plate-overhanging capricciosa, shivering and muttering as I refuelled. It's usually the case that practice makes perfect, so why was I getting worse at travelling? At least, I reasoned, it had been good training for the two-day Coryate walk I had vowed to do at some point, only not just yet. Four hours' walking today, and four yesterday – and neither of them a ruminative stroll. A lean, mean, walking machine . . . I was already the second of these, albeit in the wrong sense, and this combined with my usually accidental efforts at becoming the third was now bringing about the first. I switched into idle mode, lips slightly parted, arms loose by my sides. After an indeterminate time Mr Punch appeared, and asked if I'd finished. We both looked at the disfigured mess on my plate, strongly reminiscent, I thought, of a photo I'd once seen of a web spun by a spider injected with LSD. '*Si*,' I said.

As is often the way, I was too exhausted to sleep. My room was on the third floor at the back of the hotel, overlooking a corner of a park that led down to a stagnant canal. Lying on my bed with the window slightly open, left-right-left conversations between others lost in Padua's covered mazes came up to me from below: *'Sinistra, destra, destra; no, sinistra . . .'* Then a long silence, ended by a solitary whistle.

I got out of bed and looked down: there, under a tree at the edge of a circle of street-lit grass, someone was settling down for the night. I couldn't see much – the tree concealed all but the legs – but there was a drizzle-shiny blue sleeping bag on a sheet of cardboard, and beside it a pair of filthy trainers and an embossed-cover blockbuster paperback. A twentieth-century Coryate, I supposed, a self-contained traveller following the canal to Venice as he had done.

But then there were voices, and through a gate in the park wall came two men, one bald, one in a long leather coat. There were muted greetings and some sort of exchange, then the bald man sat down on a little stone bench while Leather Coat talked to the still recumbent sleeping-bagger. Suddenly I knew what was going to happen. Baldy did something complicated with a lighter; then he rolled up his left sleeve, flexed his arm a couple of times, and jabbed something carefully into the crook. After thirty seconds or so, he stood, wandered round the bench, sat down again and repeated his earlier action, only this time puncturing his forearm just above the watch face. He stood again, rolled down his sleeve, mumbled a bored-sounding farewell noise and departed the scene on the pushbike he'd left just outside the gate.

Was that it? I mean, if I was going to acquire a hazardous and time-consuming class A drug habit, I'd expect a bit more in the way of helpless ecstasy. I'd want to be slumped on the bench, the glow of a thousand fires on my face, the wisdom of ancient civilisations rushing through my head. I'd want to stare glassily at my pushbike, appraising its place in the world in general and my heart in particular, not just climb on it and pedal off into the night. I'd want it to be hours before I could even trouble my orbiting brain with anything as prosaic yet complex as bloody cycling. What stupid arses these people are.

Coryate spent more time in Padua than any city since Paris, attracted in particular by its university, then arguably the world's finest and consequently a splendid place for him to notch up some intellectual credibility points. He soon made the acquaintance of three English scholars – Mr Rooke, Mr Willoughby and (hooray!) Dr Moore – who kindly gave him a four-day guided tour.

But by the time the Grand Tourists started arriving, the university was in decline, the streets were dirty and they couldn't wait to get to Venice. Lord Balgonie found a scorpion in his bed; others were awoken by children 'naked but for little petticoats' crying in the courtyards below.

I wasn't quite sure where I stood on Padua. It was a wonderful morning, but it had been rather a trying night. I yawned hugely as I walked into a sunny market place, barely recognisable as the haunted arena I had blundered through so many times the night before. If I got lost again, how would the *carabinieri* piece together my last hours?

'So, Sergeant, what do you notice about this hotel room?'

'Well, sir, there's a chair, a television, blood all over the pillow, walls and sheets . . . My God!'

'Steady on, man. What am I always reminding you to do?'

'Destroy all evidence of the kickbacks we get from the smack pushers in the park, sir?'

'What else?'

'Not to jump to conclusions.'

'Correct. If you notice, the bloodstains on the pillow match those on the walls. We are dealing with someone who was bitten heavily by mosquitoes, and exacted a terrible dawn revenge on his nocturnal tormentors.'

'I see, sir. And the sheets?'

'No self-control, Sergeant. This is a man who scratches bites raw.'

'A man, sir?'

'Didn't they teach you anything at police school?'

'Only the stuff about kickbacks.'

'Not the poems?'

'Poems?'

'"*A missing hotel guest is male,*
If while on the insect trail,
He executes a reckless flail,
Then trips and busts the towel rail."'

'I see.'

'And there's more. The guests next door have reported hearing him make extensive use of the hairdryer in his bathroom, and all of the complimentary toiletries and a roll of lavatory paper are missing. We're looking for someone who's always keen to extract his full money's worth – too keen, perhaps. Any ideas what this might be?'

'Hmmm . . . a load of fluffy, dirty lint. You're not going to make me eat it, are you, sir?'

'Don't be an ass, Sergeant. It's not a Wednesday. No, the scene-of-crime boys scraped it off the rotary shoe-polisher by the lift. It's the result of someone attempting to clean a pair of pale suede desert boots in a device clearly intended only for buffing black leather.'

'So, sir, to recap: we're looking for a man covered in fresh scabs with idiotic bouffant hair and filthy, bald footwear . . .'

✦ ✦ ✦

Even so, I soon decided I liked the place a lot. As I had established during the very early stages of the night before's refugee march, Padua is a lovely city to walk about. The main market places, hemmed in by Venetian winged lions and Renaissance colonnades, were the Piazza della Frutte and the Piazza dell'Erbe, Fruit Square and Herb Square, and both were crowded with appropriate vendors. Cabbages were arranged in little cannonball pyramids, bunches of shiny grapes lolled decadently over tables – even a stall selling nothing but rice somehow contrived a cornucopian splendour. It was just the sort of place that Keith Floyd goes to when he's buying his ingredients.

And of course all the locals were acting like they were being filmed: a man whisked a bunch of roses from a flower stall and presented them to a passing nun; two girls in yellow-lensed sunglasses giggled conspiratorially in front of a butcher's shop window boasting enormous columns of Barbie-pink mortadella. An army of house-wives prodded and bargained, and I suddenly wondered if the whole mamma-mia kitchen culture had been created by the astonishing fertility of the countryside around here and the consequent variety of fresh produce. In England there would have been turnips and barley – not much scope for even the most imaginative cook. But here there was everything, leading even humble families to expect convoluted gourmet dinners, and so requiring the mother of the household to spend all morning in the market and all afternoon in the kitchen.

Separating the two squares was the Palazzo della Ragione, the Law Courts, a slightly asymmetrical block of loggias and colonnades. Inside, it was like being in the hull of a huge, capsized ark, bare timber beams curving high overhead. There was some sort of exhi-bition of bland nineteenth-century local art going on, but I had come here for two things, and that wasn't one of them.

Coryate's habit of pacing out the dimensions of public buildings was beginning to develop into an obsession, one that mirrored my own fascination with our respective fitness levels. How did the length of Tommy's stride compare with mine? He had measured the palazzo hall at 40 paces by 110. I couldn't do the full length – the end half of the hall was boarded off – and the width was made awkward by restoration workmen half-heartedly scanning the walls in a way that suggested they were on a full-time standby contract to check for and deal with structural defects as and when these might appear. Three times I had to stop, mid-crossing, my path blocked by a man in a hard hat staring up and waiting for the roof to start leaking. But I did it in the end, ignoring the curious stares of a seated curator clearly convinced I was a cat burglar who would go to any ends to satisfy his lust for bland nineteenth-century local art.

For the first time I had trodden definitively in Coryate's foot-steps. And I had won: my score was 37½ (slight blow to the nose on that last stride). Gone were the images of Coryate relentlessly eating up the ground with huge, low-slung paces, like an athletic Groucho Marx. And with it went my hopes that he was a freak, a man whose body was uniquely adapted to superhuman feats of ambu-latory stamina. He was clearly just a slightly short man in tights. I had no excuse.

I didn't expect the second attraction to be there, but it was, and right where Tommy said it would be. 'At the West end of the hall neare to one of the corners there is a very mery spectacle to be seene: a round stone some three foote high on which if any banckerupt do sit with his naked buttocks three times in some public assembly, all his debts are ipso-facto remited.'

I went up and touched its smooth, grey surface, hoping that after a bankrupt wiped the slate clean, someone did the same to the stone. Without Coryate's help, I'd never have found it. There was no identifying sign, and the little English pamphlet I picked up on the way in made no mention. Perhaps the locals were winding him up. The concept of allowing people to write off debts with a display of public nudity seemed too good to be true, and Coryate speculates that introducing such a custom to England would have led to great queues of bare-buttocked bankrupts lining up outside 'Westminster hall'. But I think it would be a fine scheme – not so much as an optional humiliation for bankrupts as a compulsory one for Michael Douglas, Il Professore and randomly selected officers of the Parks Police.

It was only fitting that minutes after fondling the stone of shame I was peering into a courtyard where a woman in a leotard and a huge laurel wreath was running through a forty-strong human arch having her buttocks manually belaboured. She was in her late twenties; the belabourers, male and female, largely in their sixties. And it was even more fitting that none of my fellow passers-by seemed to find this performance in any way remarkable. Every time I established incredulous eye contact with a passing housewife as a means of sharing my discovery of this secret world of depravity thriving under her nose, she blandly appraised the scene and its concomitant slaps and whoops, then looked back at me with a defiant indifference that said, 'And?'

It was only when the exuberant celebration moved out into the street and the leotarded lady stood on a bench, donned a mortar board and to geriatric jeers unfurled a large topless caricature of herself squeezing a nipple in one hand and brandishing a phallically rolled-up diploma in the other that I finally understood. She was a medical student; they were relatives come to celebrate her graduation.

I thought about all the GPs whose surgeries I have patronised, and tried very hard to imagine them up there semi-naked on the bench, doing the can-can before their in-laws. This difficult but rewarding mental task served to confirm two suspicions. First, that English people have more in common with a whole host of inanimate objects than they do with Italian people. Second, that Dr Fowler did indeed have 'Suffer the little children' daubed in blood across her shoulder blades.

As Coryate had found, every Italian town I had been to so far trumped the last. Just as I was beginning to think that Padua had everything except a big, airy square I emerged from colonnaded claustrophobia into the Prato della Valle, a huge oval of statuary, foliage and water features. At the corner was the eight-domed Santa Giustina, a state-of-the-art church in Coryate's day that was now smothered in scaffolding so entrenched that six-foot trees sprouted from its upper reaches. Somewhere there's probably a quango working round the clock (one of those special civil-service clocks that start at 10.30 a.m. and stop at noon) awarding contracts to scaffold up the scaffolding to those building firms which offer them the nicest holidays.

Coryate had got quite excited by the church's star attraction, a lead coffin said to contain St Luke's bones. 'That coffin I touched, but with some difficulty: for it was so farre within the grate that I could hardly conveigh the tops of my fingers.' Luke was still there in his sarcophagus, having recently been exhumed for the first time since twenty years before Coryate's visit (for tests which proved the bones were indeed probably his). I thought of Tommy stretching his arm through the bars for a crafty feel, and again felt a little quiver of childish empathy.

But the big draw in Padua is St Anthony, whose bones are entombed among a sea of tourists in the Basilica del Santo. 'His name is invoked in the search for mislaid objects,' said my Michelin guide, 'and he is represented holding a book and a lily' (so *that's* where I put them). But as a Premiership saint, St Anthony's fanbase is what one could call, if one wanted to make a really bad joke, a broad church. Coryate found 'a certaine Demoniacall person praied at the Sepulchre upon his knees, who had another appointed to attend him, that he should not irreligiously behave himself at so religious a place . . . a Priest walked about the Tombe to helpe expell the divell with his exorcismes, but the effect thereof turned to nothing.'

Nowadays, as I discovered, Tony is a big hit with those who have survived big hits. His huge marble tomb was plastered with blurred Polaroids of rolled Suzuki Jeeps upside down in Sao Paulo ravines and Peugeot 205s wrapped round Parisian lampposts, all with heart-felt messages of thanks from the lucky occupants. I'm always jealous of such genuine religious faith. It's certainly a lot more fun than crediting salvation to the patron saint of crumple zones.

Opposite the church was the Associazione Universale di San Antonio, which I can only describe as a club shop. I don't think I've ever seen such a wide range of merchandising: die-hard Tony fans could choose anything from a thermometer (8,000 lire), to a calendar and pen desk set (15,000 lire), to a splendid saint-in-a-teapot twist on the ship-in-a-bottle theme (20,000 lire). Scarves and baseball hats will be available when the saints go marching in.

I returned to the Rolls to find that someone had stuck a pigeon feather in what I will have to describe reluctantly as the silver lady's hole. I left it *in situ* – the car was in such a state that it hardly looked out of place – and it was still fluttering as I drove along the River Brenta, down which Coryate and almost all subsequent Grand Tourists had sailed to Venice. The banks were lined with villas built by Venetian merchants keen to escape the summer stench of the city, 'goodly faire houses and palaces of pleasure' in his day but now largely shuttered and run-down. At Mestre, the brazenly hideous petrochemical port clearly designed for optimum contrast with the floating city on the horizon, I left the Rolls in a seedy long-term car park whose youthful proprietors fought over the keys the moment I dropped them on the counter. I tried not to hear the winner flooring the throttle with a backfired roar; I tried not to imagine the loser chalking up 'Limousine hire' on a board by the gate.

Then it was a dark, drizzly train ride across the causeway, a scrum of hotel touts at the station and a very wet but very splendid view of the Grand Canal by night. This is what Coryate had come for, and after summarising his journey to date ('The total summe of Miles betwixt Odcombe and Venice is 952') he took a big literary sigh and provided a future generation of copywriters with the quote that introduces about a third of all tourist brochures on the city: 'The most glorious and heavenly shew upon the water that ever any mortal eye beheld.'

FOUR

Venice

There isn't a low season in Venice. Every year six million tourists visit the city, outnumbering the locals a hundred to one. So though it might not have been full-on in November, off it certainly wasn't. After a dispiriting encounter with the accommodation bureau in the station, I'd been forced to go along with one of the hotel touts, a little Inspector Clouseau with a harelip. Half an hour later, having accidentally caught exactly the right water-bus and wobbled off at exactly the right stop, I was sitting in a room half the size of a Formule 1 cell and four times the price.

No bathroom, no telly, mosquito-graveyard walls, a floor tiled with frozen nougat and eight students playing what I eventually decided was musical Twister in the room next door, which must have been rather distracting for the ninth and tenth who were respectively putting up a set of shelves and teaching a large dog to swim. I lay on the bed, noting that the sheets, like the towel, smelt of pipe-smoke and shepherd's pie, and listened to those astonishing noises, now joined by the first qualifying heats of what I correctly predicted would be an all-night running-up-and-down-the-echoing-stairs competition.

The wardrobe was wedged up against my feet, and I kicked at it disconsolately. Being made of balsa wood, it keeled over, knocking my toiletries into the rusty sink and disgorging from its interior a spare pillow which was clearly the missing piece of forensic evidence in a torso murder case. I went out, drank rather a lot of wine, came back and slept in a position designed to maximise the volume of my snoring.

Coryate went slightly mad in Venice. In six weeks he spent almost all his money, rushing around the city in a great frenzy of inscription-copying and hall-pacing, now even hugging columns to estimate their circumference. And then it was back to his room to write up notes: in a letter written two years later he recalls the late nights, 'scarce affording myself an howres rest sometimes of the whole 24 by reason of my continuous writing'. Over a sixth of the *Crudities* is devoted to Venice, and Coryate can be credited as the man who inaugurated a British obsession with the city that endured right up until Dirk Bogarde copped it on the Lido with black hair dye running down his face.

For the British aristo with a cultural inferiority complex, the Grand Tour was about becoming a man of the world in all senses of the phrase. Venice, with its maritime panoramas and disorientating east-meets-west culture clashes, broadened a visitor's horizons liter-ally, just as the anything-goes sense of bacchanalian recklessness did so figuratively. It was a Grand Tour theme park – no other city offered such a complete package. The trading capital of the world, half a millennium of artistic splendour, a fortress of Christianity against the heathen Orient – all this and plenty sexy girl. Venice offered saucer-eyed Brits what Coryate's biographer called 'all the allurements of an older and richer civilisation', a self-contained pleasure island so stubbornly independent that they even had their own daft system of weights and measures which dictated that a pound of coffee was lighter than a pound of butter.

What I hadn't realised was that even in 1608 Venice was past its prime, new trade routes round the Cape and developing links with the Americas already eroding its fearsome mercantile power. But that's not to say that they weren't short of a few bob. And being Italian, as Paul Sadka had told me, they knew how to enjoy life. Those winged lions still looked over town squares right across northern Italy and on islands as far away as Crete, but as its empire and influence began to shrink, Venice shrugged its velvet-wrapped shoulders and partied. In a two-hundred-year orgy of decadence they dressed up, whored, gossiped and gambled. The words *casino* and *imbroglio* are Venetian inventions; Coryate estimated that of the city's 500,000 inhabitants, 20,000 were prostitutes – 'the brothel of Europe' in the words of an eighteenth-century tourist. (Mind you, there was a lot of it about by then: one in eight adult females was on the game in Georgian London.)

Sleeping with your wife or husband was almost a taboo; while their men were off with the courtesans, women of status were escorted everywhere by *cicisbei*, 'auxiliary husbands'. Repeated rows with the Vatican meant the city was unfettered by religious morality – Pope Gregory XIII said, 'I am Pope everywhere except Venice.' Even nuns were considered fair game – Casanova once had a fling with a novice who was anything but, and another bride of Christ fought a duel with her abbess over a man's affections. And a slavish obsession with idiotic fashion trends got hopelessly out of hand: there were 850 wigmakers in the city, and a noblewoman was expected to spend at least six hours every morning doing her hair and make-up.

By the eighteenth century, the city was living off tourism and the revenues provided by casino taxes and levies on prostitutes. The locals were wearing masks not just to the odd ball but for an officially sanctioned six months of the year. As the Cadogan guide to the city says, 'There are many astounding things about Venice, but this may astound the most: for half the year the whole citizenry played at make-believe in wonderful costumes, incognito and single-mindedly devoted to fun, debauchery and cheating at cards.'

You can see why the Grand Tourists loved it. When, in 1763, the Marquis of Tavistock warned future British visitors that 'Venice is the most calculated for luxurious idleness of any place I know and therefore very dangerous to you,' he made the same mistake as Mr Heyworth when he told me and the rest of 4T not to go into the Popular Book Exchange on King Street because they sold second-hand pornography to minors.

Venice was perfect, because its lavish heritage of art and history offered the ideal cover for a few months' debauchery. In honest moments, the Brits confessed that many aspects of the Venetian environment left much to be desired: 'barbarous, inelegant' public buildings, streets that were 'much too dark and dismal', gondolas like 'coffins', 'old and in general ill-built houses, ruined pictures and stinking ditches'. Ah, the smell: Gibbon called it 'more noisome than a pigstye', and Walpole bemoaned the 'nauseous air'. The fact that they put up with all this shows the extent of their determination to enjoy what they'd really come for – the astonishing populace.

> In the evening, there generally is on St Marks place, such a
> mixed multitude of Jews, Turks, and Christians; lawyers,
> knaves, and pick-pockets; mountebanks, old women and
> physicians; women of quality with masks; strumpets barefaced;

and, in short, such a jumble of senators, citizens, gondoliers
and people of every character and condition, that your ideas
are broke, bruised and dislocated in the crowd.

Writing this account in 1790, Dr John Moore must have felt like
Luke Skywalker going into that bar full of aliens. And if it seemed
that exciting in the late eighteenth century, what must it have been
like for Coryate almost 200 years earlier?

Of course, with moral and religious disapproval shouting only
distantly from the mainland – and then in Italian – it was those
barefaced strumpets who held the most foreigner-friendly appeal.
One tourist wrote of the fate of his friend Mr Wynn, 'who has been
2 or 3 years at Venice, enchanted with a mistress', and our old mucker
Boswell could hardly keep his breeches up. Reporting on his encounters with the 'glittering . . . Venetian Courtesans', he boasts that he
'fought, not without glory', despite picking up fresh 'battle wounds'.
He even managed to get the Prime Minister's son a souvenir dose
of clap: 'My Lord Mountstuart saw that I was excited [did he, indeed?]
. . . I told him I was going to take a look at the girls, to taste the
pleasures and get to know the world . . . A pretty dancer was our
common flame, and my lord catched a Tartar as well as I. A fine
piece of witless behaviour [from] the steady young man who was
to help Lord Mountstuart to improve himself.'

What with that and the parties and the gambling, it was almost
too much. One tourist complained in 1794 that 'the opera does not
begin till eleven and lasts till three or four; and what do you think
must be the spirit of the public balls which are given after? Now I
could forgive people's turning water into land, but when they come
so completely to turn night into day they make too great a change
in the old system.'

But decadence by definition decays, and when the kids get involved it's time to call a halt. Elizabeth and Eugenie Wynne, visiting the city with their parents in 1790, kept diaries which give a definitive insight. 'Went to the opera at St Benetto,' wrote eleven-year-old Elizabeth on 15 February, 'and run about the boxes always masked in the Italian fashion . . . They made us a present of three pigeons.' Her twelve-year-old sister's entry for the same day is even better: 'Dressed very soon [as] a Shepherdess. Walked in the place of St Marc . . . Papa was dressed in weomen's clothes.'

By the end, Venice was a party run by gatecrashers. The last Doge to rule Venice passed out when told of his appointment; eight years later, in 1797, he and his fellow councillors heard guns in the bay and immediately voted to end the thousand-year republic before running away, unaware that the noise was actually a farewell salvo from an allied warship. When Napoleon arrived soon after, he met no resistance.

And in every sense of the word it's still sinking. To use an expression that may evoke harsh laughter from the residents of Venice's ground-floor flats, the city has long passed its high-water mark. A population of half a million had dropped to 150,000 by the 1950s, and now it's less than half that. There are only 4,000 children in Venice – the lowest proportion of any city in the world and hardly an encouraging indicator for the future.

Coryate, for his part, was appalled by the debauchery and narcissism. 'Almost all the wives, widowes and mayds do walke abroad with their breasts all naked even almost to the middle . . . a fashion me thinkes very uncivill and unseemly,' he splutters, going on to rant about the women who 'anoynt their hair with oyle, or some other drugs to make it looke faire' and then spent all afternoon in the sun with their tresses spread over special wide-brimmed hats to maximise the bleaching effect. The platform shoe was invented in Venice: initially a device for keeping skirts out of the high-tide mud, it soon developed into the ultimate triumph of form over function. Coryate saw women tottering about on eighteen-inch 'chopines', clinging on to servants to keep their balance. When he saw one wearer fall flat on her painted face while crossing a bridge, he refused to sympathise: 'it is a pity this foolish custom is not cleane banished and exterminated out of the citie'.

So why did he find it so hard to tear himself away? Hypocrisy is one answer – like a good tabloid hack he knew his readers would be titillated by accounts of Venetian excesses, but at the same time he was always careful to express his deep shock before making his excuses and leaving at the right moment. A genuine sense of awe at Venice's art and architecture is another, something that sets Coryate apart from the legions of debauched philistines who followed him – he was apparently one of the first Britons to include the names of painters in his descriptions of their works. Of all the cities he visited, Venice was the most culturally active. El Greco was in his prime, Tintoretto had only just kicked the paintpot and the villas of Palladio, whose Classical revival is credited with changing the face of British architecture, were still springing up on the Venetian mainland. The Renaissance had arrived late in England, but its spirit of can-do creative enthusiasm, still very much alive in Venice, was what had fired the parson's son from Somerset into believing he could not only undertake this journey but write a book about it.

There was a small British community in Venice in 1608 – the ambassador, Sir Henry Wotton, and perhaps three dozen merchants – and Coryate arrived keen to inveigle himself. He presented Sir Henry with a letter of introduction from Richard Martin, an MP and lawyer who was presumably a contact of Coryate's old associates the Phelipses of Montacute. Unfortunately, this double-edged endorsement ('he is more pleasant than a Dutch waggon') was subtly worded to depict the bearer as a rustic bore who didn't know when to shut up. It was the same old tragic story: Coryate's social superiors ganging up to humiliate him with their arcane wit. I thought about poor old Tom gratefully folding up this letter outside Richard Martin's grand house in London, stuffing it carefully down the back of his tights and carrying it all the way to Venice, blissfully ignorant of its coded insults. I was learning that Coryate had a habit of glossing over indignities, and though Sir Henry – having read Martin's letter – didn't invite him to stay, he vaguely insinuates that he did, talking of his 'friendship with that noble knight, which I esteeme for one of the best fortunes that hapned unto me in my travels'.

Breakfast wasn't included with my horrible bed, and I went out into a windy grey morning, wandering about dark alleys in search of food. Public urination has obviously long been a scourge in Venice – most quiet corners of the sort favoured by practitioners of the art were protected by a variety of downward-sloping slabs, which jutted out of the wall at a height and angle guaranteed to deflect the flow on to the shins. Unfortunately, of course, when your population shrinks to a tenth of its original size, the number of quiet corners increases. As the stench proved, you can't stop all of the pee-people all of the time.

It wasn't an ideal start to a day I had been hoping would lay bare Venice's enigmatic wondrousness, allowing me to feel and do the things that awed Englishmen in Venice have traditionally felt and done: swimming across the Grand Canal like Byron, hugging columns *à la* Coryate. Because the night before, blundering about the dark alleys among all the other lost tourists, I had confronted a shaming truth: I didn't really like Venice very much.

Through what I hoped was circumstance and misfortune, I found I had no truly uplifting memories about the place. Visit One: student InterRailing, sleeping on the station steps, being awoken at 5.30 a.m. with a truncheon in the kidneys, staying in some god-awful hostel with iron-bedded Florence Nightingale dormitories, heat, crowds, Japanese couples in gondolas, getting lost. Visit Two: with parents, siblings and grandfather, expensive horrible hotels, cold, crowds, Japanese couples in gondolas, getting lost. Visit Three: accompanying wife on business, heat, crowds, Japanese . . . well, actually, that was an all-expenses-paid job, so a big tick there – especially as Robert Maxwell was picking up the tab, which may have explained why we went everywhere by private speedboat, including a trip to Harry's Bar, where we – or rather he – paid £130 for one cocktail, half a bottle of house wine and two plates of pasta. Bob was probably looking at our bill when he jumped overboard.

After completing a typical Venetian detour that wasn't so much two sides of a triangle as eleven sides of a dodecahedron, I found a café, got ripped off by just too little to make a fuss about and set off after Coryate. By limiting myself to his itinerary, I hoped at least to overcome the headless-chicken panic that had governed my previous blunderings along the Venetian culture trail. Maybe, I reasoned, a more systematic, studied approach to sightseeing would help my eyes sort out the Byzantine from the baroque, my ears make sense of the bells and yells, my nose distinguish over-priced espresso from under-treated sewage. I would refine my senses, and leave Venice as an educated gentleman of taste.

From Ca' d'Oro I walked south, following a couple of grandly moustachioed German Village People who seemed to know where they were going on the grounds that they only stopped every other minute to unfold, rotate and squint at a vast map. And sure enough they took me in a more or less straight line to San Marco, past the shops selling lurid Murano glassware and gold plastic Pierrot masks, over the bridges where unseasonably T-shirted youths were dragging fridges, beer crates and grandfathers off seesawing barge decks.

Being an eminent Italian landmark, a lot of the square was scaffolded up. But they had done something rather fun with it here, covering the poles and boards with an enormous blown-up photograph of the unscaffolded exterior, so that the Doge's Palace was still the Doge's Palace, only slightly blurred and billowing in a way that initially suggested someone had slipped Quaaludes in my coffee. The blow-up was a real photo, with real tourists caught mid-stride walking across the bottom. One had a camera pressed to his face, and as I stood among the pigeons and postcard sellers I saw a tourist taking a photograph of the photograph of a tourist taking a photograph, which probably sums up Venice in general and San Marco in particular. It had been a tourist trap even in Coryate's day – they charged him 'a gazet, which is not fully an English penny' to climb the campanile. And for every one of today's souvenir stalls there was a quack-doctor mountebank, bellowing out 'an oration to the audience of half an houre long, wherein he doth most hyperbolically extoll the virtue of his drugs and confections, though many are very counterfeit and false'.

At least with *Coryats Crudities* for a guidebook you get some juice to enliven the visual clichés. While he was checking out the Doge's Palace one morning, a technician inspecting the bell of the huge clock above the gate to the Mercerie tarried slightly too long and was brained by one of the mechanical 'wilde men' who struck out the hours with brazen hammers: 'such a violent blow that therewith he fel down dead'. The sawn-off column at the south corner of the cathedral, 'almost two yards high, and of a pretty broad compasse, even as much as a man can claspe at twice with both his armes', was used to display the heads of traitors, 'though the smell doth breede a very offensive and contagious annoyance'. And there was a nice story about the two huge columns ('I was not able to clasp them with both mine arms at thrice') by the canal: there had originally been a third, but it fell into the water while they were dragging it off the barge (and nearly 900 years later, it's still down there somewhere). The architect who successfully oversaw the landing and erection of the other two was granted a wish, and chose to ask the Doge to legalise dice playing between the pillars, so inaugurating Venice's first casino.

I went into the cathedral, which was dark and wobbly floored. I went into the Doge's Palace, where Coryate turned the tables on me with a 55–63 courtyard-striding victory which made a mockery of the pigeon-paced form he'd shown in Padua. Bits of this, too, were wobbly floored from the effects of subsidence, and had been even in his day, 'chopped and cloven and very uneven'. While crossing the Bridge of Sighs, adding my own as a gondolier passed beneath playing 'Tulips of Amsterdam' on the accordion for the benefit of his Japanese passengers, I realised that part of the problem with Venice was sensory overload. Every vista rammed world-famous tourist sights and a thousand years of concentrated culture into your brain. There are no havens in Venice offering respite to the sightsore sightseer with a sprain in his rubber neck, no parks or shopping malls. And it would have been far worse for the Grand Tourists – today, because of Napoleonic looting and distress sales to tourists, only about 6 per cent of the city's artistic legacy remains.

Overwhelmed and dislocated, I walked away up the windswept waterfront, away from San Marco and the crowds. In the same way that Coryate paced out piazzas to tame the daunting scale of history with prosaic mathematics, I found myself doing calculations to bring him closer to me. If Tommy had lived until he was seventy-five and suddenly found true love with a young wench of child-bearing age (unlikely, I know, but bear with me), and if the resulting son had done the same in his time and so on, then . . . then I could be Thomas Coryate's great-great-great-grandson.

It was a stupid thought, but somehow it kept up my spirits as I leant into the wind and shivered along to the Arsenale. Nowhere in Venice symbolises the city's decline more effectively than this enormous boatyard, its name another Venetian coining. Within its 2-mile-long walls, local shipbuilders perfected a production-line system so effective that to impress a visiting monarch, Henry III of France, they once completed an entire galley during the course of a state banquet. In the fifteenth century over 15,000 men laboured here, the largest workforce in any one establishment before Victorian times.

Now? Well, in a country that has made neglecting heritage its national sport, the Arsenale wins the league and cup double. This was the heart of Venice's 1,000-year republic, the home of the city's first Renaissance building (the Great Gateway) and a whole pride of looted lion sculptures, a unique piece of industrial history. I walked up to the entrance; a couple of spotty naval ratings in ill-fitting white uniforms raised their heads with the shifty sloth of lazy people worried they might shortly have to do something.

Since 1918, the Arsenale has been home to obsolete naval equipment and young sailors watching weeds grow on the rooftops, but it's still a military base and therefore out of bounds. Imagine my surprise, then, when one of the ratings stood, turned and beckoned me with a slouch to follow him in. Well, what do you do when a sailor offers to take you up the Arsenale? I pursued him wordlessly along the quayside, past Great War concrete bunkers and semi-glazed warehouses housing Marconi-era electrical substations. Some sort of trawler rotted at its moorings, the only craft in a dock five times the size of the square at San Marco, but when I stopped to look at it my guide turned, smiled, shook his head and beckoned me onwards.

When Coryate visited the Arsenale, 'the eight miracle of the world', 250 galleys were in the dock. And galleys need galley slaves, tens of thousands of them. Coryate heard of the fate of one, an Englishman named Thomas Taylor, who had deserted from the Venetian army (a multinational mercenary force) and was now being punished. His appeals on Taylor's behalf fell on deaf ears.

After ten minutes, we got to the end of the quay. All the older buildings were opposite us, flaking damply into the vast square of water, but we clearly wouldn't be going there. The rating leant back against a huge, mortarless old brick wall, put his hands in his pockets, then abruptly thrust his hips forward and with a tut began furiously brushing four centuries of filth off the seat of his white trousers. For a brief moment I wondered if our mysterious excursion was an elaborate pretext to procure my assistance in this intimate activity, but then, with a final tattoo of self-administered slaps and spanks, he was off again the way we had come. Back at the gate he resumed his position, smiled away my thanks and left me happy that I had seen inside the place but still clueless as to why I'd been allowed to.

It was getting dark, and succumbing to a heavy physical and spir-itual fatigue I went into a bar and had a grappa. This handsomely succeeded in invigorating me, but the side-effects were unfortunate: one minute I was walking happily among the early evening crowds, the next I had bought thirteen calendars and a bell-riddled jester's hat. (It could have been worse. The Grand Tourists considered their stay a failure unless they went home with a souvenir Canaletto.)

A big slice of cake restored my financial metabolism, but not my sense of direction. Still, by night, Venice was much better. Twilight smudged out the crumbling seediness; when I peered into the canals I saw watery street-lit reflections rather than polychromatic diesel swirls and semi-submerged litter. As had happened to so many British Grand Tourists, my crash-course in cultural self-improvement had crashed; like them, I now found myself contemplating instead Venice's baser attractions. The grand *palazzi* looked splendidly louche, a sensual bordello glow outlining the pointy-topped Arabic windows that are the most obvious legacy of Venice's trading links. I stopped beneath the sauciest, a four-floor triumph of balconies and pink stucco with the shadowy fronds of huge and exotic houseplants playing across the tall ceilings. Here, I decided, was where a courtesan had entertained a parson's son from Somerset on a rather warmer evening 391 years before.

As pictured in the *Crudities*, Coryate's encounter with the bare-breasted Margarita Emiliana appears to be business rather than pleasure. He doffs his hat, leans into a bow and presses a hand to his chest in a madam-I-couldn't-possibly show of honour; she has one arm round his back while the other beckons him towards her meticulously presented chest with an oh-go-on-big-boy intimacy. But you can read it any number of ways.

> *Tommy*: This is only supposed to be an interview.
> *Maggie*: That's a coincidence – I was about to offer you a couple of jobs.
> *Tommy*: What do you think of my doublet and hose?
> *Maggie*: Like I always say, sweetheart, show me your hose and I'll double it.
> *Tommy*: Look, love, I'm flat broke.

Il Signior Tomaso Odcombiano.   Margarita Emiliana bella
                                  Cortesana di Venetia
                    Gu Host sculp

Maggie: Tell you what, dearie, two gazets for a quick feel – or make it three and I'll put my beard on.

Ultimately, of course, he didn't have the cash. Venice's courtesans, reported Coryate, paid enough taxes to maintain a dozen galleys, and the most successful of them – a category which would certainly include Ms Emiliana, judging by her rap-artist jewellery – lived in the plushest *palazzi* in town. But he still behaved like a kid in a sweetshop, even though he had to keep his hands off the marshmallows:

> As for her selfe shee comes to thee decked like the Queene
> and Goddesse of love . . . For thou shalt see her decked
> with many chaines of gold and orient pearl, gold rings
> beautified with diamonds & other costly stones, jewels in
> both her eares of great worth. A gowne of damask with a
> deep gold fringe, a petticoat of red chamelet, stockings of
> carnasion silke, her breath and her whole body, the more to
> enamour thee, most fragrantly perfumed . . . Moreover shee
> will endeavour to enchant thee partly with her melodious
> notes that she warbles out on her lute . . . Also thou wilt
> find her a most elegant discourser . . . And to the end she
> may minister unto thee the stronger temptations to come to
> her lure, she will shew thee her chambers of recreation,
> where thou shalt see all manner of pleasing objects, and
> generally all her bedding sweetly perfumed.

Well, now. It is quite easy to see how this encounter caused such sniggering back home. Or encounters plural – how else could he know that the courtesans 'generally' perfumed their bedding? Inigo

Jones, the finest architect Britain had yet produced and a man you might think above such things, wrote in the introduction to the *Crudities*: 'And in his Atticke rage, He trod a rough hen of thirty years of age.' (A bit rich considering Coryate and Jones were both well past that – standards had changed a bit by 1817, when Byron 'enjoyed' an affair with an enormous sixty-three-year-old courtesan who stuffed wodges of polenta down her bodice to keep her going on the job.)

So did he or didn't he? The frontispiece illustration of Tommy

fleeing in a gondola while a tart pelts him with eggs is footnoted with: 'For he did but kisse her, and so let her go.' The implication: aroused beyond self-control by the perfumed chest and all those clockwork vibrators, he couldn't resist a quick free-sample grope with Margarita.

Certainly the courtesan passage is the only time he gets saucy with his prose – describing their enthusiasm, he notes, 'they open their quivers to every arrow', and raising the question of offspring, writes that 'they have but few, for according to the old proverbe the best carpenters make the fewest chips'. But was this just general ribaldry, being lewd for lewd's sake in the world's lewdness capital?

There's no doubt that it sits uneasily with his priggish distaste at the sight of non-tarts walking about Venice in a state of semi-undress. But then at Milan, he had reported: 'Near to one of these Rivers I saw a pretty amorous sight; a woman naked from the middle upward sitting at her work.' Try as I might, though, it was difficult to find further passages that might shed some light on Coryate's opinion of women. The only other comments were on a procession he witnessed at Vercelli: 'I never saw in all my life such an ugly company of truls and sluts as their women were.' At best ambiguous. Did he find just those women repellent, or all women, or all women except high-class tarts? You can see what I'm getting at. Despite my best intentions, which weren't actually much cop to begin with, I had long ago succumbed to a prurient obsession with Thomas Coryate's sexuality. And in Venice, where gossip and intrigue have always been practised with religious fervour, what choice did I have?

He never married. He never – despite the bawdy illustrations – admits to female-oriented lustful thoughts or deeds. Michael Strachan's biography, as might be expected from an academic work published in 1962, was hardly riddled with speculative innuendo. 'It is not difficult to conclude from a simple Freudian analysis of his obsession with hugging columns that Coryate was an eager and prolific homo,' is all I could find, and of course I just made that up.

What, though, of a very good friend he had made a few weeks earlier: 'In Padua, a certaine Italian Gentleman assisted me, a Student of the Citie, one Signior Paulo . . . He shewed himselfe very affable and courteous towards me, and desirous to embrace my friendship. For confirmation whereof he sent me six Greek verses from Padua to Venice, as a pledge of his love to me . . .'? And, as circumstantial evidence of some sort, here is William Lithgow's verdict on the students of Padua, written following a visit to the city in 1771:

'They are notorious for their beastly Sodomy . . . a monstrous filthiness, but to them a pleasant pastime, making songs and singing sonnets of the beauty and pleasure of their Bardassi, or buggered boys.' In Greek.

If he was the first, he wouldn't be the last. A desire to experience the fruits of tolerance led many Grand Tourists to come out of the travel closet – homosexuality was despised by British society as 'the Italian vice', but even in eighteenth-century Paris there were 'boys that walked about in the evenings to be picked up, as women do about the playhouses in London'. And there was something about the anything-goes decadence of Venice that particularly egged visitors on: William Beckford fell in love with a youth there in 1780, and . . . well, I dunno, what about *Death in Venice*? And I'm sure there was something similar with Anthony Andrews in *Brideshead Revisited*.

But having shamed myself and my profession (whatever that might be) with this hotchpotch of baseless tittle-tattle, it has to be remembered that Coryate spoke no Italian, and in 1608 it would have been tough to find a woman he could have conversed with. And God knows how you'd go about chatting someone up in Latin. Mind you, the morning-after banter wouldn't have been so tough: I saw, I conquered, I came.

Away from the pleasure palaces, I blundered across a little marble jewel box of a church, Santa Maria dei Miracoli, and then the Ospedale Civile, whose fanciful fifteenth-century façade I was astonished to find still concealed a real hospital, with real dressing-gowned patients joining real white-coated doctors for a fag by the fluorescent-lit reception desk.

And the church next door, the Santi Giovanni e Paolo, was a bit of a find, too. Here Coryate had found an epitaph, to a Marcantonio

Bragadin, that he was unable to survey 'with a dry eye'. I found it soon enough, high on the brick walls as you went in. But of course it was in Latin, and as Signor Bragadin had lacked the foresight to be killed by Caecilius's polyspaston, I scanned the gold lettering with slack-jawed imbecility, unable to survey it with a dry chin.

Miraculously, though, my Cadogan guide had the full story, which I read an hour later over a plate of *spaghetti vongole* to take my mind off two niggling worries: that the crumb-templed waiter had used my breadsticks to clean his ears, and that I had no idea how to get home. Bragadin was the Venetian commander of Cyprus, whose fortress had been besieged by the Turks in 1570. For a year he and his 350 troops held out; finally the Turkish commander (with an army ten times the size) proposed an honourable surrender. Bragadin agreed to hoist the white flag under these terms, but while he was signing the accord the Turks suddenly turned on the Venetian troops, butchering them all.

Except Bragadin: noseless and earless, he was tortured for two weeks before being stripped naked, lashed to a gallows and flayed alive, somehow maintaining a dignified silence throughout. His skin, lovingly stuffed with straw, was sent back to the Sultan in Constantinople – there's one answer to the question of what to give the man who has everything – where it hung for twenty years before being nicked by a daring Venetian POW and brought back to the city. The memorial, only twelve years old when Coryate's damp eyes scanned its inscription, is topped by an urn containing Bragadin's 'neatly folded' skin – an improbable claim that was astonishingly proven true after a recent investigation financed by one of his descendants.

Having consequently lost my appetite I paid up, went out and lost my way. Somewhere up there the stars were out in force, but it was fiendishly cold now and more than a little lonely. In Coryate's day gangs of stiletto-wielding 'braves' lurked under the bridges, knifing passers-by through the ribs and throwing the pillaged bodies in the canal. Hauling my hat and calendars through tiny black alleys, silent but for an occasional echoing dungeon drip, I thought how glad I was that I hadn't looked then in *Don't Look Now* when Donald Sutherland was being chased down just such thoroughfares by that anoraked dwarf.

Another of the problems with Venice, I was beginning to see, is that although there is an undeniable poetry about the place, it's in a minor-key melancholy honed by 450 years of slow decline. I'm a miserable enough git as it is. When I go on holiday I want vibrant cities astir with firework displays and unicycling clowns, not some gilded ghost town sliding mournfully into a putrid sea.

It was easy now to see why Venice was being slowly abandoned: apart from the once-a-decade plagues that killed 600 a day, apart from the stench and the long-standing rising damp problem, apart from the bloody tourists, getting around was such an unutterable pain. Twice I nearly strode out of a dark alley and into a darker canal. Close your eyes and take four steps in any direction and five times out of six you're up to your neck in raw sewage or spread-eagled in a gondola, face down in a Japanese lap. No wonder there aren't any kids left. It's hardly the kind of place where you can send them outside for a kickabout with their mates. I suppose water polo just doesn't quicken the adolescent pulse; the polar opposite here, in fact, when you think what's in the canals.

I was woken by an insistent chorus of off-key church bells, seem-ingly eleven minutes after I'd finally found my way back to the hotel and up to bed. A very short time later, with sightseeing autopilot engaged and the last dregs of a litre of supermarket milk dribbling down my chin, I was crossing the Rio San Girolamo. There, on the opposite bank, were the teetering, seven-floor tenements of the Ghetto, scene of Coryate's most shameful encounter.

Ghetto, of course, is another Venetian derivation, and because I seem to keep blithely trotting that out without bothering to explain further, it's from the foundry, or *geto*, that occupied the site – actually a small island – until 1390. For centuries, persecuted Jews from all over Europe took refuge here, lured by reports of Venetian tolerance. That this tolerance expressed itself in imprisoning Jews on the island from midnight to dawn, guarded by an army whose wages they were forced to pay, and in obliging them to wear identifying badges and red clothing to demonstrate their guilt for Christ's blood, indicates the sort of conditions they were fleeing from. The reason the ramshackle buildings are the tallest residences in Venice is because 5,000 of them were squeezed on to the island, which as I looked at it seemed about the size of a tennis court. So, that's the set-up. Now cue Tommy . . .

At the synagogue: 'The Levite doth pronounce before the congregation by an undecent roaring, and as it were a beastly bellowing of it forth . . .'

Outside the synagogue: 'I said to my selfe our English proverbe: To looke like a Jewe (whereby is meant a weather beaten warp-faced fellow, sometimes a phrenticke and lunaticke person) . . .'

By the gate: 'Many of them doe raise their fortunes by usury, in so much that they flea many a poore Christians estate by their griping extortion . . .'

But these were just warm-ups for the main feature. Striking up a conversation with 'a learned Rabbin', Coryate embarks on what by any reckoning must be termed a bold endeavour: the conversion of the Ghetto's 5,000 residents to Christianity. 'I asked him his

opinion of Christ, and why he did not receive him for his Messiah
. . . Withall I added that the predictions and sacred oracles both of
Moyses, and all the holy Prophets of God, aymed altogether at
Christe as their onely marke . . . and at last descended to the pers-
wasion of him to abandon and renounce his Jewish religion and to
undertake the Christian faith, without the which he should be eter-
nally damned . . .'

Here's a multiple choice. Using your skill and judgement, decide
which of the following scenarios most accurately describes what
happened next:

(a) The rabbi nods thoughtfully, then stands forward to plant a
lingering, tearful kiss on Coryate's forehead while a crowd of forty
or fifty passers-by hurl their skullcaps into the canal with a grateful
whoop of liberation.

(b) The rabbi politely begs to differ while a crowd of forty or
fifty passers-by queue up to thank Coryate for his contribution to
a thought-provoking debate.

(c) The rabbi calls Jesus a silly poor wretch that once rode upon
an ass, while a crowd of forty or fifty passers-by flock about Coryate
and begin to threaten he who durst reprehend their religion,
offering violence, hurling missiles and driving him back towards
the canal edge.

It all defied belief. Coryate was only saved from being lynched
and/or drowned by the chance appearance of Sir Henry Wotton's
gondola; the ambassador despatched 'Gentleman Master Belford
his secretary' to bundle Coryate on board. Here was the origin
of the knife-wielding pursuit pictured in the frontispiece ('flie
from the Jewes, lest thy circumcise thee'). 'Thank fuck I never
asked that nutter to kip at my place,' noted Sir Henry in his diary
that evening.

Still shaking my head, I paced around the Ghetto's courtyard, a cultural centre for the few hundred Jews whose parents managed to hide from the Nazis. Even allowing for the rampant bigotry of the time it was difficult to explain Coryate's actions. I could only suppose it was an exaggerated form of the belligerent arrogance that seems to affect a certain sort of Briton on the Continent, the sort who sees a holiday as a military campaign, from our friend who sought not to spend more money in the country of our natural enemy than was required to support with decency the character of an Englishman, to topless, sunburnt England fans torching Tunisian flags in Marseille.

It was in a bid to build bridges with the local populace that I went straight into a bookshop and bought a pocket Italian–English dictionary. Not for me the boorish shout-and-they'll-understand insolence of the defiant monolinguist, I thought, haunted by Coryate's awfulnesses. But if a little knowledge is a dangerous thing, I am now obliged to report that a tiny bit more is lethal.

'*Sport e lavoro – Noleggio di nave*' said the sign down a pungent alley opposite the Ghetto. 'Sport and work – charter of ship' said the dictionary. Pleased with this success, I turned my attention to the grubby plastic plaque by the door beneath the sign. I had soon established that ships could apparently be chartered for as little as £25 for an afternoon, and an exciting idea was born. If the proprietor of this nautical man-and-van operation was amenable, I could wangle a chauffeur-driven cruise through the real Venice, Coryate's Venice, away from the tourists – and all for the price of half a cocktail at Harry's Bar. Straddling an enormous dog turd, I rang the bell.

The door opened, and in its place, filling the frame almost as completely, stood a huge, sweating, bald-headed buddha of a man. '*Prego?*' he said in a voice that suggested his larynx had recently been given the Bragadin treatment by some Turks with long memories and longer chisels. Using most of my new words, I managed to agree a deal with surprising ease. An afternoon's charter arranged for four hours starting from now, we walked into his gloomy, quiet boat-house. '*Lavoro?*' he rasped, aiming an oily, nailless thumb at a stunted barge suspended from the roof. That didn't look like much fun. A slightly racier hull boasting a powerful-looking outboard was harnessed up to a winch, ready to be lowered into the canal below. I nodded at it. 'Sport.'

A minute later, I was squatting in the centre of this open boat, gripping the sides with my hands and wondering how we had avoided capsizing when Buddha leapt heavily aboard. My job, it seemed, was as lookout and navigator, or so I gathered from a cursory lecture involving hand signals and many instances of the words for left and right. Then Buddha started up the outboard with a fat-armed, gladiatorial yank, and above the chainsaw buzz began to bellow mechanical information. At least so I assumed from the way he would periodically complicate some already unintelligible point by pressing a button or consulting a gauge in a 'Fig. 3.11 – decoking the camshafts' fashion. I supposed if he fell overboard or – odds-on with the bookies – suffered a massive stroke, I'd need to know these things.

When Buddha clumsily jumped back on to the tiny pavement

quay and climbed up the fire-escape stairs into his boathouse, I presumed he was off to get some dockets or some such. After all, I hadn't yet paid for or signed anything. Then, however, the boathouse's roller-blind shutters clanked and ratcheted down, followed seconds later by a door being bolted and receding fat-man's footsteps echoing away down an alley. I waited until the considerable lateral motion caused by Buddha's deck departure stopped, somehow seeking to hold on to the last vestige of his presence. The motor buzzed away on idle. The backwater canal lapped gently at the hull. Around me, dunked-biscuit buildings crumbled soggily into cold tea. For five long minutes I kneeled there, still holding the sides of the boat, before accepting that the big feller hadn't gone to make me a sandwich, or to get me a photograph of his parents, or to change into his Captain Canal outfit.

I felt very, very sad. The first time I manage to dump the sod-buttocking Rolls, and I find myself in a self-drive horror with scope for even more memorable disaster. How could he do this to me? I had signed nothing, and so presumably had no insurance, no collision damage waiver, no idiocy exception clause. Charter, it had said – I've been on dozens of charter flights from Gatwick, and haven't yet had to sort out an ugly argument among the passengers about who puts on the peaked cap and epaulettes and who gets lumbered with restocking the trolleys. I couldn't have made it any plainer that I knew nothing about boats than if I'd turned up dressed as Buzz Lightyear.

Humming improvised melodies in an unsteady falsetto, I weighed up the options. The most appealing was to clamber ashore, leaving the engine running, and inch my way to freedom along the brick-wide path. Just behind came repeatedly slapping myself about the head and neck while emitting throat-ripping peacock shrieks. But gradually, very gradually, I found the Tango-ad hysteria melting into a Hamlet-ad calm. The tiny part of my brain that had not instantly capitulated to the combined forces of panic and paranoia reported a total absence of other craft, or indeed other people. Public safety might not necessarily be compromised; public shame might not necessarily be confronted. I unfolded my map, which was unwieldy but detailed. Ahead was a dead end: maybe − big inhalation, big exhalation − màybe I could just turn around, drift down to the junction behind me, hang a right, have a quick peek at the Grand Canal and return.

As the canal I was currently in seemed about two inches narrower than my boat, the difficult part of this plan seemed to be the U-turn. I repositioned myself on the bench by the outboard, and gave the throttle an experimental twist. In a great explosion of noise and froth, the front of the boat shot forward and upward while I toppled backward and downward. By the time I had righted myself and released the throttle, the boat, using the single rope that tethered the front to the quayside, had pivoted round in a precise 180-degree arc.

Well. I was clearly a natural. Looking around the dishevelled, shuttered buildings to acknowledge the applause, I untied the rope, threw it with a stevedore's flourish on to the fire-escape stairs and weaved away up the Rio della Sensa in a steady drizzle.

I was just getting the hang of the push-right-to-turn-left thing, and had even yoo-hooed under an echoing low bridge, when my tiny sliver of water T-junctioned with something rather wider, and substantially busier. I released the throttle and coasted towards the Grand Canal. A big *vaporetto* water-bus ploughed across in front of me, and indeed above me, and as the small tsunami of its wake washed over my bows I decided I'd seen enough.

Only then an irritated imprecation barked out from behind, and

I turned around to see my world filled by a substantial barge, a world ruled by a man in monogrammed overalls who stood on the cement bags piled up in the bow angrily waving me forwards. Devil, meet deep blue sea. With the barge almost nudging my propeller and a single, complicated obscenity fluttering reedily from my lips I yanked the throttle and surged forwards, feeling like Butch and Sundance at the end of the film.

I like to think I brought a little colour to Venice's waterways that afternoon. There were so many highlights to choose from: the apoplectic gondolier jabbing at my throat with his oar, the three laughing American boys who bodily lifted my bow off the semi-submerged staircase I had somehow mounted, the collisions. Ah, the collisions: bridges, walls, fellow canal users – my proudest moment was a thumping blow which finished off an abandoned dinghy (or anyway a very dirty one) in a mercifully quiet canal round the back of the docks. It was while trying to extricate my craft from the resultant wreckage that I somehow reversed on to a sunken doorstep, an audibly memorable marriage of stonework and rapidly revolving metal, and one whose messy divorce had a drastic adverse effect on my subsequent progress. The 1:1 scale map flapped soggily about my wet and trembling feet, but to even steal a glance at it would have been like thumbing through the room-service menu to see how much you're going to be charged for the pinless grenade you just found in your minibar. I could, of course, have tied up somewhere. Just as I could, of course, have not thrown my only rope on to the boathouse stairs when I cast off.

As a result, as well as not knowing what I was doing, I never knew where I was going. One minute I was sobbing gently along the Rio della Misericordia, the next I was out in the bloody open sea, with car ferries and barnacled buoys and foghorns and an enormous gale straight in my teeth, and the boat which had seemed so enormous as I ricocheted from one crumbling palazzo wall to another suddenly seemed a stupid child's toy, complete with stupid child. And try as I might – to the extent of regularly defying one-way signs and gesturing boatswains – there was just no avoiding the brutal maritime anarchy that was the Grand Canal. Gondola ferries criss-crossing, *vaporetti* zig-zagging, barging barges full of builders' rubble and beer bottles, and the pilots of all bellowing, '*Sinistra! Destra!*' and calling me all the names under the rain.

My crowning glory came after I wedged the boat between a *vaporetto* pier near the Rialto and a gaily barber-striped gondola mooring post – while kicking myself free, I somehow got a limb entwined in the motor's safety cut-off string, thereby disconnecting it and sending me spinning in serene silence towards the very centre of the canal. I actually came very close to doing a Byron and diving in, still aware that Buddha had taken no deposit and no details. Only on the fifth yank, one accompanied by a howl so bestial that every face on every boat rotated to see what was going on, did I finally fire up the outboard. Craft of all sizes were now log-jammed around me in a deafening, ugly mess. It had been like defacing a Canaletto.

At least I was now beyond caring. Cowed no more by the vicious taunts of Venice's white-boat men, nor by their flamboyant, inch-perfect manoeuvring, I steamed blindly through the confusion across thirty-two lanes of traffic and into the nearest side canal, idly pondering that as this was clearly just a bad dream, I might as well make the most of it and throw my clothes overboard. I might even have done so had I not discovered that my right hand was immovably locked in a deathly embrace about the throttle grip.

White of knuckle, dry of mouth, I had at last manufactured the narcotic unreality that had infected so many Brits in Venice over the centuries. But it was a bad trip in every sense. All I can remember noting was that even the Grand Canal was studded with sad, abandoned homes, and that along the more distant waterways nearly all the buildings seemed empty, unloved and on the verge of throwing themselves into the water in despair. It's daft – if the locals don't want to be there, but six million tourists do, even in bloody November, surely there must be a way of tarting these places up as heritage timeshares. I don't know. And to be honest, I don't care. Live a poetic life, die a poetic death. Rot in heaven.

I did find my way back to Buddha's place, completely by accident and long after I'd begun looking forward to abandoning the boat. I had even found the perfect place: a cul-de-sac off the Grand Canal, where I could quietly disembark before wedging the throttle slightly open and the rudder slightly tilted, sending her out to create merry hell. By now I was convinced that my progress around the waterways would have become a live local-radio event, with witnesses phoning in to report my latest mishap, and when I saw Buddha's bare, big-eared skull leering out above me as I banged into his quayside and killed the motor, it seemed inevitable that a pair of police caps would shortly be bookending it. And I'd have gone quietly: most of my useful joints were welded to inarticulation by stress and fatigue, and cold, moisture and exhaustion had reduced my mental resistance to that of a drugged puppy. If they'd given me a prepared confession admitting sole responsibility for Venice's mercantile decline, I'd have signed it without question.

But unbelievably, ludicrously, Buddha didn't inspect the ravaged hull and chewed-up propeller; barely less credibly, after more or less carrying my rigid, foetal form ashore he didn't even charge me for an hour and a half of unused charter time – especially kind as I had in fact been in his boat for almost twelve years. Buddha's only karmic payback was provided by a visit to his grotesque footprint latrine, which when flushed soaked me up to the shins in a barely diluted solution of predictable constituents.

Well, that was that. I was all done in. My plan had been to stay another day, perhaps two, and try to tame Venice's overbearing flood of history and culture by visiting every place recorded in *Coryats Crudities*. (Later, in fact, I realised I more or less had – of the 120-odd pages he devotes to Venice, a generous proportion is devoted to Latin inscriptions copied down in churches.) A flabby and distended adrenal gland squirted its last weary dribble into my bloodstream, just enough to keep two kneeless, goose-stepping limbs moving until I got back to the hotel. Too hungry to eat, too tired to sleep, I lay fully clothed on the bed and tried to stop thinking.

FIVE

Garda, Bergamo and Como

'Thus much of the glorious citie of Venice' was Coryate's fond farewell as he bobbed away in his gondola back to the mainland. That night, sleeping in an abandoned farmhouse just past Padua, he must have felt a terrible melancholy at the abrupt change in his surroundings, at the realisation that as he'd now spent all his money during those six weeks, there would be many more nights like this ahead. The Grand Tourists, too, would have left Venice with a morning-after sigh, though as most of them now branched away from Tommy and me, heading off to Florence, Rome and Naples, there would soon be plenty of distractions to take their mind off it.

The good thing about the distressing finale to my own stay in Venice was that it made everything non-Venetian seem wonderful. As my train rattled back along the causeway, Mestre's petrochemical flares and red-and-white striped chimneys acquired a thrusting, space-age boldness, the sun came out and I beamed so broadly at the middle-aged French couple opposite that the wife involuntarily grabbed her husband's arm. I was even glad to see the Rolls, at least initially. When I got inside, it was clear that things were awry. I looked ahead: the Paduan feather had gone. I looked up: the rear-view mirror reflected a clear view of my shoulder. I looked down: my knees were buckled up double. Someone very small had been sitting in this car, making drastic ergonomic adjustments to the driving position. Then I remembered I had noted down the mileage when I left the car, to record how my Dover to Venice distance compared to Coryate's (1,421 to his 952). It had been 186,649. Now it was 186,665.

In a way I was flattered, trying to wink knowingly at the stunted grease monkey manning the payment hut. But that didn't stop me from waiting until he'd gone before snatching a handful of small, plastic-poled pennants from a hefty cocktail-flags-of-all-nations display on the table, smothering them in my jacket and roaring off with features set in grim satisfaction.

With three days of repressed progress suddenly uncorked, I got rather carried away that day, driving halfway across northern Italy: a wet lunch in Vicenza, a wet coffee in Verona, a wet supper by Lake Garda. This was Palladio country, home to the hugely influential Classical villas that the Venetian architect built in the decades before Coryate's visit for wealthy merchants desperate for a rural haven away from Venice's pungent claustrophobia. The most famous, the Villa Rotonda near Vicenza, was designed in 1551, but this festival of symmetry was still being copied around the world (from Chiswick House to Thomas Jefferson's Monticello) two hundred years later. And I'd like to put my man down for an assist: his detailed architectural description of the villa is credited with inspiring his 'friend' Inigo Jones (of rough-hen-treading fame), the man who changed the face of British architecture with his Palladio-inspired buildings (most notably the Queen's House at Greenwich).

Coryate also inspired the Grand Tourists: by the Tour's heyday, a trip to a couple of Palladian villas was considered essential, usually by those en route to Venice keen to chalk up some aesthetic-education points before they went and blew the family fortune on roulette and tarts.

Of course, the Villa Rotonda was closed for the winter when I got there, its dome peeking distantly at me from the smooth, green 'eminent hillocke' like a Classical Teletubby Land. I ate in the car, parked by the side of a municipal pitch where twenty-two men aged from seventeen to sixty were playing attractive football in unhelpfully damp conditions. 'Where your little angel?' shouted a Super Mario-tached defender, pointing at the hole atop my grille as he trotted past to retrieve the ball. Again I wondered what Coryate must have thought as he strolled through all this breathtakingly advanced culture, a glimpse of how Britain might look to his great-grandchildren (had he not been completely gay). Though he never mentions Shakespeare (at the time busily finishing off *The Winter's Tale*, his penultimate work), he must have walked into Verona pondering the unlikelihood of a noted Italian playwright presenting his masterpiece *The Two Gentlemen of Ipswich*.

As an unavoidable economy measure, Coryate was now on foot. He left Venice on 7 August, and after his boat tied up at Padua the next day, he didn't stop walking until he got to Wallenstadt, near Zürich, on the 24th. I looked at the map. The never-ending Lombardy plain, then two merciless rows of Alps to climb and descend, followed by a long and treacherous mountain valley – and all on winding, rubble-strewn paths in the heat of high summer. It was like the route of a vicious cycling stage race, its itinerary tailor-made to push a man to the limits of human endurance. I wondered if he was punishing himself, an act of penance for whatever he'd got up to in Venice.

Economic duress had certainly made him a lot cockier. Near Vicenza he sneaked into a barn and bedded down for the night; at the Villa Rotonda he demanded a tour of the wine cellars, and was outraged when 'the cellarer had not the honestie to bestowe as much as one draught of his wine upon me'. And he was now shamelessly plundering the fields for sustenance: 'I did oftentimes borrow a point of law in going into their Vineyards without leave, to refresh my selfe with some of their grapes.' The locals had worse things to worry about: this was bandit country, and approaching Verona Coryate noted that his fellow travellers all had loaded muskets, 'because the people of the country will rob and murder passengers if they are not sufficiently provided to defend themselves'. All Coryate had was a stick. He might not have had much cash on him, but the robbers wouldn't have known that. As a man who had seen more strung-up criminals in the past couple of months than most would see in a lifetime, he of all people must have known the risks. Call it reckless, call it cocksure – but in my eyes he was proving himself the Hard Man of early seventeenth-century travel.

It was business as usual in Verona. Describing the amphitheatre, he uses the words 'faire', 'fayrer' or 'fayrest' eight times in one paragraph, and noted that the locals were already restoring the Roman seating, splashing out 66,000 crowns on new marble benches. And no Coryate account of a town would be complete without some horrible story: 'Albonius, King of the Lombards, who compelled his wife Rosamunda to drinke one day at table out of the skull of her father Cunimundus, whom a little before he had slaine'. And it was business as usual for me too: an hour of rainy laps to find a parking

space, then a dash out into the damp-but-jolly Saturday-evening
market to scoop up a fake Juventus shirt for my five-year-old and
neck down an espresso so strong it gave me hiccups. (Tip from P.
Sadka of Cremona: for an 'ordinary' coffee, ask for '*un Americano*'.)

Stuck out on the end of a 3-mile promontory that cleaves the fat
end of Lake Garda into two jowly buttocks, Sirmione is so
intriguing on a map that I can't quite understand why Coryate
walked straight past to Desenzano without even mentioning it.
There's a Roman villa, a hot spring, a splendid old castle – and, I
can report, some astonishingly cheap hotels. At least on a wet night
in November.

This was big weather: driving up the promontory, autumnal leaf
pulp was storm-blasted against the Rolls's windward flank. I parked
in front of the castle that guards the entrance to the old town, gusts
punching the car and hurling sheets of rain at the windows with
bucket-of-water slaps. The quivering lampposts were ringing, singing
wind instruments; aluminium yacht masts pendulumed crazily in the
small dock; as I flew past the moat in a wind-assisted gallop I noted
even that was storm ravaged, with swans unhappily surfing huge
breakers. But the town walls were effective windbreaks – and indeed
rainbreaks, given the horizontal precipitation – and as soon as I ran
in under the portcullis it all went quiet.

Maybe it's teeming and steamy and awful in summer, but off
season Sirmione was splendid, and it was all mine. Shaking myself
like a wet dog, I soon found a very comfortable, very empty hotel,
almost snogging the wizened crone at the desk when she wrote
down the price: a shade less than £20, including breakfast. I went
up to the room: the telly didn't work but the laundry-drying radiator did, and in reflecting I'd prefer it that way round I recognised

some sort of threshold had been crossed, probably the one into middle age. Worryingly untroubled by this, I went out into the empty streets.

Wet and winding cobbles occasionally opened up into welcoming little piazzas; up medieval side alleys lined with immaculate marble-and-chrome boutiques and jewellers were the ornamental gates of desirable holiday villas. People didn't feel the need to chain up their garden furniture as they seemed to in every other Italian garden whose wall I'd poked my nose over; everything was well tended and well mended – for once there was no seedy underbelly, no doubt because this was a tiny town inhabited by a small number of very rich people.

Along with a rather larger number of very bored waiters – in every restaurant and bar I walked past, and there were a good dozen, a group of uniformed staff sat round one of the deserted tables playing cards and smoking. One particular place had seven of them: waiters, mushroom-hatted chefs, a suited proprietor. Three times I passed it and had a quick glance at the window-posted menu; three times they all scrambled to their posts in a great flurry of dogged fags and starched linen. I suppose for some people, most notably my wife, being privately waited upon by a team of seven would consti-tute the ideal dining experience. For my part, there isn't much I wouldn't do to avoid such a fate, including traipsing about in cold circles for an hour to find an establishment with a less oppressive staff:diner ratio, even if that meant another pizza and another carafe of watered-down Lambrusco.

The wind finally conquered Sirmione as I slept, or tried to amid the amateur-dramatic cacophony of storm sound-effects. It howled down alleys, banging shutters and hurling unchained garden furniture into greenhouses; it knocked pantiles into the street and caused animals audible distress. After breakfast I went to the end of the promontory; with the dense little town cowering lopsidedly behind me it was like being the figurehead on a shipwreck. The skies were still fast-forwarding darkly overhead, and the little beach promenade had been spectacularly breached by waves that still pounded the remaining few octagonal paving slabs and the last upright streetlight. Somewhere in the clouded north the Alps came right down to the top shore of Italy's largest lake; behind, to the south-west, was the bleary smear of Desenzano, where Coryate had stayed.

I'd had my fill of the fog and flatness of the sodding goodly faire plaine of Lombardy, and the sight of hills excited me almost as much as the prospect of setting off to examine the aftermath of a natural disaster. The car was fine – only a tempest right off the end of the Beaufort Scale could budge a Rolls-Royce – but the opposite side of the car park was under a foot of water, and on the way down the promontory, waves were lapping up to hotel receptions.

The road into Desenzano was flanked by felled poplars; just outside the town my path was blocked by a huge trunk, and after half an hour of watching firemen delicately snapping little twigs off it I turned north and hoped for the best. And I got it: half an hour up Garda's last shore I arrived at Salo, where Mussolini patiently waited for two years before the partisans finally got around to stringing him up from a lamppost, and having turned left to complete my trian-gular detour I found myself outside Vittoriale, last home of every fascist's favourite playboy patriot, Gabriele D'Annunzio.

Reading him arrestingly described in the Michelin guide as 'a brilliant soldier and conqueror of Fiume, a novelist, a playwright and a poet' I parked in front of the villa and walked in. The house itself was closed, but the gardens weren't, and nor was the little office where a nice lady gave me a leaflet describing his extraordinary life, which I shall now précis:

1863: Born Francesco Rapagnetta.

Age 16: Publishes collection of poetry under new name.

19: Marries Maria Hardouin di Gallese, a duke's daughter. Does a load more poetry.

26: Now a father of three, publishes first novel, *The Child of Pleasure*, a heavily autobiographical account of a snobbish, weak-willed decadent.

28: Publishes second novel, *The Victim*, a heavily autobiographical account of a sexually depraved husband who forces his chaste wife into adultery. Divorced.

30: Has image of own penis embroidered on to favourite pair of slippers.

31: A long liaison with Contessa Gravina Auguissola gives way to another with the actress Eleonora Duse. Starts writing heavily autobiographical plays, mostly featuring himself as a Nietzschean Superman figure. An excitably poetic nature leads him to develop an exaggerated interest in extreme right-wing nationalism.

34: Is elected to parliament as an extreme right-wing nationalist.

37: Loses his seat and goes to the south of France. Sits around on the beach. A lot.

51: First World War breaks out. Remembers the old extreme right-wing nationalism. Returns to Italy and becomes celebrated propagandist and patriotic speechwriter.

53: Joins the air force. Cops one in the face during a dogfight and loses an eye.

56: Italy hands over the Adriatic port of Fiume as part of peace settlement. Declares war on Italy for this act of national treachery, then leads his own private army into the town and rules it as dictator for eighteen months.

58: Lets Italy off with a warning and comes home.

59: Watching Mussolini assume control over Italy, declares that dictators are spiritual successors of mythical heroes. Mussolini gives him a load of cash.

61: Declares that dictators embody the spirit of the nation. Mussolini makes him Prince of Monte Nevoso.

62: Finds his pet giant turtle dead on lawn after eating tulip bulbs. Has it stuffed and placed in central position on dining table as warning to guests on dangers of gluttony.

74: Dies of a stroke at his writing desk. Mussolini builds him a huge mausoleum in his villa's back garden.

Actually that wasn't all. Benito also arranged for an amphitheatre to be built in the grounds (D'Annunzio's plays are still performed there in the summer), and, most extraordinarily, for the huge Navy frigate D'Annunzio used during his invasion of Fiume to be lugged up the hill and plonked down in a rockery overlooking the lake. And he did all this not because he was especially grateful, but because he was scared of D'Annunzio's reputation. Fail to show him enough respect and even after death he might still inspire nutcase Italians into unpredictable acts of revenge. This, after all, was a man who claimed to have drunk aperitifs from the skulls of virgins who had done away with themselves for love of him.

You can't imagine any of this going on in the Third Reich. There would never have been a German D'Annunzio, just as, despite Mussolini's best efforts, there would never have been an Italian Hitler.

There was a parking ticket on the Rolls when I got back. If I'd been in Germany I'd have at least thought about paying it, but I wasn't, so I didn't.

Then it was back south, back into the plain of Lombardy and its renewed industrial emphasis. For every vineyard there was a dark satanic mill – no wonder Soave tastes like that. Still, it was shaming to compare all this manufacturing vigour with the almost total extinction of such activity in Britain. Only five years ago more motor vehicles were produced in Britain than Italy, but now we just don't make stuff any more. It had been the same everywhere I'd been, and would be in the places I had still to go, but while evidence of Germany's industrial might was depressingly predictable, and that of France's predictably depressing, I couldn't quite believe that Italy could be doing all this robustly industrial stuff-making while we faffed about selling each other timeshares and generally engaging in hot-air service activities of dubious long-term worth. Did you know the inventor of the silicon chip was an Italian?

What, in fact, did 'Britain' mean in a commercial capacity abroad? The only evidence I'd seen of any high-street presence was the occasional themed gift shop selling shortbread and Burberry teapots. Twee, cottage-industrial anachronism – I suppose the Rolls fitted in quite well (though not for long, of course, as the company is now owned by the Germans). And if it was bad for Britain, it was especially bad for England. So feeble is the selling potential of brand England, an Italian firm sells its flavoured potato crisps – one of the few products in which the English unequivocally lead the world – under the banner Highlander: Ayrshire Pepper, Caledonian Tomato and all.

I was beginning to understand TC's descent into jealous petty crime. But at Brescia, he went too far, sneaking into a chapel and pinching a 'little waxen idol': 'I had a marvailous itching desire to finger one of them, to shew it to my friends as a token of their idolatry; but I saw there was some difficulty in the matter. I stood at one corner of the Chappel while the women were prostrate before the image, and very secretly conveighed my fingers into a little basket where the images were laid, and so purloyned one of them out, and brought him home into England.' Honestly. And not just insultingly rude, but dangerously idiotic: as Coryate admits, if he'd been caught, he would have been imprisoned by the Inquisition 'longer then I could willingly have endured it'.

Brescia on a Sunday afternoon was benignly prosperous, with families promenading in a funereal calm broken by the occasional screeching scooterist. But I couldn't see anyone who looked like they deserved having their faith defiled, except maybe the kid who flicked a caramelised peanut through my window as I drove past, and I set off on a pilgrimage of Brescia's ecclesiastical outposts in a bid to find Coryate's chapel and apologise on his behalf.

My quest, though, was a dispiriting one – even on the Sabbath most of the churches were closed, no doubt due to a lingering apprehension that someone might sneak in and get sticky fingered with the waxen idols. But after an hour I saw a nun exit a quiet, back-street chapel and drive away in a very loud Fiat Panda, and having cross-referenced with the *Crudities* willed myself to believe that this was the place. It was open and it was empty – no people, and not even a lick of paint on the bare stone walls. I had intended to make a modest financial atonement, and after some searching found a slot in the wall into which I slipped a tinny cascade of lire.

I was turning to leave when there was an electro-magnetic clank from some machine in the wall beneath the slot, and my saucered eyes beheld the suddenly illuminated recumbent effigy of a yellow-faced nun, previously entombed in darkness behind a glass panel in the wall. My retreat was as hasty as Coryate's, but I had already seen too much and four nights later Ol' Yeller starred as a shoplifter in a nocturnal vision of my future life as a Milanese store detective.

Taking the motorway to Bergamo was a cop-out, but it was a lovely drive anyway. To my right, snow-slathered Alps pierced sunset-bruised clouds; to my left, poplars swayed above the twilight ground mist. Old Bergamo was perched on top of a huge rock, and hoping it was better than the fantastically bland new Bergamo I slalomed the Rolls up to its summit.

Though only a day after I'd visited them I was already having difficulty telling my Veronas from my Vicenzas, I can still recall Bergamo in loving detail. It was a shame for the Grand Tourists that hardly any of them came through here, or indeed any of the towns I'd passed through for the last day and a half. They wanted Venice, Florence, Rome and Naples, and if your town wasn't on the way there, tough.

This was my last night in Italy, and it put on a great farewell show. A two-floor, three-telly hotel suite for the price of a Venetian hovel; a moonlit market under the Renaissance colonnades; cobbled, hilly streets lined with late night confectioners; a basement restaurant packed with babbling locals where the waitress gamely mimed her way through the entire menu, earning cellar-wide acclaim for a definitive interpretation of Full-Cooked Donkey with Kidney Beans of the Dead. (Preferring my donkey medium rare, I had spag bol.)

Even Tommy did me proud, the *Crudities* leading me through a gorgeous pocket-sized piazza where a drunk was awkwardly recumbent beside the centrepiece marble fountain, under a robust Gothic arch, and straight up to an unbelievably embellished hexagonal tower, flush up against the cathedral but hopelessly outclassing it.

Its floodlit multicoloured marble accessories – plaques, pediments, pillars – jostled in polished profusion, and I was reminded of my years as an Airfix modeller, and how it sometimes seemed a shame not to use up all those decal decorations left over from earlier kits, even if that meant a John Player Special-sponsored Apollo 11 plastered with swastikas.

Inside this 'work of admirable sumptuousnesse' lay the body of Commander Bartolomeo Colleoni, history's most successful mercenary, a man who made one of the Renaissance's largest fortunes by running a grandiose protection racket. Having proved his tactical nous fighting on behalf of both Milan and Venice in the early fifteenth century, he signed a golden-handcuffs deal with the latter, its astonishingly generous financial terms negotiated after he nonchalantly pointed out how awkward it would be if he were to defect back to the Milanese. With the whole of northern Italy apparently scared shitless of him, suddenly no one wanted to start a fight and his last twenty years were spent flitting about various Venetian cities in lavish idleness.

It was clear looking at his chapel that here was someone not to argue with. As well as brazenly humiliating the rather more spartan cathedral, his hexagon was studded with the busts of his favourite Roman emperors. Not just arrogant, but heretical – as Coryate says, 'the images of prophane heathen men . . . ought not to be placed upon Churches were Christ is worshipped'. But there was more. You can get away with a lot when you're rich and scary, and the decoration on the railings around his chapel was what I had really come to see. Cathedral or no cathedral, Colleoni saw no reason to be ashamed of anything, and there, proudly cast in bronze that shone dully between alternate iron spikes, was his coat of arms: three bollocks rampant.

It's an interesting sign of the times that Coryate saw nothing amiss with this motif, merely stating matter-of-factly that 'in the middest of this his armes are finely wrought, which are three testicles. The reason is, because nature gave him three stones, one more than other men have.' (Actually, it may be more to do with the fact that 'Colleoni' is very close to '*coglioni*', Italian for bollocks. But still.) What was particularly noteworthy – and shame on all my guidebooks for glossing over the whole issue – was that the central trio of cobblers had been buffed up to a shine by generations of saggy-scroted Bergamese hoping for a little spiritual assistance, something for the weak end.

History, culture and smut in one compact scenario. It was this sort of thing that made Italy so entertaining, I thought as I stood on my balcony looking down at Lombardy, breath steaming into a starry sky. Just as it was that sort of thing – on the south-western horizon, beneath a *Close Encounters* halo of smoggy sodium, lay Milan – that made it such an ordeal. Tomorrow I would be in Switzerland; while I was wondering if that thought cheered me, I went back into the warmth, turned on a couple of tellies, poured a hefty tot of Abbeville brandy into a coffee cup and lay down on the noisy leather sofa with the *Crudities*. Coryate had  arrived to find Bergamo packed out for St Bartholomew's fair; having failed to locate a bed he'd been helped out by a priest who found him a barn (here I nestled down a bit in my sofa and took a smug slug of brandy). The priest kindly agreed to show Coryate round Bergamo the day after; when he failed to turn up, Coryate learnt that 'a certain bloudthirsty Italian' with an undisclosed grudge had 'shot him through the body with a pewternell'.

Oh. I put down the *Crudities* and went to the window. I'd hoped that my humbling epiphany before Milan Cathedral might have heralded the start of an authentic aesthetic awakening, my own personal renaissance, but authentic filth and fear had crowded out more noble sentiments. Culturally, Italy had the full set of baggage, but if you tried to peek inside it too often you'd turn round to find your own gone. A long way down the hill below the hotel three shiny-haired youths shiftily unzipped a big sports holdall under a streetlight, and in trying to see and hear what they were up to I succumbed once more to paranoia. 'Go on, Gianni, give us a hubcap. All I got were these stupid velvet trousers and a pair of wet pants.' Thus much of Italy. Wind up the cuckoo clocks.

Actually, I didn't make it to Switzerland. It was a day of highs and lows, some literal, many more figurative, and it began with me failing to notice that the Alpen-packet peaks cutting crisply into a perfect blue sky were rather whiter than they had been the afternoon before.

I had wanted to see the splendid interior of Commander Bollocks's chapel, but it was closed on winter Mondays, which delayed me a little and denied me the opportunity of doing as Monsieur Michelin urged – in italics – by ordering the deacon to display and illuminate the marquetry ('in the middest of this the armes of Timoteus Moore are finely wrought, which are one testicle. The reason is, because the deacon of the chappel did answere Moores robuste demande for marquetrie illumination by booting off one of his stones into the gallerie').

But it didn't matter soon, as I swished up the shrinking SS470 towards the San Marco Pass, shades on, splendidly cheesy accordion blaring out of the radio, the minty-fresh River Bembo churning downhill alongside. I sailed through San Pellegrino, past the mineral-water factory and an abandoned Harrods of a spa hotel; soon after the traffic all but disappeared and the only markings on the road were emulsioned exhortations to competitors in a long-gone cycling race. And then there was a sign.

PASSO SAN MARCO – CHIUSO

I don't know much Italian, but I know what I don't like. I was at a fork in the road, 20 kilometres from the top of the pass, and the rusty enamelled panel dangling from two poles beside the junction was intended to discourage further progress up the left turn. Wondering whether I should start sobbing gently straight away, or save it up for a single, concentrated howl of rage and anguish, I looked at the map. To turn around would be to embark upon an enormous backtracking detour, back down two folds of map, across another, back up two again – perhaps 120 kilometres on slow roads. To proceed, hoping that because the '*chiuso*' sign was the responsibility of an Italian government agency it would be nineteen years out of date, would mean, at worst, a slightly more enormous back-tracking detour. Settling into a low-intensity econo-sob, I flicked the indicator stalk down, span the big wheel anticlockwise and carried on up the mountain.

It had been a tough climb for Tommy, three days' slog from Bergamo, the last stretch a painful scramble up near-vertical paths paved with 'extreame hard stones'. But at the top he had found a little inn, with the winged lion that gave the pass its name set into the wall. This was the boundary of the state of Venice, and an inscription beneath the lion marked the opening of the path up to the pass only fourteen years before Coryate's visit.

I drove on. The road twisted and rose, but it wasn't closed. It went up through tiny villages where shrivelled old men wandered about the tarmac with huge cheeses under their arms, but it wasn't closed. Its shadier hairpins began to sport snowy patches, sending the Rolls's rear flailing slushily about as the wheels span with a frictionless turbine whine, but it wasn't closed. It tightened into a freshly snow-ploughed corridor, my wing mirrors scooping grooves in the narrow white walls, but it wasn't closed. Finally, with the road flattening and a radiant beam of delighted wonder making its debut across my face, I rounded the last corner and there, alongside a cosy little chalet-cum-café, was a messily hand-painted sign: '*REFUGIO DI SAN MARCO 1985m*'.

It was as I gingerly eased the car towards the chalet that I noticed, or rather slid obliquely into, the large wall of snow created when a plough stops, reverses and turns back. For a very short while I sat there with my hands on the wheel, staring at the white world ahead of me, the radiant beam folding inwards as I gradually slumped and crumpled like an inflatable doll with a slow puncture.

Leaving the Rolls with its face wedged in the snow, I robotically opened the door and more or less fell out into a deep drift. It was cold, I supposed. It was windy, I supposed. If I didn't move I would be dead in ten minutes, I supposed. Now beginning to keen like a bereaved Iranian, I dragged myself towards the chalet, noticing before too long that it was boarded up. Why had the snowplough driver troubled himself to clear a dead-end path all the way up here? I wasn't quite sure, but soon enough I would formulate a theory based around him being a really enormous twat.

Up to my velvet knees in snow I set off back to the car, the painfully blue sky and bright sun irrelevant in an arctic hurricane so fierce my whole head hurt. I'm still not quite sure what made me look along the gentle, scooped-out valley on the other side of the Rolls, or what made me set off for the desolate stone cottage that lay marooned in the snow about a quarter of a mile down it. But as I approached it, my hypothermic shuffle slowly accelerated into a St Bernard bound, for there, set into the wall just above a shuttered window, was a gleaming white winged lion. And just to the left was a marble inscription. The first bit was in Latin, but the second wasn't. I still don't get half of it, but then I don't need to:

Epigrafe posta sulla casa nel 1596 rilevata nel 1609 dall'Inglese Tomaso Coryate 'My Observations of Bergamo' che percorse la strada priula nel viaggio di ritorno in patria.

Mr Coryate, I presume. It was astonishing. I barked a single incredulous laugh into the empty mountains, then raised two blue fists to the blue heavens, then laughed some more and posed for a series of childish and lopsided self-timer photos. I read the words again and again, sniggering every time I got to 'My Observations of Bergamo'. Eventually I grasped the gist: the old inn had recently been restored, and the lost original Latin inscription, as copied down by Coryate and marking the pass's opening in 1596, had been found in the *Crudities* – the page on which it appeared had been, in typical fashion, headed with reference to the last major town he had visited. Hats off to someone's historical detective work, to my tundra-trekking exploration, and above all to Tommy's painstaking inscription-copying. He had now taken to introducing these passages with 'Blame me not if I am something tedious . . .'

221

and I thought how often I'd mocked him for this, imagining the locals chortling behind his back as he scratched away with his quill. But here was proof that it had paid off, that without his home-spun scholarship these words and a part of history would have been lost for ever.

I still can't get over it. You probably won't find the name 'Thomas Coryate' carved in stone anywhere else in the world, not even in Odcombe. But here, on this empty, frozen Alp, I was alone with him, just me and TC.

This heart-warming encounter was just as well, of course, because in the final analysis I was still facing a dead end up a huge fucking mountain. A slippery U-turn somehow effected, I turned back down the snowploughed Cresta Run corridor, my knuckles tighter and whiter around the wheel with every spirit-sapping retraced mile. I had to go right back to the outskirts of Bergamo; then, following the SS36 up the eastern bank of Lake Como, I became enmeshed in a jam that at 3.15 p.m. can only have been the civil-service rush hour.

For two hours I crawled along the lake, late afternoon sun Grand Canyonising the mountains that plunged straight into it, and it was gone six before I conceded that making Switzerland that night was unrealistic. Another morning in Italy would, I told myself, give me the chance to purchase things that would cause me real physical pain at Swiss prices, like a car wash and a pair of walking shoes (I had rashly vowed to retrace Coryate's round-trip hike from Mainz to Frankfurt on foot).

And another night in Italy would give me a last chance to experience the sort of accommodation where you find your tooth mug loosely wrapped in a freezer bag full of pastry flakes and desiccated woodlice.

SIX

Switzerland

Looking at the literature, it was clear that in electing to go directly north through a load of extra Alps, Coryate once again put himself in a different league. It would be almost 200 years before Grand Tourists even considered tackling Switzerland and its ruthless peaks head on – and even then those who did were either pioneering mountaineers, boiling kettles on the peaks to estimate altitudes, or earnest types like Wordsworth, whose idea of largin' it big-time on holiday was to wander lonely as a cloud.

As a result, most people's experience of Switzerland was limited to shaving across its south-western border with France in order to visit Geneva – the ideal cool, civilised city in which to take a calming rest cure on the way home from the reckless excitements of Italy. 'After the various toils of a fatiguing journey . . . there is no more agreeable place of repose,' said one British visitor.

Even so, it still tended to be the more mild-mannered tourists who visited a country notorious even then for its intolerance of after-hours recklessness. This, added to the fact that it was possible to learn French here without mixing with too many filthy Papists, is what encouraged so many wealthy Brits to send their daughters to what we now know as Swiss finishing schools.

But if the contrast with France was noticeable, that with Italy remains astonishing. It is an unending source of wonder that two so fundamentally different nations can share a continent, let alone an open border. If the Michelin guide to Italy described the native as 'Dark-haired, black-eyed, he is all movement and romance', what would the Swiss one say? 'Grey-haired, grey-eyed, he is all watch movements and finance.'

Yet the contrast between cold Swiss profiteering and Italy's cheap-and-cheerful slapdash hedonism has not always been an apt one. Coryate found his meals north of the border cost less than anywhere else, with excellent wine poured out of buckets and beef served on huge wooden plates 'at least an inch thicke', and for the first time in weeks stayed at inns that were both comfortable and modestly priced. In those days the tables were turned: down here, the Swiss were in the main lonely goatherds, denied participation in the Renaissance by the Alps, the lack of a sea port or much in the way of goods or produce with which to create the necessary wealth.

All this may have been because the area just above Como was in Coryate's day known as the Grisons, or 'Grey Confederates', a cluster of tiny independent republics which were split between Italy and Switzerland 200 years later. (Now a canton with its own 'GR' number-plate prefix, the Swiss Grisons still retain hints of their isolated past. Almost 10 per cent of the locals speak Romansch, a really peculiar Latin-based language that would have gladdened Coryate no end.)

The one link with their Swiss descendants was an unimpeach-able honesty, impressed upon Coryate by a priest he met in an inn: 'He told me that had I a thousand crownes about me, I might more securely travell with it in their country without company or weapon, than in any other nation whatsoever.' I couldn't reasonably expect bargain beef platters and wine by the bucket, but a lingering dearth of criminals was a decent enough legacy for a man who knows he is 2–1 down in the sleeping-rough stakes.

The sun warmed the last whitewashed walls and pantiled roofs I'd see, driving up to the tip of Como and the plain that's still marked as the Piano di Spagna, site of the last Spanish fortress which the doomed priest of Bergamo had warned Coryate to avoid. 'They would lay their Inquisition upon me, as soone as they should perceive that I was an Englishman, and so consequently torture me with extreme cruelty . . . and at last put me to death,' he notes with the jauntiness of a bigot striding away from outwitted enemies towards his spiritual brethren, continuing, 'Chiavenna ministered some occasion of comfort unto me because it was the first Protestant town that I entred.'

He had been accompanied that day by an English-speaking Italian recently returned from Cambridgeshire, where he had been in the service of a man whose entry in *The Companion to British History* suggests some quality gossip along the stony Alpine valleys:

'PALAVACINO, Sir Horatio (?–1660), a Genoese, was appointed Collector of Papal Taxes by Q. Mary but when she died, he abjured R. Catholicism and appropriated the money, with which he laid the foundations of a European-wide business. From his huge fortune, he lent money to Protestant govts., including England, the Dutch and Navarre and supplied them with information through his contacts.' (A footnote in Strachan's biography reads: 'For a full account of his life as financier, speculator, secret agent and international intriguer, see Lawrence Stone, "An Elizabethan: Sir Horatio Palavicino".')

At Chiavenna I joined the Swiss shoppers stocking up with wine, forgot to wash the car and in anticipation of my vague plan to recreate a day-long Coryate march paid £18 for a pair of walking boots, or at least brown shoes. I also discovered to my slight amazement that the Splügen Pass, Coryate's route into Switzerland proper, was 'Aperto – Ouvert – Offen – Open'. Splügen was 500 feet higher than San Marco, and the road no less thin and squiggly on the map – furthermore, I'd seen on the telly that morning that Venice had been flooded up to its chopines, heralding a new wave of bad weather that would have unloaded on the high ground during the night.

'The Splügen Pass will delight lovers of bold road-building,' the Michelin guide had said, correctly insinuating an empty and barren tunnel-and-hairpin extravaganza through grubby little villages perched impossibly on the sunny cliffs. Just ten years after Coryate's visit, 2,430 people were killed by an avalanche that swept down from the mountains above Chiavenna in what remains the worst ever Alpine disaster, a fact I was glad not to discover until after I returned. Some bends were so sharp that I had to do three-point turns to negotiate them, reversing gingerly back towards oblivion on fragmented, slush-smeared tarmac. Above the tree-line I hit the mist; the ice light came on and didn't go off for the rest of the day. Pistons battered into the cylinder head with an almost terminal thump; wisps of steam escaped through the bonnet sides, accompanied by a horrid and mysterious burning-plastic stench. How could Coryate have climbed this on foot in one day, up and down the mountain and along an Alpine valley, Campodolcino to Thusis, 53 kilometres on my roads and doubtless a lot further on the wandering paths of 1608? And to do it all without a single implication that this was in any way an arduous task. He was a phenomenon.

Ever since passing Monte Gruf in the morning I'd detected a

Germanic touch to the names, a Scrabble enthusiast's eye for obscure consonants at the expense of humdrum low-scoring vowels, and it was difficult to connect the snowstorm that blotted out the last Italian outpost, the hamlet of Monte Spluga, with the land of underarm sweat circles and sundried tomatoes. The snow-slathered mountaintop border post on the Swiss side was suitably atmospheric, one of those ones with a big *ALT – ZOLL* roundel blocking your way and a couple of humourless, carbine-toting conscripts wearing caps with earflaps. A quick 'Pisspot bitte' rap on the window and straight away I felt like Napoleon Solo was trussed up in my boot.

I don't know why I said 'open border', because of course it isn't. At least not for the Swiss – handing the guard my passport, I realised that this was the first time I'd been asked to show it at a frontier since leaving home. The Swiss, you see, are deeply paranoid about immigrants flooding in for the chance to do all the shitty jobs that it's simply impossible to imagine a Swiss doing, like digging holes in the roads and pasting up billboards, and all in return for the chance to spend three quid on a cup of coffee.

Did you know that a law passed recently in Switzerland allows local people to vote on citizenship applications? They print the photographs, names and employment history of all applicants on a ballot paper, the locals go into the voting booth, and guess what – well, actually, here's a real-life example. In March 2000, locals in the town of Emmen were asked to consider the applications of fifty-six foreigners, all with work permits. Only eight were successful, all of them Italians. Of the forty-eight rejected applicants, forty-six had Slavic surnames, including the Avramovices, who had lived and worked in the town for twelve years, raised two children there and spoke the correct brand of German Swiss.

The worst of it is that the Swiss see nothing wrong with this – even anti-racism organisations are reluctant to question the stoutly defended system of 'direct democracy' which requires locals to vote on everything, down to the locations of bus shelters. No one really wants to talk, either, about the '*verdingkind*' system under which the state took unknown thousands of children from poor homes and auctioned them as agricultural slave-labour. This system persisted until – are you ready for this? – the 1950s.

I thought about the smug Swiss shoppers stocking up in Chiavenna, and then I thought about the sodding motorway tax they make foreigners pay for eroding their tarmac, because of course as we all know Swiss cars are fitted with a special hovercraft system that is activated whenever they cross a border and so prevents them from incurring any wear and tear on foreign roads. God help us all if there's ever a referendum in Switzerland on whether tourists should address local citizens as Your Eminence and wear Marge Simpson wigs after dark.

I'm glad I've got that out of my system, because having laboriously dealt with the border guards' enquiries (how could they not speak even a word of Italian?), I remembered that I was actually relieved to be in Switzerland, back in Northern Europe. The snow was weighing down the fir trees and settling picturesquely on the silver lady's wingtips, and as the road tailed a model-railway train line around the valleys, my usual motoring entourage kept a polite distance, no longer darting about in my mirrors like pursuit vehicles in an arcade game or generally behaving the way I do when I'm behind someone with one of those silver fish on their boot. If the speed limit was 50 they went 49; if it was 20 they went 19. You somehow got the idea that if it had been 335, they'd have done their obedient best to get up to 334.

I thought of all those stories about people being reported to the police for using their washing machines after 10.15 p.m., and the one I'd read in a travel magazine about the couple who went off with their hotel key by mistake and were apprehended for the crime at the border two days later. Even in the Grand Tour days the few Brits who made it to Switzerland found themselves falling foul of insane and ruthlessly enforced by-laws: in Zürich, it was illegal for certain classes of people to own carriages.

Cleanliness and order – I had wanted it, and now I had to pay for it. I stopped in a café where Romansch-speaking (or possibly just drunk) train drivers were smoking cigars; the coffee was five times the Italian price, but I didn't have to gulp it down in a paranoid frenzy, certain that if I dawdled I'd come out and find the Rolls up on bricks. And the light came on automatically in the spotless loo, though the price of helping Switzerland to minimise its electricity bill was 20p's worth of the world's most esteemed currency. At a petrol station I was even asked to pay a whole franc – about 40p – for a dribble of tap water to fill the diminutive washer bottle; when I pretended I had no Swiss money, the oily-haired teenager at the pump demanded the equivalent in the currency of my choice, which in this case turned out to be Sod Off vouchers.

At Chur, where Coryate got his first peek of the Rhine, I got out for a wet walk to see at first hand just how unItalian things had become. And of course it was right off the scale: the Protestant cathedral he had visited was short on beggars and keening widows and people Sellotaping Polaroids of their son's appendix scars to yellow-skinned dead nuns, and long on Teutonic Victoria Woods in nylon housecoats vacuuming under the pews and scrubbing away any stubborn patches of individuality. Outside, students looked like special constables were filing out of a library that looked like a police

station; next door was a white-tiles-and-steel delicatessen with all
the salivatory appeal of an optician's.

It was all so lacking in style, which actually suited me down to
the ground. I don't seem to have mentioned that in Venice I'd started
wearing my purple suit again, and was still doing so now – except
that the day before I'd worn my last proper shirt, forcing me to team
the suit with a wrinkly yellow T-shirt in a manner that – particularly in conjunction with my increasingly windblown and multi-
dimensional hair – irresistibly recalled the look championed by Leo
Sayer. In Italy I would rather have died – in fact, scratch the 'rather'
– but here I simply didn't care. This was the sort of place where
you'd expect to hear a student quietly humming 'I'm A One Man
Band' – three hours in the country and ELO had already been on
the radio four times. I had half a mind to go the whole hog and
hook my thumbs into my belt loops.

I suddenly knew exactly how Coryate must have felt. Both of
us were relieved to be in Switzerland: him for largely religious
reasons, me for the lack of criminal opportunism and consequent
freedom to loosen and lengthen the chain that bound me to the
Rolls. But the cultural contrast with what had gone before was
almost painfully jarring: 'A man who has not been in Italy is always
conscious of an inferiority from his not having seen what it is
expected a man should see,' wrote Dr Johnson 170 years later, and
try as you might it just isn't possible to stick Switzerland in that
sentence without laughing.

Coryate bravely tries to talk up the cathedral at Chur, but it was
unutterably drab and leaden after the majestic, shiny edifices over
the Alps. Some of the sculpture inside was new in his day, but looked
bland and crude, the sort of thing Italians were knocking out 300
years before. And for my part, actual lawlessness was now replaced

by heinous metaphorical crimes, most notably daylight robbery and being bored to death.

In hours I was rebelling. At Bad Ragaz, which may not have suggested itself to Coryate as a dated rap duo, I childishly skewed the Rolls across three spaces in defiance of the slide-rule alignment of other vehicles and strode off without paying and displaying (having first established that the entrance was too narrow for a tow truck).

It was peeing down now; by chance I had parked in front of a *gasthof*, and in I jogged, still sneering defiantly. I knew I was going to be fleeced, but I wanted them to know that I knew. The night before I'd found inspiration in William Bennet's account of a stay in a Lucerne inn during the summer of 1785: 'when our bill was produced we were struck dumb with the impudent charge of £7 9*s* for a day and two nights . . . Mr Rolle could only revenge himself by swearing heartily at the man in English, who did not understand a word he said.'

The stout *Hausfrau* at the reception did actually speak some English, but I wasn't listening. Unashamed by the Rolls's wet face at the window I tutted and moaned as she laboriously translated her room rates, resting my chin in my hands and staring wearily over her head like a rude schoolboy. It was only after she meekly pulled out a hotel directory from below the desk and began dictating the addresses of rival establishments presumably more appealing to truc-ulent tossers that I did a bit of mental arithmetic and realised that she was asking just £17 for bed and breakfast – less than I'd paid anywhere except a Formule 1. It was a long haul back to polite acceptance, and by issuing a bemused Scooby Doo grunt, holding one hand up to silence her and the other out in wordless request for a key I never really made it.

Seventeen quid? I couldn't understand it. There was even a mini

Toblerone on my pillow, and — *aaaaahhhh* — a lovely soft duvet. But they had my number now. When I went back down for supper and started asking the waitress about the spa that was somewhere up there in the wet hills, she smiled quickly and said, '*Ja*, but it is not free. *Und* . . .' and here I followed her gaze to the Rolls at the window behind me, '*und* you must pay for parking your big car.'

And then of course the only thing on their menu that cost less than my room was something called a *pagmentpäckli*, which I couldn't say anyway, or at least not without sniggering, and which turned out to be a greaseproof paper bag full of spaghetti.

The German for weather is *Wetter*, which is about right. After a slow breakfast I went out for a quick walk, damply registering that whereas small Italian towns like Pizzeghettone had barely changed in the last four centuries, small Swiss towns like Bad Ragaz were utterly transformed, from a cluster of log cabins and a rude church to model Northern European communities, all speed bumps and cashpoints. There was a giant civic chess set that wouldn't have lasted a week in Britain; the shiny buses and lorries were like life-sized Dinky Toys fresh out of the box. Oddly, though, there was a dearth of public conveniences — but at least, unlike Venice, here they didn't feel the need to erect structures to deter anyone wanting to sidle off down an alley for a quiet pee. On second thoughts they do: maximum-security hospitals for the criminally insane.

The cars heading towards me from the north all had a foot of snow on their roofs, and driving up towards Walensee, where Coryate had caught a boat to Zürich, the clouds obscuring all but the bottom few yards of 8,000 feet of mountain began to lighten their wintry load upon me. Yesterday I'd driven past Flims; today I drove past Flums, and that was about the difference. Even Coryate was in a sulk, retreating back into bald statements of distance travelled.

A dull day was briefly illuminated by the first rival Rolls I'd seen since Britain, a gleaming racing-green Shadow 2 parked outside a shut-for-lunch dealer on the fringes of Zürich's long lakeside suburbs. It was two years older than mine but priced at 30,000SF, or about 12 grand, and after parking alongside for the predictable 'holiday romance' photo, I started thinking for the first time about flogging the Rolls before I got home. ('Not in Schweiz,' said the filling-station cashier who engaged me in conversation the following after-noon. 'Holland is best – many old Rolls-Royces there, and good prices to sell.')

Shamed by the comparison, I used the opportunity to reattach mascot and hubcaps; while doing so I unearthed my haul of hot flags. It had been a random cull, and most of the half-dozen nations represented were not overly inspiring: Portugal, Japan, Ireland, Denmark, Canada. But ten minutes and 2 feet of insulating tape later, the master cutler's pennant mast was in place behind the mascot, and on it flew the mysterious sixth flag, an enigmatic rectangle diag-onally split into red and black, which I instantly decided identified me as the Burundian ambassador.

And then it was into Zürich, where over the course of twenty wet hours I'm afraid I allowed myself to sink into a slough of despond. It started when I went to park and found that the second hour was more expensive than the first, a typical low trick that smacked of a move-along-please-nothing-to-see-here attitude. And rightly so – there wasn't. After eating lunch in the car I drove off on the Coryate trail, beginning with an hour-long trek through moribund suburbs to the Church of the Martyrs St Felix and St Regula, an edifice like a Fifties sports hall which shared no more than a name with Coryate's presumably demolished Gothic *meisterwerk*. When I noted that this concrete ignominity was the only church given a Michelin star, I gave up, though not before wondering if, when St Regula was burnt at the stake, the town criers filled the cold air with shouts of 'Regula fries!'

That should have taught me not to look at the Michelin guide again, but it didn't. Did you know that 40 per cent of the world's personal savings are concentrated in Switzerland? It made my skin crawl. After reading that I couldn't look at anyone without thinking their shoes were the cumulative interest filched from that tenner Auntie June put in my Post Office account when I turned nine. Nice BMW, mate. Just thought you should know that the alloy wheels are my 1988 Christmas bonus. Excuse me, madam, do you have the time? So you do – oh, and I notice you're telling it from my one-two on the 1993 Grand National.

The last straw was paying a 50 per cent deposit on four bottles of beer, rousing apprehensions, later fully justified, of a last day in Switzerland spent on a frantic and ridiculous cash-for-empties quest. Driving around the ponderous business area, I couldn't look at a grey suit without imagining the awful secrets behind the colourless countenance, of a morning spent laundering paedophile video profits; I actually got out to inspect a bag of shredded documents on the polished granite doorstep of some bank HQ, convinced I'd be able to make out a sliver of photocopied swastika.

The trams, so clankingly wayward in Italy, were utterly silent but for the faintest hissy sparks from sodden overhead cables; people waited for buses under umbrellas, stoic and immobile; the rush-hour traffic was hornless and polite – I was already feeling like a man trapped in a model village. After almost flattening a couple of old dears I remembered it was no longer acceptable to treat zebra crossings as pedestrian skittle alleys.

Whenever I felt my depression lifting – a bargain bar of chocolate, perhaps, or the stick-it-up-your-arse-with-a-Toblerone-if-you-think-I'm-paying-that parking ticket I found on my windscreen after a two-minute coffee break – I willed myself back into it. When the Michelin guide said, 'Zürich is also known to be particularly receptive to contemporary trends associated with the younger generation,' I translated, 'Zürich is full of smack addicts' (which it is – the authorities even gave away free heroin in the early Nineties in a bid to tackle the crisis that merely attracted the wrong sort of tourist). The further revelation that 'Swiss citizens enjoy the best and most comprehensive insurance in the world' conjured an all-too-vivid insight into dinner-party banter. Suddenly imagining hotel receptionists cornering me with their favourite policy exclusions, I made an abrupt vow to sleep in the Rolls.

I needed to, anyway. Coryate's blasé account of his trans-Alpine yomps urged some riposte – by not even nicking the complimentary toiletries from my room at Lake Como (partly because the soap smelt of mustard) I had proven I was getting too soft, too slackly hotelified. But it was dark and raining brutally before I found a place to stop for the night, more or less by default after the only swimming-pool car park I located turned out to be overlooked by dozens of homes, few of which looked likely to house people for whom a filthy Rolls and a man in pants constituted ideal early morning viewing.

The road I chose, in the northern suburb of Oerlikon, was quiet, residential, flanked by tall hedges and within handy wading distance of a cheap-looking Chinese restaurant. Not actually cheap, of course – having been lured in by what turned out to be the bargain lunch menu, I paid twice the going rate for b&b in Bad Ragaz for a bowl of hot and sour soup, pork balls and an ice-cream scoop of boiled rice. Though the parade of beers didn't help. This sleeping-in-the-car business was a bit of a false economy: the only way I could face it was by getting drunk, which at Swiss-restaurant prices created its own ocean of sorrows to drown in. At least I got a fortune cookie: '*Eine neue Erfahrung wird zu einer wertvollen Erinnerung*', an eerily accurate prediction when translated as 'Intoxication and a looming dearth of bathing facilities will combine to inspire over-zealous use of the after-dinner hot towel.' It was shameful. I more or less gave myself a bed bath.

But actually, the night proved oddly enjoyable. With Dr Hook on FM and a sodium-lit Nissan Micra 1.2 Super S flush up against the pride of Burundi I felt pleasantly cocooned in suburban blandness. Sleep came quickly and was remarkably deep – I even dreamt, though nothing as ridiculous as the reality.

Dawn, however, wasn't quite so cosy. Waking with an orgasmic snoring snuffle to survey the world through frost-rimed glass, I instantly detected the 'metal nose' syndrome familiar to anyone with experience of British camping; a dehydrated swig from the water bottle almost cracked my front teeth. (I was careful to distinguish this from the other bottle – a wide-mouthed receptacle originally full of orange juice – whose nocturnally accumulated contents were rather less cold.)

At 7.45 the street was astir with commuters, cleaners and school-kids, and engaged in the complicated yoga required to get dressed in a car I earnt my first looks of unreserved disgust. Elsewhere there had always been a residual amount of curiosity, but here, where Rollers were ten-a-franc, I was sneered at mercilessly. At least I found a swimming pool, though with hire of trunks (so nylon and saggy and ridiculous I should have been paid to wear them), a post-bathe coffee and parking it ended up costing me £9 – another false economy. And inevitably I made terrible errors in pool etiquette, forgetting that all countries have their own arcane systems of changing and showering.

So I went into the boys' changing area, but as I unzipped my velvets realised it was full of just that – boys – all looking at me with tears welling up in their eyes as they contemplated a looming ordeal at the hands of this soiled roué. After having briskly relocated to the men's changing area, I walked into the loos, holding up my billowing swimwear with one hand, and shortly discovered after using these facilities that what I had imagined – having repeatedly belaboured it – to be a broken auto-flush button was in fact the emergency call. As I exited the cubicle, a duo of grey-haired *Obergruppenfraus* came jogging round the corner; knowing all too well how such a pair would react to an unflushed loo I walked briskly into the pool, bypassing the foot-disinfectant trough (and if anyone's feet needed a bactericidal soak, my damp-leather, Rolls-smelling appendages did) and ignoring the unfortunately evocative words *DUSCHEN OBLIGATORISCH*.

Aimlessly treading water amid the clockwork geriatrics and deafening schoolkids, I wondered whether German would sound so unfortunate if we hadn't had – or more precisely won – a war. Was there something inherently aggressive in those throat-stripping *achs* and *ochs*, in the way that Tannoy announcers sounded like they were about to give birth? Would the old men I'd seen being pelted with medicine balls in a sports hall the evening before have looked so scared if their Lycra instructress had been barking at them in English? Or was it just that I've read too many Sven Hassel books (one)? Certainly it was a funny language. It was difficult to imagine driving through Egg and Moosfluh or ordering a coffee at Willi's Backstuber with a straight face, and even a cursory glimpse at the map turned up a whole host of villages with names like exclamations uttered during comic-book fights: Mumpf, Gipf, Aesch.

The only trouble with swimming is it makes me bleary and fuzzy and vaguely drugged, and even after my coffee I sat slumped in the pool cafeteria for an hour, unable to move. And all around, the old folks were doing their national duty, shoving chocolate bars in their mouths like logs into a sawmill and smoking their heads off – even the Charlton Heston one who had beaten me over two lengths. Switzerland is the European base of a whole load of huge tobacco firms, most notably Philip Morris, and of course Nestlé, and the eager consumption of all related products is encouraged by incongruously low prices. In supermarkets, it's difficult to buy a single packet of fags – cartons or nothing, and all less than half the UK price. The Swiss smoke 14 billion of them a year – 50 per cent more per head than Britain – and the total grew steadily during most of the Nineties. And when I went to buy chocolate, I couldn't find it with the sweets – no, being a grocery staple, it's given huge shelf space alongside bread and tins. The average Swiss gets through 107 bars a year. And if you want to see what that does to you after sixty-five summers, go to Baden.

Coryate enjoyed himself in Zürich, meeting the author of *An History of the Errors of Popery* and transcribing what is believed to be the first English-language account of the story of William Tell, but then as now Swiss cities were expensive – supper cost him 'sixe battes, that is fifteene pence English', more than twice what he'd been paying in Italy – and he only stayed one day.

Outside Baden, unable to find any Latin-speakers, he got lost – how this didn't happen to him every single day I don't know – and had to walk back 5 miles with a Protestant scholar eager to show him the hot sulphur springs that gave the town its name. It was a well-established resort in his day, and not only for 'infirmities sake'. Coryate was prudishly appalled to see mixed nude bathing, the participants 'not onely talking and familiarly discoursing, but also sporting after a very pleasant and merry manner'. Rapunzel-plaited lovelies being covertly goosed by bearded strangers – he really couldn't get over it, 'another man's wife, and another man, both naked upward in one bath'. 'Were I a married man,' he goes on, alluding to his single status for the first time and heralding a back-ground chorus of 'yeah, *right*', 'I should hardly be persuaded to suffer my wife to bath her selfe naked in one and the self same bath with one onely bachelour.' A honeymoon spent watching you hug columns and she'd be splashing about with half a dozen of them, I thought.

No such luck today, of course. An expensive car park, an expensive coffee, then twenty minutes wandering past open-air hot tubs watching saggy-titted choc-gobblers of both sexes flatulently re-affirming Coryate's assertion that 'old folkes reape no benefit by these bathes'. Having read in the promotional literature that 'three days of full bath access with fango and hayflowers pack' would re-acquaint me with 'the pleasures of wellness', I set off up to the town, lured by a ragged trumpet rendition of 'The Lion Sleeps Tonight'.

In most countries, an enormously drunk brass band dressed up as deep-sea divers parading through the streets at lunchtime would generally be considered entertainment. But not in Switzerland. The musicians played with a sombre here-we-go-again weariness; I only noticed they were drunk when a nearby trombonist oompahed schnapps vapour into my face. And the chilled locals, watching list-lessly in front of the pebble-dashed medieval buildings, looked like a defeated citizenry ordered to witness their conquerors' triumphant march-past. It was difficult to believe that these were descendants of Coryate's bath-house orgiasts.

Sex and death: I'd done the nudes, and now I went off to find the charnel house where Coryate beheld 'a multitude of bones and skulls laid together . . . I never saw so many together in all my life'. I didn't expect any luck, but round the back of the Lego-roofed Stadtturm, with the band fading away towards the casino, I peered in through a dusty chapel window and was arrestingly presented with a huge floor-to-ceiling rack of yellowed skulls, thousands of them, all arranged to stare out at the congregation. The doors were locked, and judging by the leaves piled up in the aisle, had been for some time. It wasn't really a surprise. Right next to this chapel was the main parish church, and one couldn't imagine the modern Swiss worshipper deliberating too long when he opens his front door on Sunday morning and a neighbour asks, 'So, Ernst, what's it to be today? The nice ordinary church or the little dark one next door with all the dead blokes looking at us?'

Coryate had no idea what the bones were doing there, but it seems probable they were battle casualties from one of the many terrible wars with France, Austria and each other that blighted the country for over 200 years up to 1525 (something to remember the next time someone quotes Harry Lime in *The Third Man* pithily attributing the cuckoo clock to endless centuries of peace). And I don't know why he was so freaked out – in his day, overcrowding in British churchyards meant that the only way to make room for fresh stiffs was to dig up old skeletons and pile 'em high in the crypts. The idea of a permanent plot, marked with a headstone, only became commonplace in Britain well after Coryate's death.

It was getting colder. You know winter has arrived when church interiors start feeling cosy. I had my thermals on for the first time, but even so there was no getting away from the fact that being inside the car was a lot nicer than being outside it. The rather magnificent gorge that bisected Baden carried the River Limmat to a nearby convergence with the Rhine, which Coryate followed all the way up to the Channel. After seeing a farmer polishing the abandoned, wheel-less car by his barn I suddenly wanted to get cracking.

Switzerland didn't fit easily into a Grand Tour itinerary. It was civilised in the way that people say, 'Well, this is very civilised,' and mean somewhere with cellophane-wrapped toothpicks and urinals that flush automatically when you do your flies up. The country was very efficient at providing people – or anyway its own people – with their basic needs: I hadn't seen a run-down house or shopped in a grubby supermarket. But Alpine splendour aside, it didn't feed the soul in the way a Grand Tour was expected to. I suppose all you really need to know about Switzerland is that it is Margaret Thatcher's favourite holiday destination.

Driving along the Rhine's floodplain I began, belatedly, to understand something about the Swiss character, that low-key, I'm-all-right-Jacques self-interest. I've always thought of Switzerland as impregnable, its political neutrality buttressed by Panzer-defying Alps, but right there, through my filthy driver's window and off across the windy flatness, was Germany. Keep your head down, and maybe they'll forget to invade us. Here they could have waved at the storm troopers lined up on the opposite banks. Mind you, half of them probably did.

Basel, Bâle – one city, two names, three countries. As the red-and-white drug-company chimneys loomed ahead of me, the signs were all for 'Deutschland – Casino', 'Frankreich/St Louis', the number plates a multinational array of cross-border commuters, people stocking up with whatever was cheaper over here or headed off for bargains over there: fags, petrol, Thalidomide. I was excited. I had a plan. On the map the double-sided flags representing border crossings were as densely packed as those on that cocktail display I had de-Burundised in Mestre: red–yellow, Germany–Switzerland; blue–red, France–Germany; yellow–blue, Switzerland–France. Carefully based on my knowledge of comparative economics, I would sleep in France, eat in Germany, and lighten the jangling basket of currencies that was my right-hand trouser pocket with a chocolate nightcap in Switzerland.

Following a knot of Gallic number plates home, I made it through the border unchallenged (the Swiss guards were clearly under orders to stop only French cars, even at the expense of ignoring unkempt thieves making off with the Burundian ambassador's Roller), and immediately found that France was horrid. St Louis, butting right up against Bâle and a grenade's throw from Germany, was messy and half-heartedly prefab in a way that said, 'Oh, what's the point, we'll probably be invaded or bombed or something tomorrow.' I eventually found a shed-like but tartless motel in Huningue, just to the north and surrounded by lonely new housing estates built where the tank traps, turrets and minefields of the Maginot Line used to be.

All in all, it wasn't a very good advertisement for cross-border co-operation. The road in St Louis up to the Swiss border had been pettily festooned with huge tricolour banners; the drug chimneys were all jammed up in the top corner of the Swiss sector, guaranteeing that the prevailing wind ferried the sinister fumes off over Germany. But in a funny way I was glad. There's something rather depressing about the gradual erosion of national differences, and it was good to see them alive and well and chafing so awkwardly against each other. I'd half expected a sort of diluted blend of characteristics, so that the average Baseler would knock down every third pedestrian, demand just 13 per cent of my personal savings and only beat me once on penalties. But the only giveaway was the German speakers' habit of saying '*Merci*' and '*Adieu*'.

I switched on the telly and watched a bit of *Doctor No*, or rather *Médecin Non*, pondering that on current evidence the availability of such a multilingual plethora of channels was the only obvious incentive to live here, and curiously examined the 'feminine hygiene' disposal bags, or more particularly the legend emblazoned upon them: 'Design and Passion'. Even I could design a paper bag, and that second word surely encourages a section of society who in my opinion, and I think I can count on Tom to back me up on this one, needs no encouragement. At length, dubiously recharged by a lusty draught of my Italian wine, I set off into the curfew-empty Wednesday night for my three-nation walking tour.

Huningue was another apology of a place, so subdued that even the graffiti vandals couldn't be arsed. Wandering across the Mairie Square I finally spotted someone – a large-featured old feller reminding everybody which country they were in by letting his dog crap on the pavement – and asked where Germany was. 'Aaah,' he said, cradling his chin and closing his eyes in intense concentration, as if I'd asked for directions to the nearest twenty-four-hour alterations tailor. 'Aaah,' he said, opening his eyes, raising an enlightened finger and pointing it down a small road even I knew would eventually lead me to the Atlantic coast.

How do you react at a broad, empty and well-lit crossroads when a well-meaning old man gives you plainly erroneous directions? Having thanked him, I set off slowly down the road he'd indicated, but every time I looked round he was still there under the street-light, holding a hand up in a motionless wave while his dog and I willed him to overcome dementia and go home. In the end I had to contrive a huge detour through some wet allotments, working my way back muddily to the no man's land by the river.

It was half an hour before I got to the bridge, walking up to the gloomy customs post abruptly abandoned when most EU members abolished border controls in 1997. A rank of grimy phone boxes for drug mules awaiting their strip search to phone a tearful confession to *maman*; a checkpoint with whitewashed windows and leaves piled against every dusty door; a customs compound for naughty lorries now just a fly-tipping dump. It was definitively eerie, but at the same time, remembering the bloody religious conflicts of Coryate's day – the Thirty Years' War was just Ten Years Off – and the even bloodier political wars of recent centuries, it was impossible to believe the border would stay this way.

This was Alsace, German before the mid-seventeenth century, French from then until 1871, German from then until 1919 and French since. The EU is just a treaty, after all, and treaties are there to be broken. I notice the French had chosen to mothball their checkpoint rather than demolish it, and as I pondered this, one man and his dog strolled through the border from the other side, possibly unaware of the symbolism of taking a German shepherd for his nightly walk into the land of the French Alsatians. Still, you could have some fun here. I bet every night he storms out of his front door, shouting, 'Right, that's it! I'm off to France – and I'm taking the dog with me!'

The Rhine was as wide as a lake, the underside of the bridge echoing faintly with those lonely sounds associated with the movement of bulk items: very long trains travelling at very low speeds; foghorns from unseen barges. And then, cresting the bridge, I was in Germany, doing something I haven't done before (walking across a railway turntable), and then something I have (another nocturnal march around mattress-strewn light-industrial desolation). I cannot pretend my search for sustenance was either brief or intriguing. But I'll say this for such places: they're always good for observing covert sordidness.

The first pedestrian I encountered was a thigh-booted tart hovering about an empty car dealership; the first motorist was the silver-haired kerb crawler in a BMW 750 who picked her up. (He drove past, alone, five minutes later.) Exiting the commercial sector I traversed a low-rise estate clearly erected in nostalgic homage to the DDR and presently found an anonymous main drag that, but for the bus-shelter posters advertising live appearances by Uriah Heep and Saxon, could have been anywhere. Here, I ingested two take-away bratwursts with a rapid, self-revolted sating of base physical lusts that almost precisely matched those recently exhibited by the man in the BMW. And his service provider may well have empathised with the taste left in my mouth.

I blundered into Switzerland round the corner, and though its border post was manned no one stopped me, a shame as I was rather looking forward to explaining myself. The main traffic was Germans with slightly guilty, slightly sheepish grins filling up with bargain unleaded at the bevy of border-side petrol stations; beyond these it was all rather grimy and industrial and not very Swiss.

It was half an hour before I found a bar, and entering it through a huge, plush draught-excluding curtain like an actor striding to the front of the stage, I beheld that the audience was precisely the sort of overalled blue-collars I couldn't imagine existing in Switzerland. The brassy barmaid made great play of my nationality during the large-beer-please mime, prompting three nearby youths, one shaven-haired, to shout in unison, 'Yes! Hello, my darling!' And as I sat on a long, varnished table trying to concentrate on my beer and volume 2 of *Coryats Crudities*, the off-to-night-shift boiler-suited old timer opposite started chatting himself up, occasionally demonstrating the full range of his lunacy by pulling on one end of a huge moustache and emitting the sort of sound my children make when they pretend to die.

If it had been in any other country I'd have felt intimidated, but with yodelly accordion waltzing out of the jukebox it was impossible. At 11.30 I swept out through the curtains and into a road lined with frost-rimed windscreens, my feet suddenly pointing out that a 100-minute walk wasn't really what the chiropodist ordered. When I got back to my motel, across two borders but just short of the pain barrier, I fell on to the bed and looked at the map, dimly satisfied. I had, at last, done a Tommy.

Coryate spent two days in Basel, long enough to attend a lecture on Greek delivered by a man wearing a tall felt hat and to rave about the cathedral, and though I hadn't meant to, I copied him. With no Swiss cash left I'd crossed over to Germany, following the Frenchmen to an Aldi crapmarket that I'd recced the night before. A couple in a Porsche, an old guy in a Jag – the Rolls felt quite at home in the car park. And my word it was cheap: huge cans of lovely wheat beer for 25p, sacks of crisps for 40p – unmissable Tom-and-Tim bargains, only slightly offset by the aerosol of starch I bought, mistaking it for deodorant (not that this stopped me blasting my armpits with silicon for three days). But then, queuing at the till, I looked at my wheat beers and suddenly remembered – the bottle deposits!

I do worry about myself at times. As I drove back through the border into Basel I experienced one of those epiphanies, a snapshot preview of my tight-fisted future, of a little old man in a balding velvet suit shampooing with washing-up liquid and padding out his cocktail nibbles with MiaouMix pellets. But it was a lovely day, cold and bright, and having eventually taken the bottles back to a supermarket I stuck the Rolls in a multi-storey, found a cashpoint and whistled off into the well-kempt crowds.

Switzerland seized its unexpected second chance and belatedly endeared itself to me, chiefly by supplying a free bicycle. It's safe to say that any city which provides this service is the kind of place you could live, on the grounds that the authorities are imaginative and generous, the traffic well marshalled, and the citizens honest and responsible enough not to nick half the bikes and throw the rest in the river. Copenhagen and Amsterdam are the other two places I've found free bikes, and I have only good memories of both (though because of a slight vodka miscalculation, I don't, strictly speaking, have any memories of Amsterdam).

Leaving a small deposit with a Turkish guest worker at the nearest booth, I pedalled off with a new freedom. Yes, the trams were a bit scary, and the failure of my trailing leg to take account of the rear-mounted basket meant the first seven attempts to dismount ended in the gutter, but puffing up the steep hill to Munster, the cathedral, I was giddily content. I could stop where I wanted, go where I wanted – just as well, as whatever Tommy said, the cathedral was another let-down after Italy, the best thing being the view. A bracingly prosperous profusion of gables and spires, 175,000 wealthy homes, and the source of that wealth either struggling upstream against the Rhine's mighty current or spearing skywards from the industrial suburbs to gently fumigate the blue heavens. As in Coryate's day, the city made its money both as the inland port at the start of the navigable Rhine and from its pioneering chemical plants – which in the seventeenth century meant printing, papermaking and what the Michelin guide called 'the industry of dying'. And so I freewheeled down to the river bank, legs out and sounds of juvenile glee scaring the students, to make my own Renaissance book.

Since reading Coryate's account of Basel's proficiency at 'the notable art of printing', and learning that the city produced almost half the paper used in Europe at that time, I had decided that the original fifteenth-century mill which housed the Paper Museum was the birthplace of the *Crudities*. I was the only visitor, and after explaining my pilgrimage the kindly staff gave me the run of the place. Down in the basement, where a waterwheel drove tree-sized hammers into buckets of wood pulp, I was allowed to make my own fifteenth-century paper, panning a frame of mesh into the pulp and hanging the resultant soggy page up to dry (astonishing to think that all paper was produced this way until Victorian times). Upstairs I presented my page to the matronly printer (okay – so we'd dried it in a Corby trouser press), and under her aegis I lined up the metal type, inked it and stamped it on to the paper: THOMAS CORYATE NOVEMBER 1999.

It was corny, but it was a throat lumper. Coryate had departed the city saying, 'By Gods grace I will one day see Basil againe,' and standing out on the cold quayside in front of the museum, waving my piece of paper like Neville Chamberlain, I looked at the Rhine and thought: Actually, no, you won't.

I should have gone then, but I still had a tenner in francs left, and for some reason decided to spend this on a haircut. Coryate was scrupulously above such things, but to many of the later Britons, fashion and foppery were obsessions, sometimes even the inspiration behind an entire Grand Tour. Charles James Fox came back from the Continent with his hair powdered blue; Horace Walpole danced on Florentine bridges wearing a dressing-gown and a straw hat; many others bought red shoes, green gloves and had their hair elaborately curled in what some sniggering barber had convinced them was the latest style, or visited one of those 850 Venetian wigmakers.

Aside from the occasional bout of idiocy with ruffs the size of cartwheels, there hadn't really been any men's fashion in Britain until the Grand Tourists brought it home. Tailoring barely existed. Coming back dressed up like a dog's *dîner* was the most obvious method of showing everyone that you'd been abroad, the suntan of the eighteenth century – the same principle, in fact, that inspired Coryate after returning to ostentatiously wave his fork about whenever someone offered him a sarnie. Striding through the crowds, it occurred to me that I had yet to acquire a fitting souvenir, if not sartorial then tonsorial. Suddenly I felt a spiritual affinity with those pioneering dandies, the men who risked humiliation by striding down the gangplank at Dover in a haze of hairpowder, laying down their dignity so that future generations of Englishmen might inherit the right to snag the billowing nylon acreage of their five-button-waistband Birmingham bags in the chain of a mate's Chopper.

In fairness, there may have been parallel motivations leading me to the unisex salon in the department store above which I'd parked – notably the surprising discovery, on a board outside, that I could procure such a service in such a country for such an outlay. Beneath '*Herren*' were a range of styling procedures, starting with Trend and proceeding down to Junior via Top, Super and Budget. I had seen more than enough Swiss people to picture the Thompson Twin awfulnesses conjured by Trend, which in any case was 70SF, or about £28. Junior it was to be.

The all-female staff were monolingual but friendly, and having laboriously established that even a great big man like me qualified for a Junior cut, sat me down with a numbered catalogue featuring styles from the appropriate range. Naturally these were uniformly ghastly, all pictures of night-club bouncers trying to look sultry (a challenge for any Swiss man) under Elton John fringes, or uncomfortable teenagers sporting heavily gelled variants of the universal German haircut, *Das Mullet*. A unisex staple since the early Eighties, this potent combination of beaver-tail long back and semi-spiked short top reached its apogee with Nena *Neunundneunzig Luftballon* and the German Euro '96 squad. It makes women look like footballers and vice versa. If there are any fashion police in Basel, they work undercover. Deep undercover.

After a failed attempt to persuade my stylist to adapt a No. 4 with bespoke additions from a bloke in a Versace ad I'd spotted on the back of the magazine her mate was reading, I settled on a No. 11, largely on the grounds that of all the models, he looked least like he was about to burst into tears.

An hour it took. For the first three-quarters of that time I feigned nonchalance, but as the mirror began to tell an ugly story intervention was required. As someone who has a haircut only twice a year, I didn't want to leave six months of my life on the floor of a Swiss department store in return for looking like a shop dummy from the kind of place you might have gone to buy a school blazer in 1974. The language barrier made it difficult, of course, and soon the manageress arrived, lifting up my ragged, dog-like ear flaps and muttering disconsolately to herself.

'Gel?' she enquired at length, still holding my left-hand flap.

'No! *Nein*,' I blurted in panic.

'Like zis?'

I looked up to see my fringe manipulated into a sort of centre-parted marcel wave, like a Belle Epoque French waiter. For a second I thought I would be okay; then the comic hysteria boiled up out of my guts and I snorted forth a great sneezing guffaw. The scene instantly recalled a juvenile appointment at the Royal London School of Dentistry, when two students attempting to photograph my asymmetric canines while a colleague splayed back the encroaching lips with a pair of surgical shoehorns were repeatedly frustrated by their young patient's helpless hilarity at the scenario reflected in the lens before him. I can take retrospective comfort from the image of Robert Adam, surveying himself before a Parisian mirror in his red-heeled, diamond-buckled shoes, embroidered-gusset tights and 'Frenchified head of hair', and having the rare honesty to 'burst out a-laughing'.

Relaxing her grip on my fringe, the manageress politely waited for my unsightly mirth to subside. Then the young stylist pushed her pierced navel up to my right ear, bent over me to examine the left, now being re-exposed by her superior, peered into the orifice and at length deliberately and carefully grasped and extended a strand of hair whose lonely, unloved follicle lay somewhere deep within my inner lughole. Amusement turned to horror. I'd never had one of those before. Realising I would never be able to laugh again at those seasonal commercials for the Remington Nose and Ear Trimmer, I winced in pain as she tugged slightly harder. All three faces met in the mirror. The manageress, reinforcing her own tonsorial grip, was the first to speak. Without apparent malice she nodded at the contents of her assistant's thumb and forefinger and said, 'You like to keep zis?'

It was a masterstroke on their part. The aural intruder was the last hair to go, and minutes later, I was corkscrewing the Rolls squeakily down the multi-storey ramps, heading out into the rush hour to find a sign for Frankreich. If John Belushi had been beside me, I'd have sparked up a half-price Marlboro, chucked the lighter out the window, turned to him and said, 'It's 110 kilometres to

Strasbourg, we gotta full tank of gas, half a punnet of unwashed grapes, it's dark and I'm wearing a shop wig. Hit it.'

SEVEN

The Rhine and Germany

It had taken 2,000 miles, but that night I finally did some Grand Touring. I'm not sure what made the night drive to Strasbourg so evocative – the road along the Rhine was flat and straight and no man's landish. Possibly it was that the Rolls, free at last of slush and inclines, was happy for the first time in weeks, eating up the miles rather than choking on them. We raced the Germans on the bank opposite, all speeding home from their tax-free jobs on the auto-bahn or in double-decker commuter trains, the Rolls lolling serenely along the empty French tarmac, alone with me in the misty dark, the ice warning light burning fiercely orange and the faint blue glow of the dials reflecting off the veneer and picking out the jagged contours of my handaxe-crafted caveman fringe. The cruise control even started working, which was good and would have been even better had this occurred at my behest.

The Rhine's silent blackness concealed an Alpine might that ferried Coryate to Strasbourg in just over a day, the scenery passing at what would have been a blur at 1608 speeds. And then, after an hour, the river was gone, hidden behind escarpments and embankments that I realised at length were more remains of the Maginot Line, France's 200-kilometre white-elephant defence against a Nazi invasion. I mean, how were the French to know that Hitler would be low enough to invade them through Belgium? After all, it was almost twenty-six years since any other Germans had done exactly that.

For another hour there was nothing, just earthworks to the right and forest to the left. Then, abruptly, I found myself surrounded by chimneys and steam, by huge steel spheres and ranks of pylons floodlit like cathedrals, the heaviest of heavy industry, a petro-chemical theme park. And even this seemed eerily wondrous, at least all apart from the disturbing odours wafting snidely towards Germany. You may be interested to learn that the worst stench, a sort of eau de Paris Métro with overtones of old swimming towel, emanated from the Wrigley plant.

And then, having passed a compound where 50,000 new Peugeots were getting cold, the road turned inland through the Ersteins and Plobsheims of Alsace's Teutonic past – Coryate calls the area 'the garden of Germany', and *choucroute*, more familiar as sauerkraut, remains the regional speciality – and before I realised it there I was, circling Strasbourg city centre with the Friday-night cruisers, being stared at again for the first time since Italy. Things went smoothly; without trying I found an underground car park. And it even had a special 8F overnight rate, a tempting if overly fluorescent accommodation option which I vigorously spurned the moment two Clios came screeching down the spiral, parked sloppily across three and a half spaces and disgorged four handsome young couples who ran off towards the stairs in a great clattering echo of stilettos and laughter.

This was what had been missing in Switzerland, this vibrancy, this style, this cocksure, spur-of-the-moment sense of fun, and I wanted to be part of it. Yes, so Coryate had slept in his boat just outside Strasbourg, and for once moaned about it ('having for my coverled the cold open aire which did not a little punish me . . . I comforted my selfe that I did not deserve the sweet junkats of my little experience without some bitter pilles and hard brunts of adverse fortune'). He doesn't say where he stayed in Strasbourg, but it would have been somewhere nice in the centre. And the night before he'd treated himself to a 20-pence supper, the most he'd ever spent on a meal, and standing in front of the cathedral's overwhelming façade, jostled by students, Eurocrats and German day-trippers, I was more or less shoved backwards by the sheer force of Gothic architecture into a plush hotel lobby.

'Can you recommend a good place to eat – one that doesn't serve chew-croot?'

As soon as I heard that, drawled to the receptionist in middle-aged Midwest, I accepted that the Hotel Cathedral would be very expensive. But in the end, after a bit of haggling that I'm convinced is the way forward for such establishments (at least those keen to see their breakfast buffets laid waste with locust-like efficiency by guests with stolen face flannels shoved down their pants), I bagged an 800F suite for 500F. It was up in the hotel's medieval attic, which gave me a chance to bang my head on the very same beams that Coryate might easily have done, but it was huge, heavily cushioned and gadgeted, and the first place I'd stayed where they fold the dangly bit of the loo paper into a chevron (so guaranteeing contact, albeit indirect, between the chambermaid's fingers and your sit-upon).

My extravagance was apt in that at Strasbourg I was meeting up again with the Grand Tourists I'd waved goodbye to at Venice.

Connected by good roads to Paris, the city was a popular stopover for those either heading home or setting off towards Germany. A reputation for gourmet dining didn't do it any harm, either – after pancakes 'resembling a cow dung with mushrooms sprung through it' in Geneva, they found 'incomparable tench at dinner and exquisite perch at supper', drinking 'good hock, and we find it medicinal'. 'Here we begin to live like ourselves again,' wrote Philip Francis in 1772, so impressed with the food in Strasbourg that rather than go to a 'spectacle' he spent all night eating.

Another attraction was the occasional presence of the philosopher Voltaire, who was mercilessly pursued by British tourists all over Switzerland and France. No Grand Tour, it seems, was complete without an audience with the greatest living Euroceleb, who in his dotage had to become accustomed to looking out of his windows at crowds gathered outside hoping for a glimpse. In Strasbourg in 1753, William Lee knocked on his front door and found it answered by a man 'emaciated and weakened with ill health', though this didn't stop him barging in and demanding the philosopher's thoughts on the King of Prussia. 'He always changed the conversation and seemed to dislike it,' said an aggrieved Lee.

Decamping to Ferney, just outside Geneva, didn't help Voltaire escape his foreign fan base. 'Ferney attracts more of the truly devout today than the Vatican,' said one tourist. Persistently harassed, the drinking man's thinker soon took to insulting his visitors. John Cosyer found that 'talking to ladies he was inclined to be rather indecent'; one such visitor was told she had roused the old man from his tomb before having the door slammed in her face. Boswell, for once keeping his hands above the table, got the full nine yards. Having lured the seventy-one-year-old Voltaire out of bed, he attempts to engage him in conversation about Scottish art, a gambit rebuffed with 'To paint well, it is necessary to have warm feet.' After trying to get him to speak English ('No. To do this one must place the tongue between the teeth, and I have lost all my teeth'), Boswell signs off with a cheery aside about his own planned tour of the Hebrides: 'Very well. But I shall remain here. You will allow me to stay here?'

The excellent truth was, the ruder he became, the wittier and sharper his foreign visitors found him. When he eventually snapped and bellowed out of the window, 'Well, gentlemen, you now see me; did you take me to be a wild beast or a monster that was fit only to be stared at?', the crowd of Englishmen gathered below probably applauded.

The tourists might have driven Voltaire away from Strasbourg, but the weather can't have helped. It was so cold outside that I couldn't stop stuttering 'Jesus'; even with gardening gloves on, my hands were curled up into fists across my chest. But it was lovely all the same, all pale-pink Christmas illuminations (with the odd left-over witch) and well-dressed window shoppers breathing steamily on to well-dressed shop windows. The cathedral was almost too big for its square, intimidating the steep-roofed, half-timbered medieval houses cowering in its shadow, but there were plenty more generously proportioned rivals, off one of which, behind Barclays Bank and Marks & Sparks, I did indeed find a place that served me chew-croot, and sausages, and mustard, and beer, and with no third party to suffer the nocturnal aftermath I devoured it all with a clean conscience.

Cleaner, anyway, than the conscience associated with my activities back in the room, when in an attempt to maximise my waking hours in a flash hotel I stayed up watching some prodigiously appalling Hulk Hogan film, fiddling with the spotlights in my antechamber along with the whole gamut of complimentary appliances from trouser press to climate control, eventually creating such a power surge that at 1.45 something blew and I was plunged into black silence.

It didn't matter so much then, but proved a bit of a bind the next morning. Have you ever had a bath in the dark? Soapy and distressed was the man who phoned reception to confess his blighting addiction to wattage; prompt and merry was the handyman who arrived to redeem him.

The breakfast room overlooked the cathedral (mine overlooked a courtyard full of smoking chefs), and I sat down between a table of Italian and the chew-croot Midwesterners to admire it from behind a plate of food stacked to a height that Scooby Doo and Shaggy would have been proud of. Any place that lets you eat gherkins for breakfast is okay in my book.

It was astonishing to think that the red sandstone tower shooting upwards out of sight was completed 300 years before Coryate's trip. At 465 feet it's still taller than all but half a dozen buildings in twenty-first-century London. In 1305 people must have looked at it and cried with disbelief. The Italians were babbling animatedly and craning their necks for a glimpse of the summit – they were clearly looking forward to their day in a way that the Midwesterners, still grumbling about last night's catering, clearly weren't.

Leaden with calories, I checked out and stumbled the 15 yards to the cathedral entrance. It was teeming with schoolkids and Germans inside, but I got a good look at the towering astronomical clock that impressed Coryate so much he had an engraving of it included in the *Crudities*. It was a triumph: as well as all the moon-phase dials and stuff, there was a splendid little skeleton who came out of an arch to ring out the hours by battering a femur on a bell. None of your jolly wee men in umbrellas here. And

again, even though it was already fifty years old in his day, Coryate couldn't believe its hi-tech wondrousness – his detailed description, along with the engraving, was intended 'as an encouragement to some wealthy Fraternity to erect the like in St Paules Church'. I thought of last night's space-age petrochemistry, of the TGV and the RER, of the silent, bullet-train trams here in Strasbourg, of the animated adverts projected on to the streets and the digital displays outside even inconsequential towns that told you precisely how many spaces were left in each car park. History was beginning to repeat itself. We were once again at the periphery of Continental innovation, peering across the Channel in gormless, backward wonder.

Out in the streets, wandering among the Germanic half-timbered townhouses, cold people were doing the usual Saturday things: queuing up at cashpoints, standing about wondering why they'd bought three bagfuls of designer clothing and a standard lamp, not yet realising it was because they were hungover. Stamping about in the cold, I kept retreating blindly into any cosy-looking establishment regardless of its browsing potential: one-hour photo shops; opticians'. At some point I blundered across a flea market, but if I was expecting a repeat of the medieval bazaar in Lyon I was to be disappointed: this was all the sort of stuff no one wants when their great-aunt dies, with a heavy emphasis on ceramic fauna. And the prices! One bloke had simply emptied the contents of the kind of bottom drawer you might find somewhere in most houses out on to the cobbles: old keys, encrusted batteries, a couple of Seventies postcards. Yet when a woman prodded an enquiring foot at a single Bakelite door knob, he blithely requested 150F. I suppose you should expect bloodsuckers at a flea market.

On the way out of town I picked up some hitchhikers, or rather

vice versa. Rolling up to join the back of the queue at an enormous
junction, I heard a hoot and a laugh, and looked round to see two
hippy-ish teenage girls running up the pavement beside me. The more
forward, with Nana Mouskouri specs and dark hair to match, rapped
gaily on the window; I whooshed it down; she laughed and held open
both hands in a general expression of curious delight; I thumbed the
back seat queryingly; her face lit up. I clicked down the central locking
and they noisily piled in, shoving aside the tent and other rubbish at
my behest. Without quite knowing how or why, I was soon chauf-
feuring two giggling females about the French suburbs. They royal-
waved at passers-by, they swapped specs for shades and began clapping
along to the Pulp tape that was all I could find in the way of student
music. And it was great, like a pop video, especially when I started
being an idiot, caning it over the cobbles and rolling my passengers
from one door to the distant other round the corners.

But then, as I barrelled under a sign marked 'Deutschland 2', the
claps and laughter died as if switched off and a suddenly composed
voice said, '*Monsieur?*' I glanced up at the rear-view mirror: two dead-
straight faces. '*Ici, s'il vous plaît.*' Turning down the music, which
suddenly seemed stupidly loud, I eased into a Citroën dealer forecourt, and after a quiet '*Merci*' they rustled awkwardly over the
flysheet and stepped out on to the sump-stained tarmac. Waiting to
rejoin the traffic flow, I watched them retreat slowly up the road
back to the city, certain they would suddenly slump with laughter
at my expense.

Just before the border I pulled in at a self-service carwash to
exchange my last francs for a modicum of vehicular presentability,
and while grappling with the high-pressure hoses I wondered what
had gone wrong. Was it the looming border? Certainly the
whole carefree scenario might have been a little suspicious, a little

Baader–Meinhof for German tastes. Perhaps they'd just got bored. Perhaps . . . Suddenly I knew. I dropped the hose, letting it buck about crazily on the wet concrete, and flung open the back door. They had nicked something. It was the only explanation for the sudden mood shift, the sudden and sombre end to our journey. I ferreted about madly, bundling the tent out of the door, looking for whatever it was I wouldn't find.

But instead, rolling gently in the left-hand footwell, conspicuous and accusing on the Wilton, was a familiar, but for the last three days forgotten, wide-mouthed orange-juice bottle. Even in the gloom cast by the carwash awning the nature of its contents was unequivocal. Realising I'd be dining out for years on this story – though on my own, and probably not in a public place – I made a face like a man with a bad hangover awaking to find his pillow filled with scampi.

Streetlights powered by solar panels; old men furiously scrubbing their thresholds with arthritic desperation; tall, bare, crow-nested trees swaying above a cold plain: there was no mistaking Germany. And all the signs were there when I stopped for provisions at Lichtenau, where Tommy spent the night: absurdly cheap food, and a sullen and snooty manageress who stood at the supermarket doors mentally awarding all shoppers one out of ten for presentation – even those who didn't look like they cut their own hair with a broken bottle. The laundered Rolls was substantially more impressive, and as I sloped back to it across the car park, the manageress's gaze boring into me, I found myself powerfully reminded of how Keith Moon used to while away his afternoons by dressing as a tramp, standing at a crowded bus stop being smelly and mad before, at a pre-arranged time, being picked up by his chauffeur in the Rolls and gliding away through a sea of confused outrage.

My declining appearance was appropriate in that it mirrored Coryate's. After leaving Lichtenau and receiving a 'profound draught of good Rhenish wine' from a Franciscan friar in a forest-bound monastery, he found himself confronted on a lonely woodland track by 'two Boores'. They were ragged and armed; Coryate for the first time expresses real distress:

> Whereupon fearing least they would eyther have cut my throat, or have robbed me of my gold that was quilted in my jerkin, or have stripped me of my clothes, which they would have found but a poore bootie, being but a threedbare fustian case . . .

It doesn't look good, but as a confrontation looms, Tommy thinks fast:

> A little before I mette them, I put off my hat very curteously, and very humbly (like a Mendicant Friar) begged some money of them, expressing my minde by such gestures and signes that they well knew what I craved of them: and so by this begging insinuation I preserved my selfe secure & free from violence, and withall obtained that of them which I neither wanted or expected. For they gave me so much of their tinne money as paid for my supper that night, even foure pence halfe-penny.

263

If he hadn't fazed them with his Latin, and looked such a mess, it would have been curtains. What a man. And what a haul: at today's prices, he walked away with a 3-quid profit.

Still the fields were bland and cold, and flat enough to have attracted a load of NATO air bases. That was then, of course: when I drove past the vast enclave of 'Kleinkanada', the Canadian airmen had gone, their runways and barracks and hangars being ripped up and torn down to make room for a golf course and a business park. It's always seemed to me that these bases were as much a punishment to the Germans as a strategic consideration: throughout the country there are road signs every half-mile telling British and American soldiers the tank speed limit. If the Canadians had forgiven the Germans, why couldn't we? I thought with shame about the tabloid coverage of international meetings between our two nations, Gazza and Stuart Pearce in tin helmets and the headline 'FOR YOU, FRITZ, ZE EURO '96 IS OVER'. And then I thought: Hang on, it's Scotland v England today.

Twenty minutes later I was propping up the bar in a small-town sport club, watching schnapps-drinking parents watch their blue-legged ten-year-olds play football through the big picture window. After pained negotiations the chef and barmaid had understood and agreed to my televisual request – 'Ah: Schottland–England, a bath of blood, yes?' – even though, as I realised when the bar began to fill with old men who stared up disconsolately at Alan Shearer chewing along to the national anthem, they'd been planning to screen a German league game. But no one would hear of it when I attempted to rescind viewing priority, and although everyone else wanted Scotland to win, my lonely theatricals during England's 2–0 victory were tolerated with indulgence. It was when the chef started plying me with free sarnies eschewed by the kids' parents that I began imagining, superfluously, how a German tourist would have been received if he'd gone into a similar establishment in semi-rural Britain and asked, in German, if instead of showing Man U v Arsenal they could screen Austria v Germany. Sometimes, we really aren't very nice. Who actually cares about the war these days?

I got an answer soon enough. Just after full time a young man with a goatee and an old feller with bulbous features and muddy carpet slippers came in and sat down beside me; it was soon established that the former, named Christian, had lived in England for fourteen years (doing some sort of Ph.D. in neuro-something – the kind of stuff I thought you'd have to go to Germany to do) and had an American fiancée, whereas the latter, who in fifteen minutes consumed two huge schnappses, a lager and three fags, was both Christian's grandfather and a one-time U-boat rating.

It didn't take long. Slamming his empty schnapps glass on the table ('He has to be quick – my grandmother thinks we are doing some garden work'), he fixed me with a rheumy eye, coughed with almost terminal intensity and then, with his grandson as interpreter, told his tale. Near the end of the war in Europe, his U-boat, sailing under orders from Bergen to Japan, was intercepted by the British in Indo-China. Unwilling to finance repatriation, the British apparently then sold him to the Foreign Legion, in whose Indo-Chinese fortresses he was enslaved for almost five years. 'He says he will never eat rice again,' said Christian as I shifted about uncomfortably, fiddling with the erratic Caligula kiss curls on my forehead. '*Scheisse Englisch!*' blurted the old man, bunching his fist near, though not quite in, my face. Christian laughed uneasily. 'Don't worry about him, please.'

What could I say? It all sounded improbable, but there was nothing fabricated about the old man's rage. Five years. As they left to face the grandmaternal wrath, I stood up, then half sat down again, and feebly attracted their attention. 'Umm . . . Listen, tell him I'm sorry. About the whole, you know, the war-slavery thing. Sorry.' Christian nodded pacifyingly and prodded the old man through the door. '*Scheisse Englisch*,' came a muted cry. 'English . . . shit.'

Soberly I returned to the Rolls, driving off into the Black Forest feeling like the Burundi flag had been replaced by a huge Union Jack and that if I pressed the horn an amplified chorus of *The Dambusters* would blare out through the grille. At Baden-Baden, in some obscure act of contrition, I drove into the tourist office, bought a keyring, asked for a room in a guest house and didn't once make the 'so good they named it twice' joke.

Wearied by his table-turning experience with the muggers, and having spent a few hours totally lost among the dense conifers, Coryate arrived tired and late at Baden-Baden (its name derives from the existence of two separate spas in the town, but as Coryate claims there were actually no fewer than sixty-five, cartographers and station announcers should count their blessings). Driving into the 2-mile tunnel that ploughs through the rocky hill separating Baden-Baden's ritzy, Euroroyal centre from its humbler suburbs, I wasn't immediately concerned with the Romanesque baths where Coryate sought refreshment. I had other plans.

My *gasthaus* room was a spartan affair above a bar, with no telly and a duvet so stiflingly weighty that I was to spend all night empathising with poor Frau Kohl when Helmut's in the mood. No matter. With waltzes thundering out of the bedside radiogram, laundered whites dripping on the towel rail and tonsorial presentability partially restored via convoluted penknife action, I brushed down my velvet, winked in the mirror and set off for the casino to be James Bond.

Oh, you must know the film, forgotten its name – the one where

Bond sweeps up in his shiny Roller to the grand casino, then swans suavely over the red carpet and through the cocktail dresses to find out that he won't be let in without his passport, and has to drive 4 miles back to some shitty little guesthouse, where he finds half his wet pants have fallen into the bog.

Why in the name of Baron von Fuck-Buttocks do you need a passport to get into a casino? I thought the idea was to have *money*. 'Right, Blofeld, let's make this interesting. I'll match your bus pass and raise you a library card.' I steamed back through the tunnel at 100, filling the Rolls with wild words, and had to compose myself before entering the casino's underground car park (I had hoped to be able to toss the keys to a valet with practised nonchalance: 'Here you go, sonny . . . Oh, and help yourself to bits of old Emmental and grape pips').

After ten minutes I was better. Determined to put on a show, I wound down the windows, cranked up the *Avengers* theme on the stereo and began circling the Porsche-laden car park, the lord high ponce, the ponce's ponce, the ponce royale with cheese. The high roller in a high Roller: it was shameless, but it was deeply satisfying. The Ferrero Rocher mittel Europeans peered and gawped as they stepped daintily out of their Mercs; a stringy-haired woman of certain years in a slit-sided red dress clapped and cackled echoingly as I passed her for the third time.

And inside, it was a proper James Bond casino: columns, shed-sized chandeliers and red damask walls, all tempered with just the right amount of flared kitsch – tinkling up-lit grottoes, a gold mosaic bar where fat men kept their bottles of Becks in ice buckets. For an hour I loved it, sauntering among the roulette tables with a worldly Grand Tour half-smile, savouring the occasional hey-it's-him nudged exchanges among witnesses to my car-park performance, searching for a frightened blonde whose evil sugar daddy I could wallop at *chemin de fer*. It was only after watching a haughty-looking Oriental woman with black nail varnish lose 3,000DM – over a grand – on four spins of the wheel that I belatedly realised that this place was the antithesis of all I stand for, my own private hell.

Suddenly, everywhere I looked people were throwing away enormous amounts of money, and without complaint or distress. Of course, it helped that most of these were awful wankers. A man in a white suit and a teenager I took for his son, both of what a policeman would describe as 'Middle Eastern appearance', found themselves a gap opposite Shanghai Lil, bought 2,000DM of chips and lost it all in one go. And again, and again. And then they walked away laughing, joshing, in precise emulation of people emerging from an exhilarating fairground ride. I wanted to squeak, to ululate, to bench-vault up on to the baize and shout, 'Listen up, you stupid arses! You! You there with the green chips on 25 – I could have had 700 cans of wheat beer for that! And you – yes, you, you silly fat pig with the flock-wallpaper tie! Put those blue ones back in your pocket and go and buy your wife something, a pearl-handled Luger, an ear and nose hair trimmer, I don't know, anything! Away! Away! *Raus!*'

This, I realised, was what really set Tommy and me apart from the Grand Tourists, this phobic horror of waste, expense and extravagance. I'd long since begun to enjoy our shared obsession with cost, how he'd go into a church and come out muttering: 'Their tabernacle upon their high altar is a very costly thing. For it cost them two thousand duckets, which is two hundred thirty three pound six shillings eight pence sterling.'

Now seething for two, I looked at everyone with a horrid fascination, like someone watching a fairground freak mutilate himself.

The Arabs aside, most of the clientele looked like they had earnt their money through hard work and shrewdness – so what were they thinking of? You could see what kind of people the casino wanted to attract by its promotional literature – a leaflet I'd picked up at the tourist office had featured the following travel information: 'By car – Baden-Baden to Frankfurt – take motorway A5. 180km. Approx travel time – 70 mins.' You need an expensive car to average almost 100 miles per hour on a journey between two city centres, and you also need to be a recklessly idiotic prannet. Maybe the only way these people unwind after making a lot of sensible business decisions is to pop out and make some really shit ones.

And apart from the Arabs, no one looked happy. If someone did enjoy a short-lived moment of triumph, the rule was to affect profound boredom. The only way you could tell whether Shanghai Lil had won or lost was that when she lost she took a little boiled sweet out of her purse and popped it into her mouth with those black-tipped digits. Actually, there was another way, and that was that she never won.

There was an old man playing blackjack – a really, really old man, with a 30-degree squint and a turkey-tendoned neck five sizes too small for his supper-stained shirt collar – whom I'd noticed was attracting a lot of side bets. Pops was a wise old bird; toughest gamer in the world, thirty years, man and boy. He knew the score. Stick with Pops. But it soon became obvious that Pops didn't know the score, or probably his own name, sitting there blowing his family's inheritance by twisting on 17 and sticking on 12. I kept expecting his grandchildren to run in and wheel him off, castigating the croupiers.

Now the glamour was tawdry and juvenile, people trying to be cool in the way you did when you were fourteen, all menthol fags and slit skirts. I was watching a very unhappy young man trying to impress two heavily accessorised girls by losing 100 quid when I heard a familiar distant cackle. 'Hey! You play baccarat? I show you how.' My car-park fan, the straggly red-dress whom I now perceived to be both drunk and Latin American, was becoming tactile with a bald man whose body language fluently marked him out as a stranger. 'Come, come!' She now had a grip of his tie, for support as much as anything. 'Is sooo-perrrb game, so eeeasy.' He recoiled; she reeled him in; his ears went as red as the damask walls, and so did his head. 'Come – how much you have?' He muttered something I couldn't hear. 'Five hun-der-red? Five hun-der-red?' she spat in fiery disgust. 'What is five hun-der-red? You are a . . .' – and here she flicked his tie into his face – '. . . small man. Small!'

This was more like it. But as she flounced erratically away from the hapless slaphead, I realised too late that as a single man I was a target. Even as I swivelled back to the roulette wheel I knew it was too late. 'Hey! You play baccarat?' There was a tug on my jacket. I resisted the subsequent yanks and pulls until my shirt became untucked. Then I turned, adopting the wet-lipped moronic death mask that was my last line of defence. 'Hey! You play . . . Hey! Meester Rorlz-Roy! Hey!'

It was an ugly confrontation, right up there with most of the fights with drunk Latin American women I've had in casinos. As I tried to outflank her she cut me off by the croupier, barging me into his velvet stool, essaying a clumsy but determined assault on my trouser pockets.

'The keys, the keys,' she half laughed, half ordered.

The croupier gave me a tut-accompanied disapproving glare, as if I was denying my crippled mother access to her sewing box. '*Rien ne va plus,*' he said, forlornly attempting to focus his players' attention back to the baize.

'No! Wait! *Attendez!*' drawled my assailant, triumphantly holding aloft a bulky fob marked 'Pension Freudenstadt, Baden-Baden'. 'My friend's Rorlz-Roy on black!'

Frozen there it is a scene worthy of illustration in the *Crudities*' frontispiece, but as the tape runs on we see one· velvet-cuffed hand twist and grab the lofted arm while the other yanks the key free with a concentrated violence that elicits a confused 'Aiiii!' of female pain. The key is repatriated to its loin-hugging pocket; seconds later the wearer is standing under a black winter sky, looking up at a digital display above a bank to learn that it is (a) −3°C, and (b) time to run to McDonald's, rapidly stuff his face, run back to pay his second car-park ticket of the evening and return to the Pension Freudenstadt.

It was odd to discover how much Germany had changed. The casino had seemed the very embodiment of the Grand Tour, but it was built in 1821, long after the Tour's heyday. In fact, most of the small number who passed through the country in the eighteenth century found the roads appalling, the inns filthy and basic and the people dishonest. Boswell had to sleep on a table in Vellinghausen and in a barn full of livestock in Hanover. One traveller warned guests to show the innkeeper 'your firearms and to tell him, with a courageous look, that you are not afraid of a far superior number of enemies'.

And the customs took some getting used to. The Earl of Dartmouth, visiting Leipzig in 1752, found himself in a tent full of ladies, 'for the most part neither young nor handsome', and was horrified at the requirement to kiss them all after every toast. 'It was sad, clammy work,' he sighs.

Breakfasting alone in a chilled, dark bar room, I perused the spa brochures in a new light. Should I go to Baden A, the Caracella, where I would 'float on a wave of well-being' and 'share a tingly feeling with water sprites of all ages'; or Baden B, the Friedrichsbad: 'No swimming costume necessary. Creme service not available on Sundays'? If I tell you that it was Sunday, you will understand why half an hour later I was in the car park beneath the Caracella, floating on a wave of ill-being after my third encounter in thirteen hours with the exclamation mark on the multilingual 'Please pay!' displays in such establishments.

They didn't sell trunks, so I bought the cheapest pair in the gift shop: yellow and blue, more pant-like than my pants. But there were no Zürich-style changing-room unpleasantnesses, and though I've been rather spoilt by regular geothermal dips in the land of my Icelandic in-laws, the hot outdoor pools were undeniably soothing and invigorating in just the right measure. Because German people eat a lot of sausages and drink a lot of beer (a pound a week and a pint a day for every man, woman and fat, drunk child), there weren't too many water sprites bobbing about in the hot bubbles, and rather more water buffalo: hairy beasts with last night's hop-froth in their beards − and, a ha ha, you should have seen the men. But so what? At least, unlike at the casino, everyone looked like they were enjoying themselves: further corroboration of the general rule that a hot bath is nice, whereas pissing away all your Christmas money isn't.

There was an excellent waterfall under which I stood, or rather was pinned: rather like being at the bottom of one of those rubble chutes when a labourer empties a barrow of broken breezeblocks down the spout from the fifteenth floor, but marvellously restora-tive on shoulders bowed out of position by a Eurohiker bag full of books, food and chromed vehicle accessories. After I'd been battered into watery submission, my place was taken by a full-chested fraulein whose bikini top was never likely to challenge the forces of gravity, motion and male willpower. It was an arresting display, but I couldn't help thinking that the target audience wasn't quite as enthusiastic as one might have imagined.

I soon found out why. Proceeding up a spiral staircase and through a steamed-up glass door marked 'Eucalyptus sauna', I found myself in a pine-benched hothouse that stank like the devil's own Sinex and was populated by very many naked people. I'd like to say I didn't know where to look, but I did, and was frankly shocked. A man with a girl I sincerely hope was his teenage granddaughter; two fifteen-year-old blokes with wandering eyes and towels rising in their laps. Not wishing to be seen to endorse such a spectacle, I almost felt obliged to castigate the benign middle-aged participants. 'You, sir – bratwurst and two veg. Should be ashamed of yourself. And, madam – turn about please . . . Yes – just as I thought: dumplings and Black Forest.' The traditions of German public nudity and hypo-critical British prudery, established at least as long ago as 1608, were alive and well in one compact scenario.

There's only so much fun you can have watching sweat tribu-taries congregate into hairy-fleshed valleys, and when I found my overheated brain urging me to deliver a ringing tattoo of slaps upon the next fat bottom that came in through the door, I struggled to my feet, dressed soporifically and set off for the hills.

Whereas in Italy the filthy, ancient city centres were redolent of Coryate, in bombed-and-rebuilt Germany I only really felt at one with him out in the sticks. When he started talking about 'a marveilous abundance of frogs', bang on cue there was one of those comical beware-of-the-frog road-warning signs; I pulled in for an in-car lay-by snack to find two dozen huge dead hares strung up on a washing line, dripping blood over the picnic tables – an inescapably seventeenth-century still life. The damp, misty hills of the northern Black Forest were studded with venerable half-timbered houses, their roofs so steep they sometimes sported three rows of dormer windows. Villages were smothered in Gothic script and overrun with men in feathered Tyrolean hats, but as well as being twee it was neat and comfortable looking – the first places in Germany I could almost imagine spending a summer in, at least until I wondered how I'd get along with neighbours who put signs up outlawing bicycles from 22.00–06.00.

There's also a bit of an acid rain problem, most of it caused by British coal-fired power stations, which may well have accounted for the withered and sickly look of some of the big trees. And now there's a bit more of a problem, all of it caused by me. I'm sorry – blame the couple in the Opel Kadett who parped and flashed and harried me down a twisty hill road, forcing me to shift gear with such regularity I accidentally discovered that by engaging neutral and briefly flooring the gas I could expel a hugely impressive cloud of thick smog, through which my pursuers would emerge in the manner of a heavy metal band taking the stage, only with expressions more appropriate for those who find themselves on the wrong side of the road and heading towards a tree. It was great. I did it the whole time after that.

Bypassing the heavily industrial Karlsruhe, not even a name in Coryate's day, I went through Durlach without realising it was the 'Turlowe' where he spent a night, and then Weingarten, where vines still trailed up to the last fringes of the Black Forest, and then a whole load of drab, flat towns with names like mutant hormones – Oestringen, Rinklingen, Remchingen. Here Coryate had slept in another of his 'solitary houses'. Mindful of my rule that I'd sleep in the car unless the ice light came on, I gave the warning panel a hefty smack as the appealing silhouette of Heidelberg's castle loomed above the mist; it obediently illuminated.

Coryate might have been one of the first foreigners to enjoy himself in Heidelberg, but he was by no means the last. Mark Twain's account of the city made such an impression on Americans that they didn't bomb it during the war, returning afterwards to establish their European military headquarters here. I drove past blocks and blocks of barracks and sports clubs: one in seven residents of the city is a US citizen.

And my grandfather, lured by a friend's account of twopenny loaves of rye bread and halfpenny glasses of wine (must run in the family), chucked in his job on the *Birmingham Gazette* to go to Heidelberg in 1923. He spent a glorious year there, living like a foreign-currency king during the wheelbarrows-of-cash inflation of the Weimar Republic. Having taught himself German in a couple of weeks from an old dictionary and a copy of Goethe's *Faust* (must not run in the family), he inveigled himself into university lectures wearing a cloak, wrote a play and dreamt of becoming a poet. 'It was at Heidelberg that I conceived and confirmed enthusiasms that have lasted until now,' he wrote in a brief autobiography we found after he died, 'and I briefly enjoyed there the leisure to indulge them.' As quintessential a Grand Tour sentiment as you could hope to find – he came back with the excellent proposal that retirement, rather than being 'a final interlude near the end of life', ought to come instead near life's beginning, 'a decade of enriching freedom at 20'.

Despite all the military infrastructure, Heidelberg remains above all a student town – the oldest in Germany, where the university had its own laws and even a prison until the First World War, and old lecturers still sport duelling scars. Generously tolerant of the armed horseplay, Grand Tourists had a high regard for German academe – thirty years after his own visit, Boswell sent his son to Leipzig University, and the erudition of Heidelberg graduates was regularly commented upon.

That I was near a tertiary education facility became obvious when I parked in front of a suburban house with four dozen bicycles in the front garden and bad jazz trumpet shrieking out of a window in the loft. The hotel alongside was the right side of 40 quid but the wrong side of 30; downtown the weather was the right side of instantly fatal but the wrong side of bloody freezing.

Hauptstrasse must be the longest pedestrianised street in Europe; if not, it's certainly got the most bars. Many were called stuff like The House of 101 Beers and had signs reading 'Englishmenu is to have inside' in the window, but there were lots of fun-looking spit-and-sawdust student places, many buzzing even at nine on a Sunday night. I have to report, however, that the German student at play is an alarming beast. He will spend long minutes staring silently into the windows of knife shops, before abruptly donning a Pippi Longstocking wig and shrieking random sounds at the top of his enormous voice.

I compromised in the end, eating sausages and drinking a slow beer in some Café Rouge-style place that actually could have been anywhere, tapping my foot along to Nik Kershaw, eschewing cutlery and generally exhibiting other worrying signs of having spent far too long in my own company. The worst symptom was the unsightly paranoia exhibited as I carefully bundled up all my rank possessions and carted them off with me every time I went to the loo.

A donnish American couple on a neighbouring table had a copy of the *Guardian*, and when they got up to leave I swiped it hungrily – my first English paper since leaving. I had got down to the financial gossip by the time they threw me out; unfortunately I had also got down to the weather, and in particular this portentous runic statement: Frankfurt −4 25 sn.

On the long walk back to the hotel, I saw a couple of students pause to pick up one of those condomy things that sheathe handbag-sized umbrellas and place it carefully on top of a bollard. The fact that they should bother to do this; the fact that the owner of such a blatantly superfluous item would retrace their cold, wet footsteps in search of it – I was strangely affected, and immediately concluded that if only the Germans ran Italy (and they've had a couple of years of practice), you'd have the best cities in the world.

Only on an aesthetic level, though. As a people, I was regrettably concluding that they weren't quite right. Coryate had noted that the Germans drank a lot but never seemed to get drunk, and it's the same today: it's okay to drink beer at breakfast, and you always meet people who reek of booze, but not once did I see anyone being disorderly. Admirable maybe, but also somehow unsettling. The student eccentricities had more in common with the effects of electro-convulsive therapy than those of alcohol. And then there's the nudity. And the way the lavatory pans are designed with a 'shelf' to encourage detailed pre-flush faecal examination. And the TV guides that put a crucifix and the date of death beside the names of all defunct actors. And the number of shops on the Hauptstrasse selling knuckledusters and rat-traps (who actually wants to *trap* a rat?), and something called the Silvester Party 2000 set, which comprised half a dozen party poppers, some indoor fireworks and a short-barrelled revolver.

And the way they start being noisily industrious at 7 a.m. on

Monday: building things, vacuuming, even chain-sawing a car in half if the drastic cacophony in the courtyard below my window the following morning was to be believed. I opened the curtains for a bleary investigation and was presented with an even more startling scenario: on the roof terrace opposite, adding his own percussive counterpoint to the painful metallic dissonance shrieking up from below, a man was nailing an old rotary mincer to his trellis, already home to two dozen or so similar appliances. You see what I mean? Not quite right.

And yet at the same time they're a lot like the British, certainly more so than the French or Italians. In the breakfast room, conversation was funereally muted in a way I'd forgotten possible this side of the Channel, despite the robust aural intrusion of our friend in the courtyard, now clearly welding and riveting his vehicle back together in a fit of remorse. And there was a little plastic barrel on each table marked 'Breakfast remnants', into which one deposited all the butter wrappers and eggshells and beer bottles – something the Hyacinth Buckets of British suburbia will be kicking themselves not to have thought of. The reality is, all the things that bother the British – dog crap in the streets, a dodgy pint of lager, dishwashers whose doors don't shut with a satisfying clunk – also bother the Germans. Only they wake up at six and do something about it.

It was what the Icelanders call 'window weather': nice to look at from the inside. I parked at the foot of the vast castle rock in painful sun, but it was bitterly cold on the endless flight of shadowy stone stairs. In the hotel lift I'd noticed a big old poster of the castle, the road outside it strewn with finned early-Sixties cars, and was again reminded of my childhood motoring tours. There was never any problem parking then: the car was king. You could drive straight into someone's garden and park on top of their rabbit hutch and they'd consider it an honour. And now here I was, trying to outpace a dozen Japanese girls who hawked and spat all the way up the stairs, through the wrong kind of leaves, the wrong kind of frozen coating and the wrong kind of number: 330 of the buggers.

It was even more inclement on the exposed summit, but the red-roofs-and-green-hills view was splendid, pictorially captured by the assembled Orientals with the frenzy of tourists long deprived of decent photographic light. The castle itself, approaching the peak of its red-stoned splendour during Coryate's visit, was surgically ruined by the French in 1689: one of the huge round towers was halved almost precisely about its vertical axis; another, blown up from beneath by sappers who burrowed into the foundations, was neatly disembowelled. But the inner courtyards had lasted well, as had the chamber enclosing what Tommy describes as 'such a stupendous masse that I am perswaded it will affect the gravest and constantest man in the world with wonder'. Steady on, son. It's only a barrel.

Even allowing for Coryate's passion for bulk, I couldn't quite get it. It's a barrel; it's very big. It's a very big barrel. But as well as the Orientals, a large party of underwhelmed primary schoolkids had been brought in to survey the Great Tun, along with its slightly less enormous neighbour, the Little Tun. What was the educational value? I couldn't be sure, but the teacher was delivering an animated address, emphasising random words in a German-student bark and waving her arms about with increasingly wayward passion as she stood dwarfed in front of the Great Tun's bus-sized oaken mass.

'So, children, to CONCLUDE: big barrels really are big. Why do we not produce such barrels TODAY? Anybody? No? Just look up THERE for a moment, look up at its . . . Can you not see? Can you not feel something? It is fear – YES, Gerhard, our fear of these big WOODEN faces, round, angry faces that have forgotten more

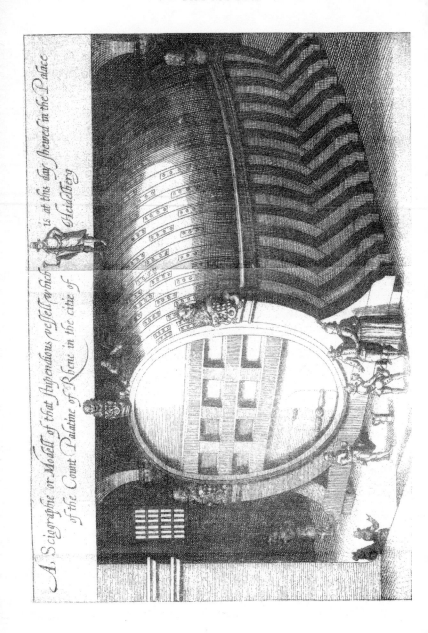

A Sciographie or Modell of that stupendious vessell which is at this day shewed in the Palace of the Count Palatine of Rhene in the citie of Heidelberg

evil than you will ever KNOW. Behold not the face, Heidi! He who BEHOLDS the barrel shall be smote down and ever forth must roam the Hauptstrasse with a HAND MINCER!'

There was a gift shop selling souvenir glasses emblazoned with 'I saw the big barrel' in languages that included Korean, and even wine with personalised laser-printed labels which people were paying good money to drink there and then, rather pointlessly as the 50,000-gallon Great Tun hasn't actually stored any wine for centuries, and is only known to have done so once.

At least in Tom's time – and there was a rather deflating moment when I learnt that the barrel he's depicted standing on top of in the *Crudities* was only a defunct precursor to those currently on view – it was always full of wine, albeit some even ghastlier forebear of Liebfraumilch. Coryate had a glass himself, noting the Tun 'containeth a hundred and two and thirty fuders, three omes, and as many firtles . . . Every fuder countervaileth our tunne, that is foure hogsheads . . . the ome is a measure whereof sixe do make a fuder, the firtle is a measure that countervaileth sixe of our pottles'. The more I read the *Crudities*, the less I was inclined to resent metrication. My favourite bit was when he asked a farmer in the Grisons how many miles it was to the next village, only being informed after the ensuing all-day tramp that 'a Grison mile is five elsewhere'.

After a reciprocal souvenir photocall with a pigtailed Californian surf dude (in town visiting military relations), I walked about the barrel for a bit, examining the ancient graffiti for traces of either Coryate or my grandfather. It was in this room, during some student bacchanal, that my grandfather had drunk his first glass of wine – relief from a diet that otherwise consisted of beer and eggs. Bread was cheaper but had no shelf life – at a time when prices could double in a week, his routine was to stock up with several dozen eggs as soon as he'd changed his sterling into marks, then go back to his room for a fortnight of boiling and frying and poaching in between brainfuls of Goethe. He ate so many they gave him appendicitis. (I forgot to take all this into account when I said he lived like a king.)

The earliest scribbles were dated 1818, but there were plenty of initials from the Twenties – had I looked harder, I would indeed have found a 'MARTIN MOORE 1923' and been very excited, at least until I'd got home and learnt it had actually been etched there by my brother as a tribute sixty years later. There was even the odd wartime 'I voz 'ere' – a reminder how good the Germans are at preserving an air of normality in times of crisis, such as penalty shootouts. In the Pharmaceutical Museum mysteriously located next door, there were official price lists of chemicals drawn up during the Weimar Republic's economic meltdown: in the two weeks after 8 August 1923, the price of a kilo of 'argent. nitric. fus. i. bacill' rose from 54,422,500 marks to 75,010,200. How could they decide on such an exact figure? It was as if they felt they could tame the problem by sheer statistical precision. And in the case alongside were details of 'the rebirth of the pharmacy', a special Nazi programme to improve the efficiency of local chemists and a reminder of the all-encompassing nature of everyday life in the Third Reich.

Back down in the square outside the university I stood in a shrinking triangle of sunlight watching workmen erecting a 50-foot Christmas tree. Two American students strolled across the cobbles in front of me, enthusing aspirationally about a cappuccino machine in a way that seemed totally at odds with the squalid, shiftless cynicism of my university days: 'It looked great, too, but it was 836 bucks.'

'So, when you win the lottery . . .'

'No! When I win the Nobel Prize!'

There was a lot of this in Heidelberg. The Americans might have come here in the first instance to practise melting Communists, but the cultured, erudite atmosphere of the place had transformed the hawks – not quite into doves, perhaps, but maybe wise old owls. Outside the castle I'd passed an elderly colonel type with a grey Spiro Agnew crew-cut and his large, fur-coated wife as they emerged from an enormous Lincoln, perhaps off to meet their Californian surf-dude nephew. The snatch of conversation I heard might reasonably have been expected to include phrases such as 'glasnost my ass' and 'Scramble, scramble, Limey homo at twelve o'clock'; instead I eavesdropped in guilty astonishment to a discourse on the Moorish influences apparent in Southern European architecture.

Working with typically efficient brevity, the workmen had finished the job by the time the cappuccino kids strode earnestly into the lecture hall. A Christmas tree . . . my word, I'd been away a long time. Homesickness suddenly engulfed me, the usual stupid reveries: my children tobogganing down Hanger Hill while my wife sighed, 'Daddy would enjoy this,' and then Colin Firth dodging a snowball and saying, 'Oh darling, must we spoil it all by mentioning that oaf?'

Suddenly I felt cold, small and vulnerable. Reading eighteenth-century reports of the places I was heading towards in Christopher Hibbert's *The Grand Tour* didn't help, except in explaining why so few Brits followed Coryate up here. Mainz was 'in a perpetual state of decay and neglect'; Koblenz 'dingy'; Bonn 'a dirty little city with nothing to detain the visitor'; Cologne 'the ugliest town in Germany'. At least I didn't have to go to Nuremberg: 'Crooked streets . . . indifferent houses . . . They wear pointed hats and monstrous bushy ruffs.'

Eating a two-for-one 'Mac Pac' (or 'Mick Pick' as I eventually discovered is the only apparently intelligible rendition) I coated most of my upper body in McRib sauce, along with the map which told me I was actually heading briefly away from home. Didn't Coryate ever get depressed? If so he never talks about it. When I got back to the Rolls I put on the face that I'd seen worn by so many passing pedestrians: what the naked arse was I doing with a car like this? I now felt ill and incapable of operating such a machine, almost giving up and walking away into the forest after I got lost on the way out of town in a maze of roadworks and US Army 'facilities'. At one cloverleaf interchange I circled every leaf in turn. I'd had enough of looking after this stupid car. Why couldn't someone come and look after me? Wearily rejoining the Rhine at Speyer, I looked at the nice *Hausfraus* cycling past with babies in their bike seats and found myself thinking, Can I go home with you? I won't be any trouble.

It would have taken a lot to cheer me up, and it was not the fault of Speyer, Frankenthal or any of the relevant villages in between that they didn't. I just drove along on autopilot, not remotely interested in seeing what remained of goodly cloister A or exceedingly eclipsed bishopricke B. The looming sunset was of the shepherd-pleasing variety, but only succeeded in garishly illuminating the return of the flat plains. Something needed to be done, and as I approached the suburbs of Worms, I did it.

'There hapned unto me a certaine disaster betwixt Franckendall and Wormes, the like whereof I did not sustaine in my whole journey out of England' is Coryate's introduction to the scene that inspired me. In Italy he'd regularly been helping himself to grapes from the vineyards; the tolerance of this theft had encouraged him to pilfer turnips and radishes ever since. These, twinned with a farthing loaf, formed a 'toothsome and pleasing' snack, whereas a meal in an inn 'might cost twenty times as much'.

Endlessly delighted with his discovery that nicking stuff was cheaper than paying for it, he soon got overconfident. Just outside Worms he nips off the road, helps himself to 'two little clusters' of grapes and proceeds 'jovially towards the citie, whose lofty Towers I saw neere at hand. But there came a German Boore upon me with a halbert in his hand, & in a great fury pulled off very violently my hat from my head, looked very fiercely upon me with eyes sparkling fire, and with words I understood not swaggered most insolently with me, holding up his halbert in that threatening manner at me, that I continually expected a blow, and was in deadly feare lest he would have made me a prey for the wormes before I should ever put my feete in the gallant City of Wormes.'

The lack of full stops was a sure-fire indicator of Coryatic excitement: a halberd, it should be stressed, is a long spear fitted with an

axe head (as illustrated in the *Crudities*' frontispiece). Caught red-handed by a large and angry man bearing such a weapon, most of us might opt for polite contrition and/or whimpering pleas for mercy. Not Coryate. Rather than attempt to apologise, he mounts a spirited verbal counter-attack, 'discharging a whole volley of Greeke and Latin shot upon him', claiming surprise when the man's ignorance of these tongues serves only to raise his fury. Eventually, a Latin-speaking gentleman on his way out of Worms passes the scene, explaining to Coryate that he 'had committed a penal trespasse in presuming to gather grapes without leave, affirming that the Germans are exceeding sparing of their grapes . . . And so at last my hat was restored unto me for a small price of redemption, which was twelve of their little coynes called fennies, which countervaile twenty pence of our English money.'

I'd only pulled up the side road to snooze and belch and generally purge myself of fatigue, depression and McDonald's. But as the electric seat hummed to the recline position and I stifled a sad yawn, there, up against the wire fence that separated me from the railway line and shimmering slightly in the heat haze wafting up from the Rolls's bonnet, was a row of twenty neatly pruned vines. And on their gnarled boughs, in defiance of the season, were dozens of bunches of purple grapes – small, but perfectly formed, the descendants of those who provided 'excellent Rhenish wine' to eighteenth-century British tourists.

It was becoming gloomy; a single streetlight above the bottle banks behind the Rolls was starting to cast shadows. I got out, looked around at the many neat and modern homes arranged about me, and boldly plucked off a grape. It was seeded, but it was delicious – a heady sweetness, like undiluted squash. I surveyed the windows: a light came on behind one set of net curtains, but nothing twitched. So I took a small handful, savouring the individual fruits and noisily spitting each pip out as I propped my arse brazenly against the Rolls's front wing.

By the time a group of mopeding youths appeared and stopped by the bottle banks, I was tearing off whole bunches and shovelling them into my juice-spattered maw with orgiastic relish. Here come the Boores and halbards at last, I thought, winking defiantly at the party as I returned for more supplies. But when I turned back, I just saw them doing what German teenagers do for kicks on a late

Sunday afternoon: depositing the family's old batteries in a special disposal bin.

This was no good. One of them, a tall fellow with a Bayern Munich woolly hat and an Adam's apple the size of a knee, briefly turned towards me: I raised my eyebrows challengingly, cocked a rearward thumb at the ravaged vines and said, 'I'm just eating these grapes here.'

Now the other three turned; all four regarded me with the clueless intensity of cattle. I clumsily ingested another palmful, and having spat and swallowed, wiped a sticky hand across stickier lips and spoke again. 'I could buy some, but this is better, because I'm not paying anything. What do you think about that?'

Not much, was the answer. The only emotion I could detect in their farewell gazes was a sort of confused pity. As they buzzed steadily away in orderly single file, I resignedly popped a final fruit and surveyed my stained digits. I was red-handed, but I wasn't caught.

Still, I'd done my bit – overdone it, in fact, as subsequent alimentary issues indicated – and I drove into Worms feeling considerably more cheerful. Who needs medication when you can nick cultivated produce? In this new frame of mind, it seemed only right that I instantly found a cheap and immaculate hotel right beneath the Apollo 11 cathedral towers that had led Coryate into the town.

We all know about the Diet of Worms, but things are a little more civilised these days and I was able to find a pizzeria. A dull joke, and a lie, as after perusing Worms's cold, concrete precincts and buying some souvenir vacuum-cleaner bags I actually found myself alone in a family-run restaurant ordering bratwurst, sauerkraut and chips.

It was while reading Coryate's account of his time in Worms and wondering why he made no mention of Luther or the Diet or any of the other keynote events in the birth of Protestantism that I first noted it, a tautness across the chest and belly. By the time I was engaged in conversation by the V-necked restaurateur, a Radio 2 presenter type whose jocularity and build irresistibly suggested the adjective 'cuddly', I fancied I could feel each grape beginning to fossilise in my innards. I bent slightly forward; speech was difficult, and he was talking in riddles.

'Zo. You are from child city?'

Pale-faced puzzlement.

'London is child city – you like it there?'

I'd learnt from my *Guardian* that Gary Glitter had just been charged; was this some sort of off-colour reference? Or worse – an invitation to swap paedophiliac reminiscences? In a frail but defiant whisper I gave him my rank and serial number.

'I live with my wife and three children in a pleasant area of London.'

'*Ja, ja*, of course.' He lowered his rounded jowls conspiratorially towards me. 'But . . . you know, it's vehr interesting for childs now. Maybe viss a new rule, a new . . . law, is possible to marry, hmmm?'

Chronic indigestion is not the ideal partner to moral outrage. I screwed up my face even further but only managed a bleat of soft despair.

'*Ja* – Prinz Childs und Camilla. Vill zey marry now?'

Relief lasted until his wife arrived with my food. Ten minutes before it was just what I'd wanted, but now I could only dunk a crisp, slender chip into a puddle of mustard and leave it there. By the time the patron returned to my table I was more or less doubled up with my head in the cruet set. Overweening one-on-one service – the curse of the close season.

'Everysing gut? Okay?'

I wanted to press a button and destroy him, to hyperspace back to my bed. But I couldn't move a muscle. It was the worst abdominal pain I have ever endured, excluding kidney stones and appendicitis. 'No,' I managed in a barely coherent, pain-fogged moan. 'I have a very bad stomach.'

'Ah!' he said brightly, as if this was the best news he'd had all day. 'My vife knows how to do viss zis!'

He returned with her moments later, both beaming eagerly. I managed a smile, which faded as I noted an absence of medicinal relief to end the misery of trapped wind. No Rennies, no glass of whitish fluid. They stood before me; I craned my neck from its lowly station. 'Zo,' said the husband with a businesslike clap. 'You stand please?'

The ensuing scenario is not one I am ever likely to recall with enthusiasm. Gingerly positioning myself as ordered, leaning forward with my hands gripping the back of a chair and a set of hot breath in each ear, terrible possibilities suggested themselves, complicated depravities I would be powerless to resist. 'Now for it,' whispered Cuddly. 'She is vehr gut – always she do zis viss me.'

Jesus. I pondered my previous dining disgraces: this was already worse than the teenage finger-stuck-in-the-Chianti-bottle, and soon it would eclipse the epic humiliation of 1989's fondue inferno. My knees were going; I thought I might cry. Then two hands linked in front of my stomach just above the groin, established a firm purchase and violently jolted up into my abdomen in savage homage to the Heimlich manoeuvre. My eyes bulged and watered, blurring my view of the tabletop with its mustard-marooned chip; then a powerful, deep-throated belch erupted repulsively from my mouth. I suppose it could have been worse.

289

'*Ja!*' cheered the pair, oblivious to the sour-grape atmospherics. Involuntarily I reprised my unwholesome gaseous performance. '*Ja, ja!*' they chorused again. 'Is gut now?' And it was. The pain had vanished entirely. Shaky of limb I took my seat with a short, uncertain laugh as Cuddly put a proud arm around his wife's shoulders. Then he looked down at my bratwurst. 'Oh – your food is cold now. We have a leedle machine to heat it?'

'No – no, it's fine. Really.' However grateful I was, the inappropriateness of our contact and its shameful denouement could not be undone or forgotten. Politely nodding my way through his incessant small talk, I ate as quickly as was decent, paid and left.

The morning was the coldest yet. When I popped outside to get the toothpaste out of the boot I found the plastic tube had frozen solid; the Rolls was covered in icy scratchings and the last of the horse chestnut leaves dropping noisily into the cathedral garden were pre-rimed with frost. Inside the cathedral it was just me and an unseen organist demonstrating his thunderous prowess; my head was still vibrating slightly as I crossed the road and found myself in the Jewish cemetery.

Worms was once known as Little Jerusalem, a Jewish community that thrived for 1,000 years despite the odd pogrom. Coryate doesn't mention it – in fact, after his performance in the Venetian Ghetto he never once refers to Jews again – but by his time their lot was gradually improving. The ghetto was opened up; in 1849, the city elected a Jewish mayor. By 1933 there were over 1,100 Jews in Worms. Nine years later there were none.

I suppose it isn't every day your government declares it a civic duty to go and smash things up, and the citizenry of Worms had clearly embraced Third Reich edicts with relish. I crunched through frosted grass between splinters of ancient Hebrew tombstones, back to the end by the railway line where Victorian memorials bore the angry imprint of furious sledgehammer blows, the cracks and chips as sharp and fresh as the morning. The most recent headstone was in German, and dated 17 November 1942 – fifty-seven years ago to the day. It had been toppled and cracked in two, but was still legible, commemorating the Spiegel family, mother Lucie and her son and daughter, aged twenty-two and seventeen respectively. All had died on that day. Was it a day as cold and heartless as this? Who had placed the stone there at such a dangerous time, and what had become of them? A whole delta of tragedy fanned out from the cracks in this one broken stone.

A train thundered past with a disorientating whoosh; I looked up to my left at the modern hospital block. What did the doctors and patients think as they looked down at this cemetery? It didn't seem possible that their parents had done all this. But then I looked up to my left, at the soaring red-stone cathedral towers, as aggressively potent a symbol as any of age-old religious intolerance. The people who built it were the same ones who threw Jews down their own wells for fun. Suddenly it was quite easy to imagine the congregation emerging from the cathedral in their pre-war Sunday best, tutting with boys-will-be-boys indulgence as their sons noisily laid waste to the tombs over the road. Coryate would probably have done the same, and worse. The inexplicable hatred had been fostered all over Europe for centuries: it was just a question of waiting for the technology and infrastructure to catch up.

Scrag-end leaves blowing off the vines on to frost-hardened soil; a groundsman brushing the snow from a penalty spot; the odd red cathedral poking its towers above the flatness – it was a bleak morning. Cold-starting the Rolls was always attritional, and when the engine finally caught that morning, the automatic choke wound it up to such a state of excitement that I was able to cruise past the Liebfrau church – original home of the devil's own vineyard – at 40 miles per hour with my feet off the pedals, a cooling-tower plume of emissions trailing off behind me over the plain.

Mainz exposed itself in the now-familiar pattern: sidings-and-silos hinterland; trim, bland suburbs; trim, bland centre with a couple of Sleeping Beauty towers the Lancasters missed. The Ibis hotel was offering special rates, and though the socks-and-cigs atmosphere in reception belied familial connections with Formule 1 – the Mondeo to its Fiesta – I stuck the Rolls (now with a multilingual for-sale note in the window) underneath it, checked in and went out.

And very nice it was too: a long, old pedestrianised main drag with at least half a dozen big Christmas trees already in place; boutique owners up ladders threading fairy lights round barley-twist fronds of holly; another red cathedral with shops and stalls tacked all round its sides and rear in authentically medieval fashion.

Though I knew it might spoil my evening, I got the map out while I waited in a draughty window seat for my bar snack to arrive. The 1:300,000 map of west Germany had been startlingly useless in estimating the length of tomorrow's Mainz–Frankfurt walk – yes, I'd been trying to forget about that, too. Every time I added up the digits between those silly distance lollipops I got a different answer, anything from 16 kilometres to 70. So I'd now acquired a cycle touring plan: much larger scale, much more detail. Thirty-five kilometres as the crow flies, but 52 as the crow dies, up and over the Rhine, down and along the Main. In the dim bar light I surveyed the map's little dotted paths and campsite symbols and knew that this time tomorrow I would be sick of the sight of it.

✦ ✦ ✦

For Coryate, the Mainz–Frankfurt–Mainz round trip was just another light stroll. He left Mainz at ten of the clocke, walked along the banks of the faire navigable Main and arrived in Frankfurt, where the famous biannual fair was currently being held, at sixe of the clocke in the afternoon. Beyond the now-familiar parade of tragicke and ruefull execution victims, it was a quiet day. In the ominous lack of any interesting sights to report on during the walk, he occupies himself by showing off his glossy new man-of-the-world intellect, quoting a Greek riddle with the snotty introduction that it 'will be very acceptable to the learned reader, but not to the unlearned', and inventing another word. Bit of a case of that-difficult-second-word syndrome, however: after the heady heights of 'umbrella', 'antipriscianisticall', apparently meaning ungrammatical, has failed to trouble the lexicographers.

Only eight hours to Frankfurt. But at 4.30 a.m, thanks to some combination of performance anxiety and bar-snack poisoning, I didn't think I'd be alive to see it. Sick as a dog and weak as a kitten, my internal organs withered and knotted, at 8 a.m. I deliriously concluded I had radiation sickness; at 9.30 I crawled across the floor, pulled back the corner of a curtain and saw the cars below smoothly sheathed in four inches of snow. A glance in the mirror revealed a deathly concave pallor – the pounds had literally fallen off. Or rather out.

Quite how I summoned the mental and physical resources I will never know, but at 10.10 – only ten minutes behind my Coryate-copying timetable – I was slushing across a huge bridge in two pairs of socks, long johns, jeans, a T-shirt, a Fred Perry, a polo neck, a corduroy jacket and an anorak, topped off with a furry Cossack hat I'd bought in Italy for my three-year-old daughter, lashed in place by a yellow Paisley scarf knotted under the chin, mumps-style. In my stomach the handful of dry Sugar Puffs that was all I could manage for breakfast had already solidified into a super-dense globule of antimatter; on my back sagged a small overnight rucksack; on my feet, the brown moulded plastic I'd forgotten to wear in was already wearing out.

Following the bike-path signs, I hit the banks of the Main, under a bridge where two old men with trilbies and binoculars were spotting barges. I couldn't tell whether it was cold – my body was randomly blotched with numb spots and heat rashes – but the snow was soon melting, ruching prettily down the windscreens to be hurriedly harvested by youthful snowballers. For some time I made good progress, my plan to expend calories before they could be expelled paying dividends.

Huge Dutch barges with the skipper's car parked on the wheelhouse, so full of goods and raw materials that their bows were almost beneath the surface; endless slopes of spidery, leafless vines; a mysterious monument to Queen Victoria by the railway line. And everywhere construction and reconstruction: cranes and distant drilling, wire-mesh Meccano towers awaiting a concrete coating.

I'd learnt that the British don't make stuff any more, and now I realised we don't build anything either: partly because governments these days seem to want 'private funding' for anything bigger than a bus shelter, partly because of the influence of conservationist lobby groups. But all over Germany, as in France, there didn't seem to be any equivalent of the not-in-my-backyard nimby or, my own favourite, the banana: Build Absolutely Nothing Anywhere Near Anyone. I'd actually whiled away one French evening composing appropriate city acronyms:

Ruin Everything In My Street
A Metalworks In Every Nice Suburb

Great: Really Enormous New Oxide-Belching Laboratories Everywhere!
Stick Those Railway Arches Slap-Bang Over Unspoilt Rear Gardens
Please, Another Runway – It's Sexy!

After three hours, I passed a cycle-path signpost: Frankfurt 32km. Twenty covered: I was on schedule. But I was also feeling weak, and when polystyrene-ball hailstones began shotblasting my face I felt myself slowing. Now there was no one: the cyclists and joggers had cut and run. Happy at least that my difficulties were no longer being exposed to the public, I leant into the hail, dragging myself along the Main's dreary floodplain with Captain Scott determination. Points of interest were rare: a muddy, carrot-nosed snowman; a huge Third Reich lock still efficiently processing the barges; an exchange of blizzardy waves with a suburban shepherd mysteriously leading his vast-bollocked rams across my path.

The shoes were becoming an issue. I thought the idea was that they would mould themselves to the shape of my foot, but their plastic rigidity meant the process was being reversed. I'm not sure if it is possible to limp on both legs, but as it started to get dark – with more than half the distance left – I gave it my best shot.

I crossed the Main at a lock; the buildings receded gradually to the horizon. For an hour or more the path skirted the kind of lonely heathlands where strange men sit in cars all day and dogs whose size or personality makes them unsuitable for the urban environment are exercised. The moment the hail abated a pale-furred polar bear of a St Bernard rumbled out of a copse and reared up in front of me with a furious red erection; moments later I was run over by two whippets. In both cases the chortling owners blamed my hat.

The scenery didn't help. As someone generally used to the idea of towns and cities showing a river their best face, it was still unsettling to see so many places preferring to greet theirs with a hairy-arsed moon. Ugly housing blocks, burnt-out cars, barge jetties clumsily decorated by generations of Dutch sailors with the names of their teams back home: Vitesse, PSV, Ajax. A boat was moored up at one: the fairy-lit waterline cabins looked impossibly cosy, the pigtailed daughter PlayStationing on the bridge painfully evocative.

It started raining and I took shelter under a motorway bridge. Through a veil of dizzy confusion I decided this was already the most painful thing I had ever done. Cycling across Iceland's arctic deserts had been more exhausting, but created no agonies to compare with the hot-iron leg braces now being clumsily nailed to my shins. As the rain lightened and I wincingly prepared to continue, something caught my eye, a message sprayed in four-foot aerosol capitals on the bridge embankment's concrete retaining wall: 'FUCK YOU, TIMMY MAROO'.

This was a bad thing to see, and this was a bad time to see it. Could Maroo be a solvent-addled interpretation of Moore? Or was it just a silly and humiliating nickname? Maybe they had been planning a reference to my purple suit, being interrupted before the final 'n'. And who were 'they'? The grapewatchers of Worms, exacting belated revenge? That shepherd? Il Professore? Maybe . . . could I have done it myself? When I found myself feeling the paint to see if it was wet, I knew the damage had been done. A small part of my identity died under that bridge. Two days later, suddenly engulfed by delayed paranoia, I checked my credit cards and passport to see if the surname had changed.

Now accepting that if I stopped again my legs would burst, I stumbled on like a drunk robot. The path veered inland, skirting around the perimeter of the enormous Hoechst chemical plant, and suddenly I was making irregular virgin footprints in the day-old snow along a dark and scary network of ring-road hard shoulders and footbridges. To my right, queues of planes circled near the airport, stacked up by the weather delays. It had suddenly got much colder: remembering a subtitled documentary on extreme weather survival I'd watched in a Formule 1 somewhere, I tried to make the Inuit symbol for 'I'm okay', linking the thumb-tip to the little finger to form an O. If you can't manage it with both hands, you're in trouble. Big trouble, Maroo. In the last dying of daylight, I looked in horror as my gloved thumbs trembled inwards with agonising imprecision. With my face buckled in effort and concentration, my right thumb eventually docked. But even looking like James Bond pulling 4Gs in a sabotaged NASA centrifuge I could only get my left hand to curl up into a claw-like fist.

Six o'clock came and went. Three hundred and ninety-one years ago Tommy had already skipped into Frankfurt, fresh as a daisy – and here I was, gazing blurrily at its distant skyscrapers through tears of distress. The moment when I passed a signpost and read by the lights of a passing barge that the city centre was still 9.2 kilometres off will go down as one of the worst of my life. In the realms of uncharted torture, on legs like burning stilts, and I still had to walk the equivalent of Oxford Circus to the top end of Hampstead Heath. Was there a limit? If I was a refugee or a soldier, could I keep going like this for days? Certainly the pain barrier was well guarded: every time it seemed I might break through a big bloke would run up from behind it and whack the backs of my knees with a scaffold pole. If I'd been a racehorse it would have been curtains.

Wearing an expression of incredulous agony and issuing a constant low moan, I hobbled through Frankfurt's outskirts, past joggers and cyclists who neither knew nor cared that this scarf-chinned Maroo character was engaged in an epic, to-the-death struggle against pain, fatigue and malnourished delirium. When the latter blossomed into full-blown dementia I embraced it warmly. A polite smile for the man in the John Lennon white suit and coolie hat who probably never was, an exchange of witticisms with the rabbits. A roped-off roadworks hole looked cosy and inviting, and who knows what I might have done if at that moment I hadn't raised my featherlight head and beheld the fuzzy, mobile outlines of the Frankfurt Ibis.

At 7.50, after more than nine and a half hours, I wobbled into the reception area, still unable or unwilling to stop my erratic forward motion, only doing so when attracted to a bowl of complimentary boiled sweets on the desk. By the time the receptionist warily greeted me I had a dozen in my mouth, most of them with their wrappers on. We stared each other out while I laboriously ingested the lot.

'I'm sorry,' I rasped, untying my headscarf to facilitate intelligible speech. 'You see . . .' and here I paused, the dramatic effect spoilt rather by hawking extraction of cellophane, '. . . I've just walked here from Mainz.'

She looked at me evenly, then cocked her head, knitted her brow and said, 'Why?'

Why indeed. What had I proven? I imagined a German tottering into the Heathrow Ramada Inn and announcing he'd just walked from Reading. And I couldn't even look back on my achievement with any pride – 50 kilometres wasn't much more than marathon runners manage in two hours with little discernible distress. For Coryate it had been just another holiday stroll. I had been physically humiliated by a short man in tights and slippers, a man who walked on rude tracks and was fuelled by stolen turnips. What had happened to render me so uselessly feeble?

Twenty years of fetid sloth suggested itself as an obvious answer, but easing myself arthritically down on to the bed I chose instead to blame my footwear. Its uppers were not of a breathable fabric, as might be expected in an £18 pair of shoes, and the plughole gurgles as I painfully eased them off indicated my feet had not held their breath. It was awful down there. Peeling away my socks was more like removing a dressing; examination of the appendages beneath, already bubble-wrapped with blisters, recalled the Milanese description of the wheel-breaking: 'a sea monster's tentacles; raw, slimy and shapeless flesh mixed up with splinters of smashed bones'.

I gently lowered myself flat. During the course of the day I'd been five of the dwarfs, but if I wanted to be Happy I'd first need Doc. My legs were twitching like a dead spider's; my pelvis felt glassy and scorched. Again I tried the Inuit hand signal; again the glacial response suggested my left thumb had donated all its blood to my socks. Somewhere above, a tiny voice in the white-noise roar of competing pains, was a headache. I started to look for the single, foil-wrapped aspirin I kept somewhere in my anorak, but then I gave up. I didn't need aspirin. I needed an epidural.

Coryate's funny little there-and-back detour to Frankfurt sticks out like a sore thumb in his otherwise direct route plan, and though he maintains he was only interested in the fair – 'the richest meeting of any place of Christendom' – it seems likely that the rumoured presence of the Earl of Essex was more of an attraction.

When would he learn? His esteemed fourth cousin, whom he'd just missed in Lyon, was hardly likely to want to be seen with Coryate, particularly in his current state. I had an image of Tommy picking the nits and burrs out of his beard as he walked along the river bank, rinsing his tights in the Main and generally trying to make himself look less like the man whom muggers gave money to.

Of course it didn't work. He did indeed meet Essex, his 'thrice-honourable countryman', but completely glosses over what must have been a perfunctory, and very probably humiliating encounter. It was the same with the various scholars he claimed to have struck up warm friendships with during his travels: of the half-dozen he wrote to after his return, only one ever replied.

But there was only one person I was going to feel sorry for that day. Waking with a tired bleat of pain, I accepted it had been ambitious to expect an overnight recovery; in fact it would be almost two months before I could break stride. I hobbled into the breakfast room like a little old pigeon-toed cripple, wondering if I would meet the fat man with a plumber's wrench in his back pocket who had sat on my shins as I slept. My first meaningful calories for thirty-six hours restored mental equilibrium, but my mobility was no better. After a tearful failure in the Gents I had to go next door and use the disabled loo.

If I'd been Coryate, I could have gone and cheered myself up at the fair. Goldsmiths displaying 'a wealth so great it was impossible to conceive'; churches full of 'wares and notable commodities'; 'an infinite abundance of books' in stalls that were the precursors of today's Frankfurt Book Fair – it was all there. Coryate even ran into a former servant of his father's, Thomas Stockfield, who had gone abroad to seek his fortune and now boasted a display of assorted wares that 'did fare excel all the Dutchmen, French, Italians or whomsoever else'.

I'd never realised how cosmopolitan a place seventeenth-century Europe was. Coryate had already met British merchants or scholars living in Padua, Venice and Strasbourg, and would meet many more in Holland – I was still amazed that the international finance system was sufficiently organised that Coryate could apparently pop into any reasonably large city and procure cash merely by brandishing letters of credit from some linen draper in Yeovil. And if Frankfurt was a Continental crossroads then, it's more so now. Shuffling along the sunlit pavements towards the station, I passed car parks full of dirty old coaches with war-torn destinations pencilled on cardboard shoved under their wipers: Tuzla, Split, Sarajevo. A shifty crowd of Polish men was negotiating dubious deals from the backs of knackered Transit vans; pausing for a nosy peer, I was almost quartered by a tram which clanked and shrieked to an angry halt in front of my stubbornly immobile feet.

It would have been all right if I'd been William *Vanity Fair* Thackeray, who found Frankfurt so 'beastly' that he spent his time there in his room, 'sleeping, smoking, reading and eating raw herring and onions'. But actually I'd had plans for Frankfurt, just as I'd had plans – a-ha ha ha – to walk back to Mainz. I'd especially hoped to visit the zoo, after reading a brochure in my room which revealed that the animals were 'actively encouraged to mate'. Now I could only imagine what might have been, the leery keepers bellowing, 'Get in there, my son!' to a reluctant okapi, the Viagraed-up Bactrian camels making the beast with four humps. Now it was all I could do to wince my shattered limbs into the station, where I paid 8DM for a single to Mainz.

Less than three quid – was that really all my biblical suffering was worth? As the greenery whoompfed by, I supposed that although walking was the only way of seeing a country properly, it was no surprise that the later Grand Tourists generally avoided going anywhere on foot. Walking was slow, and it certainly wasn't grand. Your diamond-buckled shoes might never recover.

At least the twenty-five-minute journey considerately avoided most of the scenes of yesterday's sufferings, the Hoechsts and Florsheims, names that would henceforth ring out whenever men got together to discuss spineless inadequacy. I had already binned several reminders of yesterday's hateful journey – the socks, the map, my youth. But the shoes had won. It would be a week before my feet returned to anything like their normal shape, seven morning reacquaintances with the plastic tormentors whose outlandish dimensions they had been bullied into adopting.

It was a bracing blue-skied day, a kite-flying day, not a great one for mad-looking cripples to falter about the streets of Mainz trying to find their car, but ideal for the subsequent drive up the Rhine's most majestic stretch.

With road travel in Germany uncomfortable and – thanks to a bewildering variety of supplements which even included an extra charge for wheel greasing – expensive, sailing up the Rhine was a popular way home for Grand Tourists. The glorious scenery between Mainz and Koblenz – castles, gorges, vineyards – was a bonus. 'The beautifullest river in Europe,' sighed one tourist, nibbling strawberries aboard one of the early cruise ships.

As ever, it was a bit tougher for Coryate. While these days the Rhine mixes business with pleasure, in 1608 it was very much a working river, and those who travelled on it were expected to pull their weight. The walk back from Frankfurt was to be his last major hike, but even so there was no respite. How did he unwind after it? That's right – by rowing all the way home down Western Europe's longest river. He finds a passage on a small boat voyaging the 100-odd miles to Cologne in the company of Dutch and British merchants returning from Frankfurt, wondering why his ticket was so cheap until he learns that 'the customers must exercise themselves with oares and rowing'.

As my Frankenstein club foot shifted clumsily from brake to accelerator – if the car had been a manual I couldn't have coped – I pondered that once again he'd out-endured me. Not many people would have appreciated a ten-day stint as a galley slave, but Coryate was clearly pining for his endorphin rush: 'This exercise both for recreation and health sake I confess is very convenient for man.' Oh, shut up.

At Bingen, the Rhine narrowed into an 80-kilometre gorge, and for once the local populace embraced the river and didn't flaunt their industrial suburbs. The sunny cliffs rising from spruce, white-washed settlements like Scottish island ports were crowned precariously with dozens of pick-and-mix castles of all shapes, sizes and states of repair, nestling in the vertical vineyards or, memorably, defying the currents mid-river. Here were the custom towns, run by 'divers Princes Spirituall and Temporall', descendants of medieval robber barons who thought nothing of opening fire on any ship who forgot to stop and pay its toll.

Tourist attractions come and go, but the Rhine flows on. The sightseers started arriving in numbers during the nineteenth century, and they haven't stopped. In the summer at least: a couple of months ago the river would have been jostling with pleasure cruisers and the road buried beneath motorhomes. But now it was just the barges on the water and me on the tarmac – so empty that I once waited for five minutes at a red light before someone arrived behind me to parpingly point out that the signal was actually relevant only to train drivers on the railway track alongside.

In a very golden November I passed the Goldener Oktober winery – birthplace of the first wine I ever drank, as a nine-year-old whose parents found themselves burdened with a crate of Rhenish syrup unsuitable for adult consumption. I may have fulminated elsewhere against the perry-like horrors of Liebfraumilch, but it's only fair to point out that the eponymous wine exported to Britain has been artificially sweetened to cater for the tastes of our prepubescent drunks. Blue Nun: alcopop of the Seventies. One can only hope it was different for Coryate when, at St Goar, he found himself involved in an ancient initiation ceremony where, in exchange for release from an iron collar, he was obliged to pay for and be force-fed 'a competent measure of wine'. You can't help thinking there was no ancient initiation ceremony, that they just made it all up on the spot. He had that sort of face.

Just past the town I stopped. Barges laboured against the current or were chivvied along by it; the water spiralled up against the opposite rock that Tommy and I only realised later was the home of the Lorelei, a beautiful blonde who lured sailors to their doom with her eerily compelling knockers. It was real off-season stuff: a couple of promenading old dears in fur coats, a shuttered-up bandstand, drifts of leaves and a sprinkling of snow on the hilltops. Around the next meander deranged hang-glider pilots taunted my manifold spiritual and physical failings with suicidal clifftop take-offs.

Koblenz, where Karl Baedeker published his first guide in 1823, is the final stop on most of the tourist cruises. I liked it. Any town with a lot of funny coloured buildings deserves respect, and the number of pink towers and bulbous turrets casting long afternoon shadows over the strolling locals immediately won me over. Why don't we promenade in Britain any more? Don't tell me we've *all* mashed our feet into a bloody, disabling pulp. I can only assume there are sound socio-historical reasons – 'promenade' is another Continental word the Grand Tourists brought back, meaning 'a leisurely walk for pleasure or display'. I think the last word is the key. British townspeople had nothing to display until returning Grand Tourists introduced fashion, but most still felt uncomfortable at the idea of poncing up and down the high street showing off. This is not the British way. Poseur is a French word used by the British as an insult. Still, it's a shame. In France and Italy, the picturesque evening promenade could be excused as a Mediterranean thing, something that excitable, gregarious people were genetically disposed to. But now, even in Northern Europe, even in *Germany*, I'd noted the locals spent at least a couple of hours a week just hanging out together in a proudly civic fashion that was utterly alien to me.

As indeed were the astonishing, spindle-limbed motorway bridges I found myself vertiginously negotiating after I followed the wrong river, the Mosel, for half an hour after Koblenz. In consequence it was pitch black when I blundered into a guesthouse-cum-bar in Mehlem, a distant suburb of Bonn. 'Is your car?' queried the moon-faced proprietor, peering in mild astonishment through the shutters. In the end he made me park it in his beer garden, a complex manoeuvre rendered more demanding by my numb-footed impre-cision and a window-filling audience of kitchen staff and regulars.

'You have pain, as I see?' said the proprietor, re-erecting the three parasols I had run over as he watched me shuffle indoors.

'Too much walking.' I smiled palely in between theatrical gurns of distress. If I was at home I'd be in bed, if not traction. But what could I do in a modest German guesthouse? 'Listen, Dietmar – the old pins are giving me a bit of gyp. Be a good feller and bring me up a light supper and a couple of elasticated ankle supports.'

So half an hour later I was in a Balkan restaurant with my pain relief lined up in front of me like a set of traffic lights: a glass of Serbian red, an amber Pernod, a bottle of Becks. The waitress –

certainly an East European judging by her water-based Barbie make-up – was too busy batting an Abba-shadowed eyelid at this shameful alcoholic parade to detect the appalled wonder in my voice as I heard myself ordering the mixed grill *Belgradespiess*.

Five years ago, no one would have thought twice about such an establishment flaunting its ethnic heritage, and it was to the Germans' credit that they clearly still didn't. Remembering the Sarajevo buses in Frankfurt, I was reminded that Germany is home to over a million refugees – more than a third of the European total; here, near the capital of the old bring-me-your-huddled-Commies West German regime, there would have been an enhanced tolerance. Even a little commuter town like Mehlem was a melting pot: on the agonising march from bedroom to Balkans I'd passed a Greek-run café, a Polish hotel and a falafel takeaway. I suppose there must be an element of obligation to atone for the Third Reich's poor showing in this sphere, but it was still difficult to imagine ordering a Belgrade Grill in Britain without being named and shamed in the *Sun*.

So I was probably alone in putting down half the restaurant clientele as robustly moustachioed warlords and their sturdy warladies, and the rest as pallid UN peacekeepers. What wasn't in doubt was my position in no man's land, the *maîtresse d'* steering away all new arrivals to distant booths with an indiscreet shove that said, 'What about here, away from the drunk tramp?'

As a result I never got to see the Scottish faces behind a marital exchange that began 'How do you think that makes me feel, hearing you say that?' and had got up to 'Well, I've still got 12,000 pound in the bank and you're not getting a penny' by the time I was necking my reluctantly proffered complimentary banana schnapps and heading out to belch grilled kidneys into the cold night sky.

Successfully anaesthetised I walked down to the Rhine, where a moon that was a day off being full struggled to break through the freezing fog. Behind me were rows of grand, white-stucco mansions, Holland-Park-on-Rhine; ahead, high above the silent river, were the misty silhouettes of a trio of castles. A chrome-and-Formica Fifties pleasure boat creaked forlornly as I clumsily stepped over a chain that guarded its jetty. Out here, watching the river rush blackly by, it wasn't hard to imagine Coryate rowing past in the thick of night, as he had done on 19 August. And after a heart-punching nearby owl hoot, it was easier still to picture the execution victims strung up in chains along the banks, 'more then ever I saw in so short a space in all my life'.

These were Freebooters, lawless mercenaries enlisted by the Dutch rebels to fight the Spaniards and vice versa in an ongoing struggle for religious and political control of what in 1608 was still the Spanish Netherlands. In between battles, huge gangs of Freebooters – up to 3,000 strong – sacked towns along the Rhine: the few that were caught were always executed in the most public and grotesque fashion as a deterrent. And if it was bad then, it would get worse: by the time the Thirty Years' War wound down in 1648, the population of what we'd now call Germany had fallen from 21 million to under 13. Villages like Mehlem lost half their inhabitants, and it had been worse further south: in a huge swathe of countryside from Heidelberg to Mainz, over two-thirds of the population either fled for good or were slaughtered. If Coryate had nicked those grapes forty years later there'd have been no one to stop him.

But what had happened to the religious zealotry that started such wars? Coryate would no doubt mock the Catholics Blu-Tacking their car-crash Polaroids to St Anthony's tomb, but at least they kept the faith. I remembered switching on some sort of Euroculture channel on the telly in my hotel room in Heidelberg, and seeing a multilingual caption explaining that *2,000 Years of Christendom* had been postponed in favour of live coverage of the international match between Norway and Germany. And it was only a friendly. Tommy would have kicked the screen into a massy pyle of fragmenttes.

The regulars were still *in situ* back in my bar, quietly ingesting lager after lager, Moonface marking each down with a little Biro notch on the drinker's beer mat. One elderly couple had twelve notches each, but you'd never have guessed it from their composed deportment. I suppose it just wouldn't be the done thing. Even here, in sub-suburban Nowheresville, everything was done with a sense of propriety and decorum, from the humidor-stored cigars to the fluted schnapps glasses Moonface kept frosted in the freezer.

At least so I imagined until my exit up the stairs sparked off a bierkeller gale of raucous merriment, and then of course it was open season for paranoia. I drew my curtains and double-locked the door, but still the harsh laughter rang out, marshalled by what sounded like Moonface's amplified voice. It was only a matter of time before I knew what was going on down there: Moonface whipping up the crowd from behind the bar, manipulating a large black-and-white CCTV screen with a remote control in one hand and a mike in the other. 'Okay – he's loosening his belt: switch to Bog Cam 1!'

I woke up and discovered that my left leg was better, whereas the right was worse. This was ridiculous – I was supposed to be on holiday, not rebuilding a shattered life and learning how to walk again. I had to go down the stairs backwards, and seeing my faltering progress to the exit, the woman who'd served me breakfast took my arm. I only understood the thrust of her concerned babbling when she opened the door and revealed a white world. Oh. I looked at the Rolls, wrapped up under a 25-tog snow duvet, the silver lady alluringly cloaked in ermine. Oh.

If you've ever tobogganed down a black run in a cast-iron bathtub, you'll know what it's like to drive a Rolls-Royce in thick snow. And if the bathtub was filled with telephone directories and had its underside buttered, and you were blindfolded with barbed wire and had a leopard sitting on the taps, you'll know what it's like to drive a Rolls-Royce in thick snow on balding budget remoulds. I have never been party to such a graphic demonstration of the forces of resistance and momentum. At the junction with the main road into Bonn, an ill-timed, numb-footed blip on the throttle sent me spinning gently but unstoppably across three lanes of furious commuters. It was like losing control of the space shuttle in a melee of orbiting satellites. I had not heard a horn used in anger since Italy, but now every slithering degree of my more exciting rotations was accompanied by a full-blooded brass chorus.

If I'd dared to look up I'd have seen a sky fat with snow, ready to drop a further foot of thick Dickensian flakes. That it did so just after I parked – and you should have heard my crowing whoops when I realised that a snow-buried windscreen meant there was no point in paying for what couldn't be displayed – saved me from participation in one of the many cameos of slow-motion destruction I savoured during my hobble/skate into the town centre. A Mercedes taxi pirouetting gracefully into a lamppost; a BMW's frictionless descent down a car-park entrance ramp cut short by full-blooded contact with the barrier.

Bonn has something of a reputation for tedium, and now that it's been abruptly dumped as the seat of government in favour of Berlin I fully expected a ghost town full of empty offices, with a sprinkling of residual dullards wondering how to look bitter. But no – there was a lot of new building going on, and the streets thronged with shoppers happily watching their city centre being transformed into a winter wonderland, perhaps relieved that the civil servants and journalists had all buggered off and let them return to a more straightforward existence in what John Le Carré described as *A Small Town in Germany*.

It was lovely: wooden-chalet stalls selling handcrafted tree decorations; red-cheeked fatties roasting *wurst* in huge, coal-fired woks; fairy lights and spruce fronds; an ice rink. And still the snow came: everywhere people were doing 'God – it's snowing!' stuff, like buying four pairs of woolly mittens and falling over on their arses. But everyone was happy, particularly once they'd noticed me. I suppose it was my child's black-fur hat – after a glimpse at myself in a shop window, I'd noted this was now topped with four inches of snow for that 'pint of Guinness' effect. Not much, perhaps, but in Bonn this was enough to cause a sensation: the sea of Christmas-shopping mothers parted in front of me with the merry smirks reserved for a local 'character', like the hairy-legged transvestite who used to hang out in the Broadway Centre during my youth. But I simply didn't care; indeed, I was quietly proud to be contributing to the festivities.

Even for someone of such a pfennig-wise–mark-foolish mentality, it was going to be difficult to resist the lure of crass seasonal commercialism. Before I knew it I was Christmas shopping for my children with the borrowed-time frenzy of a credit-card fraudster, hobbling about a department store under slot-car racing sets, infant snow-wear, a sledge and stupid bits of Little Mermaid rubbish. I have to say, though, that the gloss was rather taken off the experience by the stern 'shoplifters will be broken on the wheel' notice by the door, or more particularly the fact that it was translated only into German, English and Turkish. No offence to Turkey – well, maybe just a bit – but it was shaming to be bracketed alongside them as the only other nationals likely to put on a bit of in-store weight. Weren't there any sticky-fingered Frenchmen? Larcenous Latins? Whither the wicked Walloons?

The snow started melting as I ordered the day's 4.99DM special in a swish café, hoping '*2 stk. Butterstollen nach Dresdner Lebensmit*' wouldn't in any way involve glacé tripe. Soon, great sheets of slush were sliding off shop awnings, and being in the land of *schadenfreude* I knew I would not be able to leave until I saw at least one passer-by cop a headful. In fact I bagged a pair, two dustmen dragging wheelie bins past one of the many shops commemorating Bonn's other claim to fame as the birthplace of Beethoven with a gratuitous display of that familiar big-haired, glowering visage. I laughed, and so did they, or at least the one who retained his balance. Karma buffs may wish to know that on my return to the car I dropped all my shopping into a slushy puddle. Twice.

The snow, so deep and crisp and even at 11 a.m., was gone by the time I drove into Cologne through the worst industrial suburbs yet, a stinking Rhineside copse of chimneys dating back to the days when companies were proud to plaster their names all over the sides. And it wasn't much better in the centre: standing above my multi-storey car park in a dreadfully heartless Sixties plaza, I decided the melting brown slush suited Cologne as well as the Mozart snow had suited the city of Beethoven. Even the Dom, the tallest building in the world until the Eiffel Tower went up and still Germany's most visited monument, failed to inspire. Marooned at the edge of a concrete plain bordered by wet and windswept arcades the cathedral looked depressed and somehow squat, as if sinking to its Gothic haunches in misguided urban planning.

In 1608, those huge towers weren't there: one was only half its planned height, the other a stub. 'It is a great pity that it is so imperfect,' says Coryate, choosing not to explain that it had been that way for over 50 years (and would be for another 250), a symbol of the decline of Cologne as a city state, one whose close trade links with the Dutch led Coryate to place his description of the city after the subtitle 'The Beginning of my Observations of the Netherlands'.

He wasn't about to complain, though. Bits of Wise Men in the cathedral, 11,000 murdered virgins in a church dedicated to the daughter of an Anglo-Saxon prince, a market place measuring a hundred threescore and sixteen paces long by threescore and three broad – you can see why Tommy stayed at Cologne an extra day. Describing his encounter with the bones of the Maccabees, who 'had their tongues and the utmost parts of their bodies cut off, their skinne pulled over their heads; and lastly were fried', he finally confesses: 'I love to see these things as much as any man living.'

And oh, the inscriptions! After an eleven-page plaque-transcribing marathon in the cathedral, he even had his own Christmas-Day-football-match moment of reconciliation with a Catholic canon who, impressed by such scholarly stamina, invited Coryate back to his place and 'entertained me with much good cheare' – especially kind-hearted in Cologne, a city where earlier that same year Protestants had been deprived of their civic rights. (Four pages later Coryate is on again about 'the grosse vanities of the Papists'.)

The Bonn shopping had exhausted my daily allowance of ambulatory pain, and it was only as I shuffled slowly back to the car park that I realised Cologne was full of Brits. A snatch of conversation blown over by the cold wind caused me to look up, and suddenly I was surrounded by people who were vaguely rumpled and ill-looking – my people. Trying not to think too hard about our shared ancestral role in creating the voids now filled by the concrete nastinesses around us, I walked straight up to a couple of kindly dears with faces like old nuns. 'Well, there's five coaches with us from Edinburgh and Lord knows how many more from down south,' trilled the elder in reply to my request, issued with the uncorked babble of someone who hasn't spoken face to face with a fellow countryperson for long weeks. 'Aye,' squeaked her friend, 'we're just doing the German markets. Two days' travel; two days' shopping – we did Holland last year.'

'So what have you bought?' I barked, one hand instinctively going for their carriers in a shaming victory of curiosity over manners. They drew back slightly; one glanced up at my hat, which had not coped well with the weather.

'Er, well . . . I've been to C&A and M&S,' said the squeaker. 'Same stuff, just cheaper.'

Hardly diamond-buckled shoes and Canalettos. These days, I suppose, there aren't many Continental souvenirs you couldn't buy in any British high street. Asti in Asda, Picasso in Paperchase and, who knows, lederhosen in Lilywhites. It was sad to recall that the only mementos I had brought back from Europe in recent years were those with brand names comically unsuitable for export: Prik washing-up liquid from Norway, Denmark's Spunk jellybeans, the immortal Bum cheese snacks of Spain.

'But we're not just here to shop,' blurted the squeaker's friend, sensing perhaps that I was behaving like a spoof interviewer from one of those shows that bravely set out to make elderly members of the public look really stupid. 'It's also a chance to see how the other half lives.'

Driving out through more drizzle and chimneys, the air heavy with industrial odour, Cologne and the Rhine brimming with affluent effluent, I thought about the Brit shoppers. Standing out like refugees among the leather-trimmed, well-scrubbed Germans, they were symbols of the cultural divide, of Britain's stubbornly lingering isolationism. The few Grand Tourists who had passed through Cologne had found it squalid, smelly and teeming with 'insolent beggars'; that German cities had changed as much as the British tourists who visited them was as plain as my wet nose.

But at the same time there was a sense of a slow but inexorable Europeanisation at work, that fifty years from now there would be no more talk of 'the other half', that the tradition which Coryate had done his bit in helping to establish, of British travellers touring the Continent with deluded, snook-cocking superiority, would finally be dead and buried. That's me out of a job, then.

Trying to read a map by the headlights of the lorry behind while driving in heavy rain down a two-lane motorway with no speed limits probably isn't to be recommended, and it certainly wasn't by the lorry driver, who soon hit upon the brilliant plan of sticking so closely to my rear bumper that I couldn't actually see his lights. No wonder German service stations have chapels. With that huge Mercedes star filling my rear-view mirror and the lights of oncoming traffic polarised into smeary asterisks it was impossible to read road signs or slow down, and I soon resigned myself to bypassing a huge stretch of Coryate's Rhine.

It wasn't too painful: the area in question was all built-up-brown on the map, starting with Düsseldorf and winding up through the Ruhr basin, a conurbation of six million souls and the greatest single industrial area in Europe. When the guidebooks start talking about thriving centres for the machine-tool industry and how despite everything it is still possible to photograph a flock of sheep in front of the red and purple smoke of a blast furnace, and it's raining, and your leg hurts, you just keep driving.

Particularly if you've just remembered your T Rex tape, and the song 'Children of the Revolution', featuring as it does the lyric 'I drive a Rolls-Royce, 'cos it's good for my voice', words you may be tempted to bellow in a joyous play-and-rewind frenzy from which you will only emerge in a service-station lavatory when a map above the urinal reveals you are almost in Holland.

The Michelin guide didn't have anything to say about Wesel, though it wasn't a wasted search as while looking for it in the index I discovered the Alpine resort of Wank. Panicked by my near miss with Holland – such a rate of progress was simply unseemly – I'd swooped off the motorway and headed north towards the Rhine looking for anywhere Coryate had mentioned. Wesel got a brisk paragraph – 'the fairest city of the whole Province' – and that was good enough for me.

Hosting a bridge over the Rhine and being near Arnhem weren't the best ways to ingratiate yourself with the Allied military, and one look at Wesel's unpromising tenemented outskirts suggested the place had been comprehensively flattened in the latter months of the war. With a corresponding lack of good reasons to stop there, let alone stay, I didn't imagine Wesel would be overburdened with hotels. And so it proved. That one look became two, then three, and it was not before look five that I found a guesthouse, which with pleasing symmetry following last night's meal turned out to be run by Croats.

I could tell by the state of the upstairs window frames it was going to be horrid – the crusty Dusty Springfield proprietress and the strenuous deceit with which the lobby had been poncified confirmed this. I asked to see the room first, and all the boxes were ticked: cell-like dimensions and police-station lighting; deafening traffic noise; carpet the soles of your shoes parted from with noisy reluctance; sheets made of a fat old lady's tights and a door that slammed in dismal aural homage to the opening sequence of *Porridge*.

'Okay?' said Crusty Dusty, her flat gaze ringed clumsily with cosmetic smears that were more coal than kohl. She had BO, her room had RO. The unappealing gentlemen prowling around the car park meant that my last night in Germany was the first when I'd felt compelled to remove the mascot (though there was also a parallel fear that the 'Burundi' flag might be the colours of some obscure band of Serbian cannibals). But of course I didn't have any choice, and the very small number that she wrote down on a beer mat to indicate the room's price in Deutschmarks made things a little easier. '*Ja*,' I replied.

I'd hoped for an equivalent to last night's Belgrade Grill, but there were no Zagreb Platters or Banana Splits, and in the end it was a toss-up between 'Leber "Tony"' and 'Hacksteak "Nicky"' (though Tony didn't make the cut when I remembered that *leberwurst* was liver sausage). I've always had a soft spot for such eponymous creations, wondering if the chef dreams of the day when he hears a passer-by whisper urgently to his friend, 'Hey – that was Nicky, you know: Hacksteak Nicky, Liver Tony's mate.' My favourite was the pasta dish I once just about managed to order without spitting out my Chianti: *Penne alla Mike*.

Sadly, the night-before Serbs won the food fight. Tonight's two Croat waiters looked like Bodie and Doyle, but that was about as professional as it got. Nicky's pride was more hack than steak, and came served with canary-yellow chips, a lurid shank of bacon the colour of bubblegum and some sort of pungent, curdled whey that

I was immediately able to connect with Crusty Dusty's armpits. I didn't eat much, but the oil intake was still sufficient to ensure that in the morning it took a quarter of a bottle of shampoo to get my hair to lather.

With the lights of passing cars sweeping mesmerisingly across the ceiling I lay on the bed and, examining a curious *Star Trek*-badge blister on my left foot, had a peripheral glimpse at my last night of German television. There was an *Erotikfilm* in which a man who looked like Bernie Ecclestone was ineffectually pleasuring a woman who looked like David Coulthard; there was a documentary about the Hitler Youth. Archive footage of men in shorts cheerfully forcing small blond heads into buckets of cold water; interviews with men the same age as my father, muttering in a fidgety sulk and generally looking like they were being made to apologise for something they didn't regret. The documentary was entitled *Aren't You Really Glad We Didn't Win The War?*

I had lost Coryate's trail and was hopelessly distant from anywhere a Grand Tourist would have been seen dead in (actually – scratch that), but as I heaved my bedroom door open I knew things were about to slot back into place. Bodie and Doyle were cheerful in the breakfast room, no doubt celebrating a crushing victory in the fiercely contested pan-European 'Tiniest Breakfast Orange Juice Glass' competition. But so what: I was cheerful, too – Holland by lunchtime, the country where I was going to flog the Rolls for a huge profit. The gamble had paid off: a shade under 2,500 miles covered – just another 50 before I could cash in my chips.

Did I say that? Well, silly old me. Limping splashily across the car park, bags in hand, I looked at the Rolls and accepted the sales process had become a little more challenging overnight. There, across the bottom of the nearside rear passenger door, was a long rubbery smear which became a gouge, then a dent, and finally disappeared into a hand-sized rusty hole in the wheelarch. On the floor lay many shards of bodywork filler, lacquered moorland green like sedimentary quartzite – rather pretty, I supposed, though not until four months later. My first thought was: I didn't realise there was so much filler there. My second was: I wonder what the record is for unimaginative profanities bellowed in a public place?

I didn't go up to inspect the damage for some time. First I let my Eurohiker bag drop to the tarmac, an act I would later discover had caused a small but important fracture to my bottle of Abbeville brandy. Then, feeling a cold, impotent rage spreading down from the back of my head, I walked very slowly about the car park, examining the bumpers of the other ten or so vehicles in a futile quest for tell-tale flakes of moorland green.

Finally I approached the Rolls. Picking up the bits of filler with bloodless hands I tried to assess the damage, concentrating very hard on not repeatedly battering my fists and forehead against the metalwork. The scrape was bad, but the hole was far, far worse. Now the Rolls showed itself for what it was: just another tarted-up banger, an Arthur Daleymobile, a metaphor for Britain's papered-over pomp. Beauty was skin deep, and now the skin was ripped and the corroded guts were hanging out. I'd never sell this now. Fuck-all flash for fuck-all cash.

Crusty Dusty was nowhere to be seen: the only possible witness to the scrape-and-run incident was up a ladder in the lobby – a wizened old decorator who looked like one of the Chuckle Brothers. One glance at him was enough to understand that he didn't know anything, not even about painting ceilings, but that didn't matter. I'd be doing the talking.

'My car's been smashed up out there,' I said, not quite as calmly as I'd hoped, 'and I just want to say that it's your fault.' I was holding one of the aluminium legs of his ladder; he suddenly looked confused and scared, like an Alzheimer sufferer being ordered by his evil solicitor to sign an altered will.

'*Bitte . . .?*' he faltered, but I was already halfway out the door.

This shameful exchange helped, but there was still plenty of cancerous bile to go around. Last night I'd driven past Wesel's tourist office, and had planned to pop in on my way out of town to ask what had happened here in 1945. But as I seethed past it, I knew that the questions I now wanted to ask would not be answered. 'Excuse me, I've noticed a lot of the women here smell. Is that because you lost the war?'

Feeling my features settle into a vacant scowl, I drove off, past yards where *Obergruppenfarmers* called out to their pig-dogs, through villages where Reichsmarschall von Oldfarts sat watching TV in their *Lebensraums*. Nothing would rouse me from misanthropy – not even driving through the muddy hamlet of Groin, and not even stopping to photograph its 'Welcome to . . .' road sign.

Emmerich was the last major town before Holland, and I got out to stamp the last bits of German Groin off my shoes. Here was another town that had risen, phoenix-like, from the all-consuming flames of the last war, and again the phoenix had flown in from Basildon. The only structure I could find that didn't look like it had been uprooted from landscaped cul-de-sacs all named after wading birds of the Thames Estuary was a squat and shrapnelled monument engraved 'VATERLAND 1913'. This overlooked the Rhine, which had been hidden behind dykes all day: it was the colour of cold coffee and seemed as wide and busy as the Channel.

My latest displacement activity was trying to establish whether petrol was cheaper in Germany than in Holland, in order to plan my refuelling tactics. To this end I addressed myself to a waitress emptying a huge ashtray of fag-ends down a Rhineside drain. 'Excuse me, do you speak English?' I began, using the words that had introduced so many conversations during the last two weeks. Before she'd had a chance to indicate she didn't, a scathing Germanic echo muttered out from behind.

'Do you *spick Englisch*?'

I turned round to see a middle-aged couple walking away, their faces half turned towards me in a caricature of repulsed contempt. He had the exaggerated jaw of Michael Schumacher; she was a Twenties Berlin lesbian who'd lost her monocle.

'Yes, thanks!' I blurted wildly. 'Do you speak German?' It wasn't a gambit designed to procure a response, so as they continued down the promenade with wearily disgusted headshakes, I provided my own, silent but emphatic.

They didn't turn round, which was probably just as well.

I got lost leaving Emmerich, an unlikely prelude to spiritual deliverance, but not as unlikely as the German military cemetery I found myself walking into after it caught my attention four points into the resultant five-point turn. It was a humble affair, just a few dozen crosses in a lonely, tree-ringed plot the size of a decent suburban garden. But somehow the story was more real, more affecting than that told by those overwhelming forests of white stone that line the Somme.

Pacing first sullenly, then sadly through the crosses, I slowly realised that every single man had died in the same week, 19–26 March 1945. It wasn't just the youth: for every teenager there was one born in 1885 or 1890: sixty-year-olds who'd probably fought in the trenches as young men, and had been asked to do it all again as the Allies piled over the Rhine and rushed towards Berlin. And what a stupid waste: in just over a month, Hitler and Eva were down in the bunker playing Prussian roulette. Thinking of these men, sons and fathers, all sticking on their tin hats and going out to fight for their farms, a fight they must have known was suicidally futile, was profoundly touching. These weren't baby-eating storm troopers, these were the Captain von Mainwarings, the Schtupid Boy Pikes.

I sat back down in the driver's seat and soberly contemplated my recent behaviour. At length, I was able to rationalise the morning's incident: the Rolls had felt left out by my injuries, and would be glad to empathise with some suffering of its own. It would give us something to talk about, hardy travellers comparing knocks. Ready to make my peace with Germany, I could now look forward. Stamping cathartically on the gas, I slid back on to the road with a new enthusiasm. Holland here we come – and the last one to stick his finger in the dyke's a sissy!

EIGHT

Holland

A lot of Grand Tours ended in the Low Countries. The roads were 'the most agreeable in Europe', the towns fastidiously neat and tidy, and the unattached women so accommodating that 'to make love like a Dutchwoman' was a precursor to today's rabbit metaphor. There were English-run inns in most towns, and the whole area was seen as a theme park for the productive triumphs of the Protestant work ethic. 'It is really delightful to see what industry and perseverance will do to make a country rich,' said Thomas Brand in 1787. These combined attractions made it the third most popular Grand Tour destination after Paris and Italy – the only real downer was the scarcity of fellow aristos to hang out with, most having selfishly 'been extinguished in the Wars with Spain'.

In Coryate's day, of course, I would already have been in Dutch territory for the last day and a half, so I wasn't too disturbed to find no trace of the modern border. A sudden increase in the number of cyclists was a hint, though not as big a one as the sign in a shop window reading '*voor oop ze zweegeene*'. Still riding the crest of my wave of new confidence, at the first garage I came to – an Audi dealership with a couple of old Porsches on the forecourt – I drove straight on to the pavement in front and tried to flog them the Rolls. A bloke in a suit and another in overalls came out and dealt politely with me, not laughing at the bodywork, nor when I said I was looking for 24,000 guilders, about £8,000. But then they also didn't laugh when one of them asked if I'd had the car since new and I said, Yeah, that's right, it was my fifteenth-birthday present.

As I left them my home phone number ('Maybe we find some interesting men'), a black Silver Spirit drove past with a toot, then a jovial voice rang out from a second-floor window opposite: 'That's a bicycle way you are parking in!'

Just down the road, Nijmegen was Coryate's first major stopover since Cologne. He was still in the company of the fellow row-as-you-go travellers he'd been with since Mainz, whom he now finally names as William Tassell of Cambridge, Londoners Peter Sage and James Tower (all merchants), and Richard Savage, an academic from Cheshire. That's all we ever learn about them – you'd think all those hours pulling lustily side-by-side at their rowlocks would have sparked off a few noteworthy debates, but Tom was apparently still too concerned with Tom stuff: planning it, doing it, or writing it up. Just past Wesel he reports on a prescient initiative in public execution – an English mercenary, convicted of killing a fellow countryman in a duel, is condemned by the Spanish governor to a death by firing squad, 'and to be first tied to a post or some such thing with a paper pinned upon his breast'. At Rees he measures the market place; at Nijmegen he transcribes a shiny new gold inscription, dated 1606, above a gate to 'a pretty church'.

Nijmegen was the scene of some terrible Arnhem-related fighting in September 1944 – 1,800 US paratroopers died here – and at first it seemed all that had survived from Coryate's era were the steep side streets of what is Holland's only hilly town. It was odd to think, as I opened the car door in a multi-storey to be greeted by a stench of pee and solvents, that the main Grand Tour complaint about the Dutch was their slavish obsession with cleanliness and order. Out in the precincts and main drag it was the same, the pavements litter-strewn and broken-slabbed – were these people really descendants of the maidservant whom Sir William Temple had seen throwing a gentleman down the stairs and out into the street for entering her master's house with a spot of mud on his boots?

I understood what had happened as soon as I saw the shoppers trooping in and out under the risibly dated Christmas decorations limply festooning branches of Halfords, Dixons, Etam and Dolcis; all had that familiarly individual scruffiness. The car-park smell, the knackered pavements: Holland had become Britain. I'd even blundered across the sodding *Archers* on long wave – if the bike lanes hadn't been wider than the roads you could have been in Woking.

Then again, there was the language. The apparent ease with which all Dutch people under the age of forty have acquired such disarming fluency in English is often commented upon, but looking at the Scrabble box in a toyshop window it was impossible to believe this process could ever be reciprocated by the youth of Britain. There were only two six-letter words on the illustrated opening gambit, but between them they boasted seven Es. Holland is home to the EU vowel mountain. I don't know what the high-scoring letters would be – Js are ten-a-penny and Z would be a four-pointer at best. It is still disturbing to note the very high proportion of Dutch words that look less daunting read backwards.

And if the Comprehension is bad, just wait until you get to the Oral. As I prepared to pay for some oil in Halfords – a farewell drink for the Rolls – the cashier unleashed a single noise of such astonishing complexity, a sound that incorporated simultaneous use of all parts of the mouth and throat, that I could not have reproduced it in 400 attempts. Surveying my expression – an awed amusement that would have been instantly familiar to anyone who regularly travels naked on public transport – he nodded happily, then said, 'Oh – shorry. Three ninedy-five.'

I did find some old bits of Nijmegen in the end – the main square, Grote Markt, was neatly restored in the Fifties, right down to Coryate's gilded 1606 inscription above the churchyard gate. In fact, looking at some other plaques, it became clear that nearly all the rather splendid onion domes and stepped gables and fussy spires had been either spanking new or under construction at the time of his visit. Despite that ongoing war with Spain, the Netherlands – or more precisely the United Provinces – was just entering its golden era: by the 1650s, there were Dutch colonies and trading stations in the furthest-flung corners of the earth. I hadn't realised that Henry Hudson's voyage, which set sail a few months after Coryate's return, was financed by the Dutch (nor that having discovered and explored the various American straits, bays and rivers after which he is named, Hudson was cast adrift to die by a mutinous crew). And now they can't even host a football tournament without asking Belgium to help out.

It was dark again by the time I got back to the car, waylaid as I had been by a painfully stair-ridden detour to a bicycle museum which, as I perhaps should have predicted, featured nothing more exciting than two shillings' worth of penny farthings. By the time I got to the sit-up-and-begs I wanted to lay-down-and-die.

There is only one hotel in Tiel, a small town peripherally mentioned by Coryate, and I was welcomed into it by two textbook Dutch blonde receptionists with big teeth. I wasn't sure what 50 quid buys you in the world of upmarket rep motels, but one thing was the message that burst on to the TV screen when I entered my fourth-floor room and turned on the lights: 'Welcome MOORE to our hotel Tiel.' It was curt and it was rather sinister, and having slung my smalls in a frothing bidet I headed out into another cold night.

Trying to dismiss a sort of bored agony growing up my right leg, I struggled towards Tiel's distant centre through more Britishnesses: little Sixties terraces built too close to the road, with pampas grass and ornaments in tiny front gardens and heavily trinketed front rooms where old dears in neck braces sat watching teletext. A bloke staggered past me with a knackered armchair upside-down on his head, and I thought: You wouldn't see *that* in Germany.

Nor, indeed, would you have seen the little neon sign that drew me down a quiet, narrow side street somewhere near the centre: 'Relax . . . Coffee Shop'. I hadn't realised such establishments existed outside Amsterdam, and embarked on an investigative hobble-past. There was an entry phone and a sign banning under-eighteens; through a window filled with inflatable *X-Files* aliens I could make out the dim, smoky outlines of a counter and a couple of Afros. It was like a cross between a brothel and a bookie's.

There was a kebab shop next door, and while eating half of it in a sliced pitta I walked back past the Relax . . . Twice. Then my right leg said: 'Hey – pain relief!' and I pressed the bell.

It was a shameful exchange through the intercom, a scene from the darkest nightmare of teenagers' parents. 'Hello there,' I replied to the animal sound I took to be a Dutch greeting. 'I've come to buy some . . . some of your stuff.' Another comical noise, but this time with a querying inflection. 'Your produce,' I said, looking up and down the empty pavements like the shiftiest little smackhead. Silence. 'Your . . . cannabis.' No klaxons went off; I was not pinned to the floor by a SWAT team in balaclavas abseiling down the façade.

'Can-na-bish?' said the voice, and I almost shuffled quickly away, suddenly convinced that the Afros were bobbing with poorly restrained hilarity. But I had come too far; I would see this out. 'Yes: cannabis, pot − I want to buy some drugs!' I barked, awful words to hear filling a quiet street after dark. But it worked. There was a buzz; I pushed the door and went in.

The Relax . . . was not designed to appeal to the *soignée* dope fiend about town. The Afro-owners (actually North African crusties) were playing an intense but incompetent game of table football; the Formica surfaces around them were all lopsided and sticky looking, empty but for the odd broken Chianti lamp or Coke can. It was more like a youth club than an opium den.

The sullen-looking teenage barman nodded at me, and said, 'Mari-waaaar-nuh, yuh?'

'Er, yuh,' I said. He beckoned me to the bar, whipped out a pair of big Tupperware lunchboxes from some hidden recess and peeled off the lids. Both were full of compacted greenery, reminiscent of the matter that collects under the blades of rotary lawnmowers. Again I had to suspend my disbelief, suddenly convinced I could hear scratchy walkie-talkie whispers, the prelude to what tabloid newspapers would call 'a classic sting operation'. 'Well, that's . . . a lot. Of drugs. Um . . . have you got anything, you know . . .' This was excruciating, like asking a barber for something for the weekend, and him replying, 'What are you talking about?'

'Gchcgh?' said the barman, indicating a little tray of pre-rolled reefers. That was much more like it. 'I'll take two,' I said, noticing they only cost a quid, but he didn't understand and only gave me one. In a very short time I would be blessing his soul for this act of kindness.

Out into the night I puffed, breathing drugs all over Tiel's handful of authentically gabled townhouses before winding up out by the Rhine, which, having forked in two just before Nijmegen, was now in fact the Waal. A vast Gouda of a moon presided over an epic flatness strewn with evidence of an ongoing struggle against the tides. I had to walk through a huge floodgate cut into the 8-foot Waal wall surrounding the town, and down by the misty banks bulldozers and lorries were working away under floodlights, doing the sort of stuff boys do on the beach with Tonka Toys. Ah, I thought, reminiscing about the dams I used to build with my brother. Oh, I thought, noticing he was driving one of the bulldozers. Unmbh, I thought, as the moon came down to meet me, and after that I didn't think any more.

Without wishing to upset the proprietors of the Relax . . . Coffee Shop, I am obliged to report that associating their establishment with such a verb is an act of wanton deceit. In fact, if you were asked to rank all the verbs in the English language in order of relevance to the effects of their merchandise, 'relax' would make a lowly appearance, perhaps just above 'bore' and 'recall', but certainly well behind every single other, including 'flail', 'inflate' and 'solder'.

All I can say to encapsulate the all-encompassing meltdown of my faculties is all I can remember: a single, vivid snapshot of a man, who may or may not have been me, down on all fours watching a woodlouse, who on balance probably wasn't, cross a street-lit paving stone. It may also help to imagine the tearful intensity of my surprise and delight when, at some unknown point in the small hours, I found myself in the right room, in the right hotel, in the right continent. Even if I was curled up in a ball by the bidet.

✦　✦　✦

'Welcome MOORE to our Betty Ford Clinic,' said the TV message as I tentatively awoke, lying in the sort of position you would expect to see a chalk outline drawn around. I felt like a shipwreck survivor coming to on a beach, and surveyed my surroundings with the same sense of disorientated relief. After an unsatisfactory conclusion to the laundry I should have hung up to dry when I got in, I slunk damply down to the breakfast room and soon installed myself at the self-service griddle. The concept of sizzling your own bacon and eggs was an admirable one – no pain, no weight gain – but as the only person not wearing a rep's suit I did get asked twice by people who were to do them a quick fry up. At least I now know the Dutch for 'sunny side-up, Wet Pants'.

Covering parts of my face as I paid the bill – there was always the chance I'd asked one of the receptionists to give me a piggyback up to my room the night before – I looked through a couple of fingers at the souvenir display and pondered that being called the Netherlands, or Low Countries, can't be very good for national morale. And, as Coryate told me a couple of hours later, sitting with the *Crudities* in a café in Zaltbommel, 'Holland' was even worse: it derives from the depressions and hollows left when a Dark Age flood receded. 'For which cause the old name of Batavia was afterward changed to Holland, for hol in the Flemish tongue doth signifie as much as our word hole.' Hole-land – it's not great, is it?

The morning's drive had provided further evidence of the resultant obsession with flood prevention. A rather ragged Burundian pennant flapped before me as I piloted the Rolls along the top of a lonely, meandering dyke, huge greenhouses on my right, huge boats on my left. I gave one a race – one old barge against another – and sped forward by the current he gave me a run for my money.

Not far downstream, just past Dordrecht, was one of the earliest drainage schemes, a network of dykes and channels that reclaimed a vast area of land from what was in effect the Rhine delta. Now, almost a quarter of Holland is reclaimed land, with a third of the country below sea level. I'm sorry to say this, but I never realised all those windmills were for driving the pumps that drained the water. I just thought the Dutch were . . . I dunno, really into grinding stuff. I do have a bit of a weakness for this sort of long-term stupidity – I was well into my teenage years before I noticed Donald Duck was actually *saying* things, rather than just making stupid noises. And while it is bad enough to be caught singing along to Barry Manilow's 'Copacabana', just imagine being in a public place when you burst into a chorus of 'Coal Bunker Cavern'.

It had been a sombrely picturesque day – sheep sleeping in a soggy orchard, the odd thatched cottage, wind-farm propellers with adverts plastered up their shafts – and Zaltbommel slotted in nicely. I hobbled over the cobbles, pay-back time for last night's anaes-thetised yomp, hoping that the church tower would feature the huge cannonball embedded during a Spanish assault in 1574 and still there when Coryate passed through. It didn't, but that was okay – the main square, with its hotchpotch of tall, thin houses with stepped gables and diamond-painted shutters, had won me over. And who wouldn't warm to a town of 15,000 souls that boasts its own body-painting salon?

Surrounded by landscapes so notoriously horizontal, it's not surprising that everyone in Holland is laid back. Well, actually, yes it is. How was it that though Dutch towns looked English and Dutch people spoke English, the country had acquired an entirely unEnglish reputation for easygoing tolerance? If it looks like a duck and it sounds like a duck, then, they say, it must be a duck. But what if it then takes a big puff of duckweed and waddles into a peepshow to take in some hardcore drake-on-drake action?

My theory, which is completely right, is that a country can only achieve this state of national mellowness by first experiencing world domination, then losing it and taking 300 years to get used to the fact. In 1667, the Dutch sank the British fleet at Chatham and sailed cheekily up the Thames; this may be considered as the high point of their global hegemony. Three hundred years on – oh, look: it's the summer of love. On this basis, people will be striding bollock-naked down the Champs Elysées in 2110, and openly sniffing Tippex thinners in Cheltenham about forty years later. God help us all when the Germans get jiggy in 2243.

Since my terrible rages in Germany I'd become aware of the need for interpersonal warmth with my fellow man. To an almost embar-rassing degree – never filling up the Rolls more than half to maximise those 'that'sh quite a car you've got there, mishter Ambasshador' chats on the forecourt, or – as today – having the morning coffee I'd eschewed at breakfast in a café at the next town. Sometimes it got out of hand. Later in the afternoon I saw a friendly face in an elec-trical retailers and ended up buying an iron.

The flesh-pressing walkabout wasn't a policy I'd have contem-plated in some countries, but here, where the locals not only spoke English but were really nice, it had become routine. As I paid for a(nother) Little Mermaid doll in Zaltbommel's toyshop, one of the staff delivered a merry discourse upon global merchandising, another began giftwrapping the box and the third handed over a compli-mentary chocolate (though as I eagerly tore off the clown-face wrapper and shovelled it into my gob with a sticky 'Cheers!' I realised it might not have been intended for me).

The only trouble was my lack of practice at the art of allowing a conversation to develop in an unselfconscious, organic sort of way. Some of my exchanges were consequently unfortunate:

'Hello. One coffee, please. How many people died here in the war?'

Now that I thought of it, even the car-selling plan was at least partly intended to create opportunities for making new friends. Just outside Gorinchem I spotted a gold 1978 Shadow 2, still with its British registration plates, parked in front of a converted barn. There was no answer when I rang the bell, but it was an encouraging sighting, and I drove into the next two second-hand car lots I passed. I drove out again fairly quickly ('You can forget it'; 'Maybe we do shome part exchange on dis Jeep Cherokee?'), having accepted that the Rolls's continuing decline had shifted it from the asset column to the liabilities. The electric windows worked only intermittently, the driver's seat had become jammed in a low-slung position which made me look like a sulky teenager being given a lecture, and the indicators were on the blink, or rather weren't − the only way to flash them was by flicking the stalk up and down. Worst of all, the cassette-player speed was now linked to that of the engine, meaning that Ray Davies sounded like Beelzebub about town and Papa Smurf on the motorway.

Coryate was spot-on about Gorinchem: 'a most elegant and sweet little towne, situate in a plain, hard by the goodly navigable river Waell'. Herringbone brick pavements, no cars, a quaintly crooked church tower − sweet was the word. And if you're interested, there's a very nice Greek restaurant for sale in one of the sweeter streets.

Pacing about the compact medieval alleys I came across a sign-posted historical walk, and I just about managed it, struggling up and down the dykes, avoiding cyclists with a limping dodge. At the end, by the river, was a display of pictures from the town's Tom-time seventeenth-century heyday: I sat myself down on the bench before them with my right foot up on a bollard, watching the swing bridge rise to let a barge through. I was particularly taken with one, dated 1608, showing six men with beards and hats rowing across the river, a barrel in the bow – Coryate and his gang, perhaps, with a souvenir vat of Rhenish wine he'd picked up along the way. But all the descriptive labels next to the pictures underneath were in Dutch, and for every '*waterpoort*' there was a '*zogenaamde*'. And an '*eeuw*'.

Still, he'd passed through here, and so had the Grand Tourists. However good the Dutch roads, it was still much more comfortable to glide down the rivers. The *trechschuit*, a sort of horse-drawn water-bus, was described by one awed British traveller as 'the most remarkable boat of any kind in all Europe': all were clean and cosy, and some had evolved into floating gin palaces 'divided into several apartments', serving 'a very good ordinary dinner of six or seven dishes, and all sorts of wines'. And so cheap: the fare itself was less than a penny a mile, and in 1773, James Essex paid just 1*s* 3*d* for one of those six-course dinners, including free beer. Coryate had coughed up a lot more than that for supper in Basel 165 years earlier.

Hopelessly jealous, and still not sure where I was going to stop for the night, an hour later I found myself circuiting Dordrecht's unpromisingly drab suburbs. But I got lost, it got dark, and I thought, This'll do. I parked in front of a dingy, smutted dump of a hotel where filthy net curtains flapped out of fourth-floor windows someone had forgotten to close – the sort of place you feel you ought to be paid to stay in. But – scratched head, rubbed eyes and other physical expressions of quizzical disbelief – it was full.

And thank dyke for that, because proceeding glumly ahead I wound up in a canalside quarter so wondrously appealing that without a thought for my looming accommodation crisis I stuck the Rolls half up on the pavement and got out for an eager extended ramble.

Looking at the guidebooks now, I can't find much to back up my enthusiasm. All the Michelin has to say is 'Nieuwehaven – Pleasure boats find shelter in this dock with tree-lined quaysides' – not a single laudatory adjective, let alone a star. Nor did the Grand Tourists apparently bother to stop, too excited at nearly being home. But Coryate managed a couple of goodlies and a magnificent – if only to honour Dordrecht's achievement in 'clean exterminating Popery out of the towne' – and as I surveyed the swaying forest of masts, framed by long rows of desirable and immaculate townhouses, Nieuwehaven seemed to me to combine all the best attributes of rival canal cities. Amsterdam without the dog poo, graffiti and teenage gangsters hissing 'Cokehashtrips?' in your ear; Little Venice but bigger; Big Venice but emptier.

The houses were like squashed Georgian terraces, tall and thin – but also slightly irregular, some leaning slightly forward or sideways, in a way that gave the scene a mobile, jaunty, nautical air. Crossing the canal via an old wooden lift bridge, its cranks and cogs carefully greased, I gazed longingly at the sort of varnish-decked, glowing-portholed yachts you instantly wanted to go and live on, even though to do so would instantly transform you into some awful wanker in an old Martini advert. Someone was cooking something complicated and garlicky and I realised that anywhere else in the world this place would have been transformed into a bar-and-brasserie boardwalk, but here it was just nice, smart people living in nice, smart homes. I liked it very much, and I wanted to stay. So I went back to what had once been a nice, smart car and found the perfect overnight parking place: right up by the bright red hull of the local

fire boat at the junction of two canals, and with driver's-side views
of the River Maas's spreading estuary.

Dordrecht was on the Spanish/United Provinces front line in
Coryate's day – all along the Waal he saw fortresses and gangs of
mercenaries, many of them English – but despite this it was still one
of the richest ports in Holland. I was particularly taken by the inscription he copied from the side of the Mint: 'All things are possible
with money', but I couldn't find it and in trying to do so discovered that away from Nieuwehaven, Dordrecht wasn't really anything
special. Voorstraat, the main drag, was pedestrianised but slightly
rundown, and turned its back on the canals. I walked along behind
four men and a dust-truck: this was obviously cardboard-recycling
night, and as the men scooped up neat piles of flattened cartons,
last-minute ecologists rushed desperately out of dark doorways with
a single shoebox or Jiffy bag, hurling them into the back of the
truck as if they'd been ticking.

Sex shops, everything-a-guilder crap emporia and, under the
legends Joy Party and Ali Baba, a couple of unwelcome coffee-shop
reminders of a night spent with my head stuck in the doors of
perception – it wasn't what you'd call classy. On this basis, and because
I'd just remembered that Chelsea were playing Feyenoord of Holland
in a Champions' League game that evening, it didn't seem too
unsightly to stuff takeaway chips in my mouth while undertaking a
quest for a bar with a big telly.

I'd already rejected a couple – on account of being patronised by
a very small number of very large men – when I saw a sign jutting
out of a dim establishment ahead: 'The Boozer'. I went up to its
darkened doors, upon which were displayed the entry requirements:
'If you don't speak English, FUCK OFF'. I fucked on.

The football was about to start, but I never really got to watch it. I was too busy starring in a feature-length special of *Auf Wiedersehen, Pet* – sorry, *Tot Ziens, Pet*. Only with offshore welders instead of builders, and a limping ponce instead of a Pet.

At 7.15 there were only half a dozen installed at the tiny bar, but already they were all on pints and chasers – including the young barmaid, whom I only realised wasn't a Mancunian when she answered the phone and went Dutch.

'Hello there,' said a silver-haired, bright-eyed Yorkshireman with a perfectly hemispherical beergut. 'Nice hat.' I'd forgotten the Anna Karenina headgear, and now it was too late. There were beery cackles; the barmaid lost it and brayed like a donkey. 'Over there with the hat wankers,' shouted a Black Country voice from the other end of the bar, and my attention was drawn to a three-toothed mess grinning sheepishly under a woollen Kangol. 'He's over there because of his hobby. Saddle-sniffer. Only came here because of the bikes.'

'Dreams about tandems,' came another shout, and Three-teeth rolled his eyes good-humouredly, then nodded at me amid the general hilarity and said, 'Name?' in Scottish.

It wasn't a good time to be called Tim; I expected hoots and imaginary handbags, and I got them. 'From the Smoke, yeah?' Chiswick gave up Smoking some decades back, but I was still rather taken aback by the shrillness its mention elicited. 'Lord Christ Almighty! Chiswick! *Chiswick?*'

And then of course came the exaggerated contrition, and when I raised my eyes back up from the floor I saw a little glass full of Bovril, and the Yorkshireman said, 'Jagermeister – down it,' and at the second attempt I did. Now came the introductions and hand-shakes, and one by one I received them all, the lisping Londoner with his oily-fringed teenage son, the porn-star-moustached

Brummie, every last welder and ultrasound engineer. Then everyone started setting up complicated bar tabs and buying me more drinks; the Yorkshireman kept bellowing '*Aqua vitae!*' in a mock Victorian baritone and holding up his empty shot glass. Pretty soon the barmaid gave up and started knocking back Jagermeister from the bottle.

Unlikely as it seemed, this gathering of British men getting loudly drunk together in a dark, foreign inn was the most compelling emulation of a Grand Tour scenario I had yet been involved in. 'They go abroad,' wrote Lord Chesterfield disparagingly of the Grand Tourists, 'but, in truth, they stay at home all that while . . . not speaking the languages, they go into no foreign company . . . but dine and sup with one another only at the tavern.' *Plus ça change*, as they wouldn't have learnt to say when they got home.

However, as I seemed to be enjoying myself more than I had for some considerable time, it was difficult to criticise The Boozer's clientele. Everything was a performance. 'Great Balls of Fire' came on the tape; it was cranked up to obscene volume and everyone except me stuck their feet up on the bar and did a Jerry Lee Lewis; then it was 'The Stripper', and in less than a minute two fat men in pants were pouting at me and flicking their socks in my face. An unassuming boss-eyed Dutch redhead came in with a couple of friends; I was stage-whispered at not to catch her eye. 'She's had 95 per cent of the blokes in here,' said a blotchy-faced Scotsman. 'And given half of them the clap. What do you give to the girl who has everything? Condoms.'

By nine, my final timecheck, the quality of the banter was starting to decline. Chelsea stuck a third past Feyenoord, but no one was watching. Gazes turned down to glasses, the words 'wife' and 'home' were muttered in accents spanning the length and breadth of the

British Isles. The Yorkshireman's clear eyes reddened as he talked of his ex and their three kids back in Sheffield – he'd been here fifteen years. Pornstar had a Dutch wife and bilingual kids, and said, 'You come here for a summer and you'll never leave,' in a sinister way that conjured up images of a tainted paradise from Greek mythology, or at least the Hotel California.

Things became a little fractious as the bar belatedly filled up. Pornstar told a Yehudi Menuhin/Gary Glitter joke, or at least so I assume, having only heard the 'both fiddle with kids' punch-line; a young Ulsterman with a flamboyant belching condition took exception.

'You should be barred for that.'

'Okay – bad taste, accepted.'

'No – not accepted. That is bang out of fucking order. You should be barred.'

The Yorkshireman went off to sort out some imagined slur delivered by two smiling Polish seamen in Huggy Bear hats; the boss-eyed Dutch girl made the mistake of shouting out 'Feuck you all!' with predictable consequences.

And this was just a Wednesday. Did they all have days off tomorrow? 'No,' said Pornstar, 'we'll be there.'

'What, even him?' I asked, cocking a finger at Three-teeth, now on tumblers of Jagermeister and arguing quietly with himself.

'He'll be there first,' said Pornstar, affronted. 'Quick rub of the eyes, splash of cold water and clocking on at 6.28.'

Carefully stripping my conversation of any comic references to paedophilia, I managed to get some sense out of the Ulsterman. Dordrecht was infinitely preferable to Amsterdam – 'the kind of place where people find a used condom in the street and stick it behind their ear for later' – and a lot cheaper. Flats here were £50

339

a week and you got a £300 allowance every six weeks to go home; he never did.

A pug-faced Scouse friend of his turned up and soon they were holding forth on the wonders of Dutch life, with particular emphasis on its tolerance to social drug use and lurid pornography. 'Every Thursday night on telly – not hardcore, but it does the job. And on the rigs – it's not what trade you do that counts, it's how much porn you've got.'

When the Jagermeister stopped tasting like earwax I knew I was in trouble. 'I'm as shagged as three welders,' said the Scouser before zig-zagging out towards the door; feeling as drunk as five, I soon followed him. With a lazy grin smeared across my face I made my way haphazardly down the Voorstraat, literally and figuratively all over the place. But I somehow found the Rolls, and in ninety ugly seconds had stripped down to my underwear, shoved maps and food about a bit and wrestled myself into a sleeping bag.

Then two things happened very quickly together. The first was the discovery of a note shoved under my wipers; the second was the hand that, at the second attempt, whisked it out.

'So you weren't talking bollocks,' said a familiar voice.

I craned my head at the passenger window and saw a Lancastrian pipeline engineer in a Bolton Wanderers shirt; next to him was a thin man, as gormless as Stan Laurel, as silent as Buster Keaton.

'This is my pal Johan,' said the Wanderer, whom I now noticed was holding the flag of Burundi in his other hand. He rapped on the window. 'Come on – I'm catching my fucking death out here.'

With my glass-draining draught of Jagermeister less than half an hour old, inebriation was still waxing: I clicked down the central locking and they piled noisily into the forgotten attic that was the back seat. 'Just wanted to see if this Rolls was for real,' he said, ominously liberating an unopened half-bottle of Jagermeister from Johan's jacket. 'You said by the fire boat, and there's only one fire boat.' Johan giggled imbecilically to himself; he had discovered the rear-seat vanity mirrors and their concomitant illumination. 'And speaking of which . . .'

He didn't finish the sentence, preferring instead to top up his Jagermeister levels with a long and noisy pull, but with his free hand he passed me the windscreen note. 'Fire parking ONLY PLEASE' it read.

'Well – better move then,' I announced with unusual bravado, slithering awkwardly out of my sleeping bag and delving about for my shoes.

'Oh, pardon us, my friend – didn't know you'd settled in,' he said unconvincingly, following it up with: 'Got any sounds?'

And so, with 'Children of the Revolution' booming and shrieking out of six speakers, I drove very slowly along the road that overlooked the Maas, dressed only in T-shirt, pants and untied shoes and with two drunk strangers gurning out of the back windows. But only for about 150 yards, when I swung abruptly into a space, not aware at the time that my front wheels had come to rest perhaps three inches from the quay edge.

We are now at the boundaries of recall; I remember Boltoncentric football chants, Olympic-class freestyle swearing and a Dutch-accented voice rising dreamily above the Beatles' *White Album* to announce, 'This record – my first sex.' Then, suddenly, I found that turning round to communicate engendered a certain queasiness, and moments later the lusty Lancastrian choruses of 'I drive a Rolls-Royce, 'cos it's good for my voice' went into repeat and fade, and I was gone.

✦   ✦   ✦

Coryate had established a connection between the Dutch preference for beer ('sometimes two whole howres pass before they will
let their tankards out of their hands') and the Dordrecht merchants'
notorious habit of watering down Rhenish wine as it passed through
before heading off to England. The reproachful expression worn by
the red-bearded stevedore staring at me from just beyond the end
of my bonnet implied that nothing of the sort had happened to
their Jagermeister.

The world had been busy while I slept: that huge barge had tied
up right in front of me; my back-seat passengers had departed; I had
undergone pioneering organ exchange surgery with a dead dog. I
glanced at my watch: it had been stopped in its tracks by some
unknown act of recklessness at 12.20, presumably the same act that
had dislodged the second hand, which now lay forlornly wedged at
the bottom of the face, between five and seven.

Cringingly pondering last night's terrifying and stupid drive, I
looked to my right and saw the word 'POLITIE' in painfully large
white letters on a blue background: a police van. To my left was
another. A glance in the mirror confirmed I had parked directly in
front of a police station; when, at length, I departed, I noted a large
and unequivocal message painted on the cobbles reserving my space
for its staff.

While tracking down my clothes I scanned the Rolls for signs of
theft or damage. The Burundian flag had gone, but that didn't really
matter because after I returned home I found out it had actually
been identifying me as a proud stalwart of the mercenary-hiring
regime in Papua New Guinea. Among all my rubbish on the back
seat was some of theirs: in particular the empty Jagermeister bottle,
a rather attractive dark green against the olive leather, and the foil-
wrapped remains of some sort of takeaway food. It should have stunk,

but it didn't, and then I saw why: both rear windows were wound down three inches. Noticing that somewhere in the strata of physical distress was a little seam of cold numbness, I patted and slapped and clawed at the master window control switches on the driver's door. One whooshed up; the other didn't. I tried the back-seat switch: the same result. And then it started raining.

It wasn't all bad. The resultant frosted-glass effect on the windscreen created what the makers of shower doors call a 'modesty strip', so allowing me to spare the stevedore the unwholesome contortions involved in dressing in a car. Having pulled on last night's horrible, stinking pub wardrobe, I tackled the open-window situation with a roll of insulating tape. It wasn't easy – my brain was too full of muddy thoughts and pain to have much space left for problem-solving, and the interior glazing was smeared with an adhesive-unfriendly cocktail of condiments, fat and Anglo-Dutch fingerprints.

I now had only two desires. One was a mound of deep-fried awfulness, swiftly acquired and despatched at a ring-road chip van; the second were bathing facilities. This proved more irksome. After an endless and taxing tour of Dordrecht's suburbs, one governed by imagined hungover idiocies such as the bonnet being slightly open at the expense of the more pressing issue of keeping to the correct side of the road, I eventually found two pools. Both were currently reserved for swimming lessons ('I've always been rubbish at front crawl,' I pleaded gamely to the cashier at the second, who replied with a series of keep-him-talking nods that suggested her fingers were scanning the underside of the desk for the panic button).

I even found myself walking with wincing deliberation up to the reception desk at a health club, but was put off partly by the £12 entrance fee and partly by the grey-quiffed manager who came up and said, 'Have you been to a Dutch shauna before? Mosht of our clientsh shtay for a long time and enjoy our other shervicesh.'

So, filthy and oily and unshaven and limping I gave up, and passed the afternoon wallowing biliously west on a small road along the top of a dyke, having the Rolls's flanks slapped and battered by wet wind and sheets of reclaimed mud thrown up by passing lorries. So much rain in such a flat place – I hoped no one had left the plug in. It was here, out in those fields of churned crap, that Coryate saw a sad legacy of the terrible St Elizabeth flood of April 1421, when the rivers spectacularly burst their banks and more than 100,000 people died – Dordrecht became an island and a vast reed forest, now known as the Biesbos, was created to the east. Almost 200 years after the event, Coryate was still able to look across the water and see 'many Churches half drowned, the upper part of the tower appearing very plainly above the water'.

Most of that land, and a lot more besides, has since been reclaimed – down near the sea, Coryate saw peasants building crude dykes, 'laying a great deale of strawe and earth to preserve the banke'. Today's coastline and even the routes of the rivers would be barely recognisable to him: in 1608 he sailed straight down the seafront to Bergen op Zoom; now it's all land. Driving through a load of faceless prefab towns knocked up on these new bits of Holland, I wondered if it would be possible to invade another country by stealthy reclamation. A few dykes and windmills and plenty of innocent whistling and the Nazis could have inched France across to Dover without anyone noticing.

What I hadn't realised, until I got talking to a waitress in a cafeteria in Middelharnis, is that the biblical floods had kept on coming. In 1953, a storm flood breached dykes all along the coast: over half a million acres were inundated and 1,865 drowned. Now I understood, with appropriate sobriety, the obsession with learning to swim.

Blame the redrawn map, blame the hangover – for whatever reason, I lost Tommy somewhere along the way, and didn't find him again until I drove into Zierikzee at 6.30. For a town that sounded like a Scottish offshore welder trying to say 'seriously' after dark, it had done all right for itself. 'A beautiful place' in 1608, its trim, seventeenth-century streets were still dominated by a vast, unfinished clock tower, all that remained after a fire in 1832 burnt down the attached cathedral.

A quick drive round another winning main square failed to turn up a hotel; two nice men in a bike shop directed me to the town's only relevant establishment, run as a sideline by the Chinese restaurant on the ground floor. The proprietress had a careworn look, a look that acknowledged in advance that her guests would not enjoy their stay, as well as accepting that an enormous facial birthmark would invariably make it hard for them to remember what they were going to ask her. The bed filled the room and was propped up on one leg by a corrugated stack of used beer mats; all I was fit for was watching telly, and there wasn't one. So instead I sat down, picked up the phone and tried to flog the Rolls.

Calling home to hear the predictable news that no one at all had rung about the car, I did at least manage to procure my wife's assistance in tracking down, via the Internet, the contact number for Die Mascotte – Holland's premier Rolls-Royce owners' club. A minute later I was allowing myself to become rather excited: Mr Vos, the club secretary, had thought of a couple of people who might be interested. If I would phone him back in an hour he would let me know what they had to say.

Having shaved and sluiced and scrubbed off about ten years –

how did those welders do it every night? – I went out into narrow streets wind-tunnelled by a growing gale that whipped fairy lights against shop fronts and quickly rendered my lips reptilian. But despite the disincentives of the weather, Zierikzee was lively and – at 7.30 – still open for business. For the first time since Italy I got caught up in a *passeggiata*, an evening stroll *en famille*. The main square had improved further in the last hour: the battlemented façades of many of the townhouses were outlined with gay strips of lighting, and there was even a little Italianesque arcade, home to a dozen dope-smoking moped riders sheltering from the elements. If my leg hadn't hurt, I might even have paced it.

I was happy now – the sight of a homemade bumper sticker reading 'NO NUTS, NO GLORY' made me shriek with child-scaring laughter – but the hangover lingered, and with it a legacy of wild swings of emotion. A toyshop window almost reduced me to tears; inside, I hobbled up to the woman at the till and asked 'Do you have The Little Mermaid?' with a quavering intensity that suggested I believed myself to be The Big Mermaid.

I made the mistake of reassuming my jauntiness before calling Mr Vos back. Mr van Hobgoblin was away, he reported, but Mr van Hairysluts had apparently snorted with derision: 'He says he will pay 9,000 guilders less for cars with the driver's wheel on the right side.' Then there was something about a car tax system based on weight: until the Rolls was twenty-five years old, it would apparently cost over £800 a year to license it. 'You will find it very hard to sell it from what he says.' I felt my bottom lip tremble, and then I made a fearful ass of myself. In a cracked whimper I begged Mr Vos to unburden me, to rid me of this awful millstone blighting my life. 'Well . . . maybe I can try another member, Mr van Horsekok.' Knowing he was just saying that to stop me stalking him, I thanked

Mr Vos, and then I sighed, and then I cried. Why wouldn't the Rolls just leave me alone? I'd had enough of being in a goldfish bowl, and now it was leaking, and I was stuck with it. Big wobbling silver lady flaps to everyone.

And what was happening to me? If the car was falling to bits, so was I. What unsightly method of intoxication would I choose tonight? Butane? Poppers?

In the end it was just food – a vast Argentinean steak put to the fork in a comely, candlelit restaurant run by nice young ladies who didn't mind putting me in the choice table by the window, so advertising their establishment as a soup kitchen for pizza-anoraked, chapped-face loners. I looked out at the families leaning into the wind, and then at the incongruous Sixties bus-station clocks which top the church towers here as in so many Dutch towns, and I thought: I must be awaie betime in the morning. Time to go home.

Coryate was in a hurry, too. And the wind was in his face. The day after leaving Zierikzee, still in the company of fellow returning travellers William Tassell and Richard Savage, his boat struggles all day to cross the 9 miles to Arnemuiden, now well inland but then a thriving harbour. Frustrated at his slow progress, he wheels out the 'nothing memorable' insults, and goes on square-pacing strike. The last week of his voyage, including the two-day crossing from Flushing to London, is scribbled up in just eight pages – less than he'd allotted to Cologne Cathedral.

And the Grand Tourists, even though they'd enjoyed Holland, often succumbled to an are-we-nearly-home-yet malaise as England approached. Flatness meant fertility and so was a good thing, but one that even the most enthusiastic agriculturist could eventually tire of. The fourth Earl of Essex, grandson of Coryate's esteemed relative, came to find the geometric horizons maddening: 'I do not admire this country . . . I have not seen anything like a handsome prospect.'

On this basis it was not difficult to decide, as I portentously opted to give my purple suit a final outing, that the breakfast I consumed that morning in Zierikzee would be my last on foreign soil. It helped, however, that this meal was perhaps the most melancholy dining experience of my life, sitting there alone among the soy-sauce cruet sets and plastic orchids in the dark Chinese restaurant, eating a cheese roll whose constituents had got mixed up about who got to be the soft one with a flaky brown crust.

Then it was off over a huge flood protection barrier and across more horizontal greyness, the storm blowing the wind-farm propellers so violently it looked like they were about to take off. The odd old village cowering behind dykes; church spires and shallot domes sticking up over the defences; tentative new settlements on the reclaimed bits. A race with a minibus of jeering schoolkids, then miles of nothing – no more towns, no more spindly trees, no more huge green tomatoes in huge greenhouses. The flatness, the monochrome mist, the piles of beets: it was ending as it had begun.

In Middleburg I got out for a walk. It was cold; it was largely ruined by the Germans in 1940; I bought some chips from a trailer advertising deep-fried potato snacks in the shape of the Euro symbol and ate them back in the car. Flushing – Vlissingen to the Dutch – was just down the road: I'll be home by teatime, I thought. At the time of Coryate's stay it was owned by the British – a sort of deposit for assistance in helping repel the Spanish – and one of the lingering legacies of this connection is the car-ferry service to Sheerness.

Was, anyway. An amused man at the terminal looked at the Rolls and said, 'Sure – we can take your car. But not you. Ish freight only.'

Ignoring the strong temptation to take him up on this offer, I drove on. My Michelin map had boldly indicated the existence of a year-round car-and-passenger ferry service to Sheerness, and exiting the town I fear I may have taken the Michelin Man's name in vain, loudly ridiculing his many physical idiosyncrasies. It was a pisser — after all that, I wouldn't now be able to follow Tom home.

But a miss is as good as a mile, and there were plenty of both in the hours ahead. A long wait for the long ferry trip across the Westerschelde to Breskens; traffic jams of Belgians coming north to stock up on porn and clogs; then Zeebrugge. More amused terminal staff: 'We have not sailed to Dover for six years now. But you can go to Hull!' You too, love.

So further south to Ostend, through stupendously ugly, stone-dead towns, places where it looked as if the war had gone on until 1963, and the curfew was still in place. It was now dark, but apparently not quite dark enough. 'There is no boats before 9.15.' It was 6.30. Two hours later, following an autoroute crocodile of harassed British motorists who had clearly spent their three-day off-peak breaks trying to teach the French lane discipline, I drove into the ferry terminal at Calais with all convenient speed and immediately got called a flash twat.

NINE

Home

'I arrived in London the third day of October being Munday, about foure of the clocke in the afternoone, after I had enjoyed a very pleasant and prosperous gale of winde all the way betwixt Flushing and London. The distance betwixt Flushing and London is a hundred and twentie miles.'

Typical Tom: no poetic account of his homecoming, no resumé of his trials and tribulations, no ode in praise of foreign lands – let the numbers do the talking. He goes on to list the legs of his journey and the distance between each, finishing: 'The totall of my whole journey forth and back betwixt Odcombe and Venice: 1,975.'

Then comes a final paragraph whose novel typographical alignment cannot disguise one of the most anticlimactic endings in publishing history:

The Cities that I saw in the space of these five Moneths, are
five and forty. Whereof in France five. In Savoy one. In
Italie thirteene. In Rhetia one. In Helvetia
three. In some parts of high

Germanie fifteene. In
the Netherlands
seven.
FINIS

I sat in the exclusive Motorists' Lounge, the surface of my pint of Stella swaying slightly as we headed out into the Channel, and read these words over. It didn't exactly leave you gasping for the sequel. And he didn't even get the distance right – using a length of dental floss and a big map of Europe, it was clear that his journey was more like 2,400 miles. Not a mention, either, that over half of it – in excess of 1,200 miles – was covered on foot, without including the hundreds he would have notched up legging it around Paris, Lyon, Padua, Venice, Frankfurt and all the other cities he spent more than a couple of days in.

The ferry was almost empty; a gang of removal men in blue polo shirts were celebrating their return from a Continental job by shouting at a fruit machine. If Coryate was cagey about his achievements, what of the Grand Tourists, sailing back from Helvoetsluys to Harwich on the packet boat? The ever-present Eurohiker bag was at my feet, unaware that its joyous destruction and disposal lay only hours away, and for the last time I emptied out its soiled reference library on the table.

There was a legacy, of course, in the arts: between 1710 and 1740, almost 150 mansions were either built or redesigned by recently returned tourists inspired by what they'd seen. Inigo Jones, as noted earlier, got neo-Classicism up and running, and for the next 200 years British architecture was coloured by holiday romance. Palladianism emerged, too, across the fledgling United States: as well as President Jefferson's home, Montebello, the University of Virginia and a host of plantation houses were erected at the behest of the small but influential groups of Southern landowners who had undertaken their own Grand Tours. It was the same inside and out: British gardens soon had a less formal, more romantic Continental air about them; foreign interior designers were shipped in.

Music appreciation was transformed to the extent that the royal composer of choice during the first half of the eighteenth century was Handel, a German, and the astonishing quantity of painting and sculpture the Grand Tourists brought home with them was stuffed into mansions across the country. It is no accident that the words connoisseur and virtuoso are both Grand Tour souvenirs – but then again, the sneering term dilettante also sneaked into their luggage.

Reading on as we eased over the dark, calm Channel, it seemed that an indictment of superficiality was in many ways the mildest reproach for the majority of returning Grand Tourists. For every Englishman who returned determined to 'out-Italianise the Italians', there were dozens of braying, hungover youths with Voltaire's crumpled autograph somewhere in their waistcoat and a trunk full of bronzes and busts that for them were little more than the raffia donkeys of the eighteenth century.

Adam Smith, who before discovering free trade was tutor to the young Duke of Buccleuch on a 1764 Grand Tour, stated baldly that most Englishmen returned 'more conceited, more unprincipled, more dissipated and more incapable'. Few, apparently, disagreed with him: use of the word 'absurd' crops up regularly in damning critiques of the Tour's value to Britain's noble youth. They hung out with their own kind, learnt no foreign languages, and occupied themselves only in 'the conquest of some waiting gentlewoman of an opera Queen'. And drink: Walpole complained that his companions Sir Francis Dashwood and Lord Middlesex were plastered 'the whole time they were in Italy', and others noted the difficulty of prising an Englishman abroad out of a tavern. The only knowledge they acquired was of foreign 'fashions and fopperies', strutting about Paris or Rome dressed as 'a kind of animal, neither female or male' while insulting the locals with 'an ostentatious preference of England to all the rest of the world'. They returned, said Lady Montagu, 'no more instructed than they might have been at home by the help of a map'.

Soon, in fact, a whole industry sprung up to maximise the ridicule of returning tourists. Samuel Foote wrote three plays lampooning them, and newspapers regularly published spoof letters home by the likes of Tim Shallow (cheers for that) of Simpleton Hall. 'As for this Town of Paris it is very large . . . they eat Frogs like mad and devour the Devil and all of Garlick and Onions . . . I do not believe the Romans are a bit like the old Romans; they are thin-gutted, snivelling dogs, and I verily believe we could thrash forty of them.' That sort of stuff.

Yet it wasn't the critical momentum building up against the Grand Tour that killed it, but the French Revolution. All those baskets of noble heads weren't the best tourist-board advert, and when Napoleon emerged from the Revolution's ashes it was all over bar the shooting. Most of Europe was out of bounds, Venice defeated and much of the culture that attracted the British to Italy shipped back to France. My my, at Waterloo, Napoleon did surrender, oh yeah – but it was too late to save the Grand Tour. Steamers were soon crossing the Channel, and when the railways began snaking down to the Med a couple of decades later, a man called Thomas Cook started flogging his 'Great Circular Tour of the Continent' to a different class of British tourist. Coryate's journey to Venice had been a humble one, and 200 years later things were turning full circle. The history book on the shelf is always repeating itself.

Only in America did the concept of packing off landowners' sons on European odysseys of self-improvement live on. Increasingly few Englishmen could afford lengthy Continental trips, and with the advent of railways no longer needed to. Americans were becoming the new global aristocracy, sufficiently wealthy to finance exhaustive Grand Tours and sufficiently far away from the Continental action to justify them. The works of F. Scott Fitzgerald offer ample evidence that America's gilded youth were still being sent to Europe for their final polish well into the twentieth century.

But even during the Tour's *Gone With the Wind* American heyday, for every quiet and sensitive Ashley Wilkes there was a more robust soul succumbing to the inappropriate sentiments that corrupted so many Englishmen's travels. In 1787, Thomas Jefferson rather surprisingly summed up what he had learnt in Paris and Italy by expressing the fear that 'we shall become as corrupt as in Europe, and go to eating one another as they do there'. Back at Tara, the Tarleton boys, learning that another college expulsion will lead to parental forfeiture of their own planned Tour, conduct this memorable duologue:

> 'Well, hell! We don't care, do we? What is there to see in Europe? I'll bet those foreigners can't show us a thing we haven't got right here in Georgia! I'll bet their horses aren't as fast or their girls as pretty, and I know damn well they haven't got any rye whisky that can touch Father's.'
>
> 'Ashley Wilkes said they had an awful lot of scenery and music . . .'
>
> 'They can have 'em. Give me a good horse to ride and some good licker to drink and a good girl to court and a bad girl to have fun with and anybody can have their Europe . . .'

Then again, Ashley Wilkes survived the Civil War and the Tarleton boys did not. If they'd been to France they might have learnt how to win a civil war – at least in Italy they'd have learnt how to run away from one. (On the other hand, Scarlett O'Hara fell for Ashley despite rather than because of his 'maddeningly boring' accounts of European life.)

It was secretly pleasing to learn of the unsavoury and unedifying nature of most Grand Tours. In the light of those thickarse, degenerate toffs, that 1982 Magic Bus trip suddenly seemed far less shaming, its Coryate-like asceticism a source of pride. And in my velvet breeches and stupid hair, I was merely continuing a long tradition of Englishmen returning home coiffured and clothed in slavish mimickry of the most ludicrous Continental trends.

But what had I learnt? The removal men swore in hoarse celebration as the fruit machine surrendered a noisy jackpot; the French barmaid didn't look up from her *Paris Match*. Coryate had set the Grand Tour's outward itinerary, and though together Tom and I rather lost the aristocratic trail on the way home, between me and them and him we'd seen a lot, almost too much.

Which was, I suppose, exactly what he had hoped for. Coryate might have been one of the first to view a foreign tour as providing a burgeoning stock of reputation-enhancing anecdotes, but he certainly wasn't the last. The Grand Tourists didn't have domestic access to computer-generated walkthroughs of the Sistine Chapel or *Floyd on France*, but then no one's going to listen in rapt attention to an impromptu lecture on your CD-ROM collection or what you saw on telly last night. Actually going there was the thing, allowing all one's senses to impact on the experience and so fix the memory: a cold pastis on a warm evening, the fumes of fresh espresso and old Vespas. Even the most familiar tourist sights were elevated from brochure cliché in their original settings, if only by causing the spectator to marvel that the arse-pinching handbag snatchers peopling the splendour around him were direct descendants of the immortal geniuses who created it. Not all of us have the opportunity to stand on the shoulders of giants, but by strolling through the Tuileries or across San Marco you can at least walk in their footsteps.

There was more than that, though. This isn't a terribly stunning philosophy, but it has always seemed to me that having been placed on what is by some distance the most varied and exciting planet in the known universe, it does seem rather foolish not to see as much of it as possible in the limited time available to us. Coryate certainly appreciated this, more so than most Grand Tourists, who paid lip-service to the concept of self-improvement while busily bequeathing the British abroad a reputation for boorish philistinism that hasn't gone away. He slept in barns and stole turnips, but in aim and ethos his tour was far more civilised than most of those that followed.

The whole point of travel was to experience novelty, to see different sorts of people doing different things, expand one's mental territory – in modish terminology, to develop a hinterland. I scanned my hinterland: it was a lonely, windswept place, but if I looked closely there were signs of civilisation – the roof of Milan Cathedral sticking out of the mud, a violin bow propped surreally against a sugar beet. Sadly, of course, developing a hinterland is not as exciting as going down in history as the man who brought the fork to England and coined the word 'umbrella'. Coryate's Continent had given up all its secrets long ago. The best a contemporary tourist could hope was to come back and say, 'Well, we did find this *rather special* little bistro tucked away in the Camargue.'

Then again, it had been surprising and refreshing to learn that even in Europe, people changed over time at least as much as the places they lived in. Looking back from the end of the twentieth century, it was astonishing to think that the Germans had once been bad at road building but great at making music, that for centuries the Dutch were lampooned as control freaks. The Italians, of course, had made a whole national career out of confusing historians, and were still doing so, and the French, the French . . . well, Paris was a dump only twenty-five years ago and now it puts London to shame.

And what of the British? Some lights appeared outside the window, there was a juddering application of reverse thrust as we pulled up at the Dover quayside. Wandering down the diesel-daubed stairwells and across the car deck, I decided that the Rolls – a convincing synthesis of Tim, Tom and the Tourists – might give me some clues.

Descending the ramp on to home soil at the head of a queue of hatchbacks I felt like a flash, ageing football manager leading his young players out of the Wembley tunnel – Big Ron and the under-21s. With all my lost wanderings and backtracking I had covered 3,142 miles; the Rolls was cosmetically ravaged but had somehow held itself together mechanically. For six weeks I had flown the flag abroad, pitching British engineering and history against Continental geography and sociology. And then there were all my running battles with Coryate: coward versus bore, rolling stone versus moss-gatherer, tight bastard versus tight bastard. I wasn't quite sure who had won any of these contests, but their conclusion felt like something worth celebrating: it was past midnight, the roads were empty and I gunned up the fast lane at immodest velocity, 80 motorway miles in half as many minutes and twice as many decibels.

If someone had told me then that in six days' time a nightclub bouncer would be driving JPM 455V away up the M1 to Nottingham, I'd probably have cried. But when they added that he'd have paid me in used twenties, and in fact fifty more used twenties than I'd handed over two months before, I'd probably have stopped.

Epilogue

Coryate's movements after his arrival in London are revealed in his own transcripts of those ignored letters he sent to Zürich and Padua. If he was expecting a 'hail conquering hero' reception he was to be disappointed: of the few days he spent in the capital, there is no mention of any sort of party or welcoming committee. The thousand-mile walk, the brushes with death at the hands of petty villains and religious zealots, the tarts and carts and deep-fried frogs: he had done it all to impress the nobs, and they dismissed his heroic achievement with a 'yeah, whatever'.

If that was a kick in the teeth, there was another when he got back to Odcombe. A week before, while Tommy was mid-Channel, his mother had married some local type called John Salmon about whom nothing else is known. Before this could sink in − and it probably never did, as his subsequent letters are always addressed to 'Mrs Coryate' with her other half referred to only as 'your husband' − he went straight to the church. Now came the poetic gesture: having obtained permission from the rector, he hung up his comprehensively knackered shoes, nominally as a memorial to God for his safe return, but more accurately to show off.

And rightly so – his was a unique achievement, and if no one else was going to applaud it, he'd have to do it himself, in deed if not in printed word. He was already making a point of ostentatiously using forks at meals as a conversation piece, and any mention of a foreign land got him going: 'The mere superscription of a letter from Zürich sets him up like a top,' said Ben Jonson rather pointedly. 'Basil or Heidelberg makes him spin. And at seeing the word Frankford or Venice, though but in the title of a Booke, he is readie to overfloe the roome with his murmure.' Fair enough. If I'd walked to Venice and back my friends wouldn't get a word in edgeways for decades.

The shoes hung there for over a century, and even earnt Tommy an indirect mention in the first printed edition of Shakespeare's *Measure for Measure*: Act IV, Scene III: 'brave Master Shoe-tie the great traveller'. And then he found himself a house in the village, and over the next five winter months wrote up his notes into a manuscript of 200,000 words.

Poor old Tom. Having failed to find a publisher willing to take on such a huge and groundbreaking endeavour – between all the piazza-pacing and column-hugging, this was after all the original first-person travelogue of the type we are now so familiar with – he had no choice but to go down the vanity-publishing route.

And then came a new disappointment: the funds allocated for this were the presumably considerable unspent proceeds of his bet with the Yeovil linen draper, but when he went to pick up his winnings the draper welched. A messy court case ensued, which did at least give Tommy the chance to puff on the trumpet that his noble associates had so rudely declined to blow for him. Summing up his case before the Chancery Court he provides the sort of epic language he should have stuck at the end of the book: 'Who can justly call this a small and common Voyage, to pass almost two thousand miles by land? to expose ones body to such a world of iminent dangers both by Sea and Land as I did? to passe those stupendious mountaines of the snowie Alpes? . . . & after the consummation of my travels to be thus opposed by a Vilipendious Linnen Draper?'

Anyway, it worked. He got the dosh. But before he took his manuscript to Prince Henry, whose endorsement was needed to procure the necessary licence to publish, he went back and padded it out with an enormous and unutterably tedious 'Oration in Praise of Travel' by some German history professor whose work he'd found along his travels, and, more touching but even less readable, the complete unpublished poems of his late father George. In Latin.

The Prince may have looked at the first chapter – that Oration in Praise of Travel – and then perhaps he skipped through to the last – dead dad's dead-dull doggerel. And then he may have looked up at Coryate and said, 'Tell you what, shagbatter – leave this with me and I'll get it jazzed up a bit.'

Poorer, older Tom. Even though he was paying for it all himself, Coryate had no choice but to nod bravely. If he had any worst fears, they were all realised. Suddenly every smartarse in town was interested in the book, or more particularly in contributing a 'panegyrick verse' for its introduction, as requested by Prince Henry. Nominally a eulogy of the author, these soon became first bawdy, then downright rude. In no time there were fifty-nine, half of them unsolicited, as Prince Henry's entourage succumbed to Tom-baiting hysteria.

Very few of the courtiers, lawyers, academics and MPs who contributed verses had read the book, being inspired solely by a copy of the frontispiece illustration. Coryate seems to have paid William

Hole to do the engravings that decorate the book, but their content is more likely to have been influenced by the mischievous Ben Jonson, seminal playwright, wit, friend of royalty and tireless self-publicist. It was Jonson who supplied the crude verses upon which the frontispiece illustration was based – all the puking and whores and violent slapstick – and which set the tone for the 'panegyrick verses'. It's likely that the title – and the extended fart analogy that followed it – were his too. As had happened during those after-dinner humiliations before he left, Coryate was still 'the courtier's anvil to try their wits upon'. His journey was supposed to have given him instant gravitas and credibility; instead, it merely provided more ammunition for his tormentors. Nothing had changed.

You can just imagine the scene when Prince Henry returned the 'amended' version to Coryate, courtiers sniggering behind their capes in the background. The title might have come as enough of an unwelcome surprise, and the frontispiece illustration perhaps more so. And thereafter followed precisely 100 pages of panegyric verses, almost all of them viciously offensive.

As Coryate read on, it would have been difficult for him to have maintained a fixed grin, and I guess that was the point. They were bullies, taunting their victim and waiting for him to crack. Jonson's own verse pictures Coryate as a socially inept, blabber-mouthed tightwad ('He is alwaies Tongue-Major of the company . . . guilty of a thousand impertinences . . . frequent at all sorts of free tables . . .'), and there was worse to come. The great metaphysical poet John 'For Whom The Bell Tolls' Donne mercilessly slagged off Coryate as a 'half-pinte wit' with absurd social and intellectual ambitions – 'Oh to what heigth will love of greatnesse drive Thy leavened spirit?' – before comparing him to a sebaceous cyst on the nose which outgrows the nose itself.

And so it went on. Perhaps they were jealous of his achievement, perhaps they saw a chance to show off to each other, perhaps it was just too much to see this jumped-up little yokel buffoon not only writing a book – and no Englishman had written in detail about France and Italy for over fifty years – but having the audacity to make up his own words. Those who stopped short of character assassination went for the debauchery, rhyming Venice with penis and using well-chosen phrases such as 'how glad thou wert to come and kisse her bumme', or describing Coryate drinking the Great Tun of Heidelberg dry. To be honest, most of the verses don't make an enormous amount of sense to me, but even the most surreal hardly sound polite: 'Tom's a Bologna sawcidge lovely fat, Stuft with the flesh of a Westphalian sow, A French Quelque chose farced with oilet holes.'

It must have been agonising. On the one hand, Coryate knew that having big-name contributions from Jonson, Donne˙and Inigo Jones would do wonders for the book's profile and sales potential; on the other, he was being portrayed for 100 pages as the personification of most of the English language's negative adjectives.

> At last when I saw the multitude of [verses] increase to so great a number, I resolved to detain above a thousand [lines] of them from the presse. Whereupon the Princes Highnesse . . . gave me a strict and expresse commandement to print all those verses . . . wherein many of them are disposed to glance at me with their free and merry jests, for which I desire thee (courteous reader) to suspend thy censure of me till thou hast read over my whole booke.

It is a tragic introduction. And remember, he was paying for all this himself – one of the verses gloated that Coryate had spent all his winnings from the bet on publishing the book, and was now left penniless. He had no choice but to try to recoup some money by flogging as many copies as possible, and when *Coryats Crudities* was published in March 1611 – the same year as the King James Bible – he began touring noble residences in the south of England leading a donkey with a box full of *Crudities* on its back.

No one knows exactly how many he sold or at what price (only forty copies survive), but the inclusion of all those celebrity contributors and that novelty-act donkey must have served him reasonably well, as by the end of May 1611 Coryate was £106 in the black. He was preparing to do a slim-volume follow-up cash-in, *Coryats Crambe*, featuring some rather more polite panegyric verses that had arrived too late to be included in the *Crudities*, when something bad happened.

Just weeks before the publication of *Coryats Crambe*, a cheap pirate copy of the panegyric verses at the start of the *Crudities* appeared under the title *The Odcombian Banquet*. Coryate could do nothing: having self-published, in those days he had no copyright. And worse, the pirate book was expressly designed to humiliate him: with chortling reference to his donkey sales tour, the brief introduction to *The Odcombian Banquet* lampoons Coryate as an ass, explaining that only the insulting panegyrics were worth including. The main body of the book, writes the anonymous author, contained nothing 'worthy the reading, as wold have filled foure pages'.

Coryate knew that people were probably only buying the *Crudities* on the strength of the introductory verses. With these now available at a fraction of the cost, sales dried up. He began to eat into his savings, and by April 1612 had only £6 left – unlike most of those he wished to impress he had no private means and was never given a penny by Prince Henry. And of course those who'd written the verses thought it was hilarious, particularly after Coryate defended his own bit of the book by saying, 'of the six hundred fiftie and four pages . . . at the least five hundred are worthy the reading' – admitting straight out that almost a quarter of it was rubbish.

No one ever found out who published *The Odcombian Banquet*, but Coryate's humiliation was not over. An obscure Thames waterman, John Taylor, presumably hoping to make a name for himself, realised Coryate's clumsy, easily aroused sense of outrage made him an ideal target for starting a war of words. A pamphlet of poetry including a verse mildly poking fun at Coryate's 'idle Braine' was enough: Coryate took the bait when any PR man could have told him to ignore it. He kept no records of his threatening replies to Taylor, but the self-styled 'water poet' alluded to their intensity in his own published ripostes: 'The cause, I heare, your fury flameth from; I said, I was no dunce-combe, coxcombe Tom; What's that to you (good Sir) that you should fume; Or rage or chafe, or thinke I durst presume . . .'

John Donne, Ben Jonson and now some boatman he'd never met – Coryate must have wondered who would turn on him next. He might have hoped for some anti-Taylor help from the big guns, but everyone was too busy laughing at this pathetically small-time slanging match. In the end, he wrote to King James and asked that Taylor be punished; the royal reply was rudely dismissive. It was the last straw.

The year before he had already begun to recognise that however impressive his 1608 journey should have been, somehow it wasn't impressive enough for the cynical been-there-done-that courtiers. History would remember the *Crudities* as the first recognisable travelogue, and the journey it described as the inspiration for the Grand Tour. But history was no good to Coryate. He didn't want to know that in 300 years' time, forks and umbrellas would be stalwart features of the British way of life, that in certain parts of the Lake District both were used on a daily basis, often the right way round. He wanted quick results, to be a legend in his own lifetime.

As humiliations and debts mounted, he vowed to wipe both slates clean with an epic odyssey whose achievement and resultant published description would grant him the social and intellectual credibility he craved. At a stroke he would definitively lay the 'bumptious bumpkin' tag to rest.

On 20 October 1612, seemingly almost unnoticed, Coryate set sail in an unknown boat from an unknown port, headed for the Aegean. Even he wasn't sure where he was going: Constantinople looked good; Jerusalem, possibly – all we know of his journey is contained in a handful of letters he wrote home, along with the odd account written by Brits he met along the way.

The Venice trip had been ambitious, but this was in a different league. In the early part of the seventeenth century, pirates were taking an average of one British ship a week in the southern Mediterranean – over 1,000 Christian slaves were traded every year in Algiers and Tunis. And the Ottoman Empire was so feared, religiously and otherwise, that all British church services included a prayer that included the line 'our sworn and most deadly enemies the Turks'.

We know that Coryate visited what he thought was Troy (actually 18 miles away), delivering a typical oration in which he declared himself the first Knight of Troy; and that while in Constantinople he had an ague cured by blood letting, and saw a Mohammedan who had been found drunk killed by having boiling lead poured into his mouth and ears – all typical Tommy wish-you-were-here stuff. But this time, he was in no hurry to come home. Maybe he wanted to make sure he got the right material; maybe he was still bitter. But for whatever reason he stayed in Constantinople for a year, eventually setting off for Jerusalem in January 1614.

Reading Coryate's surviving letters in Michael Strachan's biography was unsettling and increasingly poignant. There was more recognisable material – the rabbi who circumcised a young boy, then 'did put his mouth to the childs yard, and sucked up the bloud', a procession of 'the ugliest sluts that ever I saw' on the Aegean island of Mytilene – but reading in the huge gaps between the very small number of lines, it was clear that he had changed.

He was dressing like a Turk, and had already learnt the language; in Jerusalem he'd had large crucifixes tattooed on each wrist. He looked odd, and sounded it: the extreme elements of his character were becoming exaggerated into ugly caricature. That quiet confidence in his own abilities flared into monomania – he took to introducing himself to fellow travellers as 'the Odcombian legstretcher; a walker as I doubt whether you have ever heard of the like in your life', and went on to boast unrestrainedly about the astonishing work of literature his journey would produce. Recovering from a swoon, he informed those around him that it was caused by the thought that England might somehow be denied the majestic accounts of his travels.

And the bigotry was now running riot. He told a large crowd of Muslims that they should 'spit in the face of thy Koran and bury it under a privy . . . I my selfe have already written one better booke and will hereafter this write another better and truer'. It was like reading a postcard from some rather pompous friend who'd gone off InterRailing and gone off the InterRails.

His arrival in Jerusalem was recorded in a local register on 7 April 1615, and after pilgrimages to Bethlehem and the River Jordan – all the while being harried by sniping archers up in the dunes – he made the fateful decision to continue eastwards. Attaching himself to enormous trading caravans – one he estimated at 6,000 strong – he marched up to fifteen hours a day through Syria and Persia, often through the night when the desert sun burnt too hot. On the banks of the Tigris he was mugged by one of the caravan's own guards; all his money was stolen except for two gold pieces 'hidden in certaine clandestine bodilie corners'. Soon after he was conned out of half an arse's worth of his remaining funds in some undescribed incident; for the last part of his walk he lived off the equivalent of a penny a day. Every few weeks he would come upon some vast, almost mythical fortress city – Orfah, Diarbekr or Isfahan, trading centres which with 200,000 inhabitants were as large as Coryate's London. And his only map and travel guide was the Old Testament.

Finally, in July 1615, ten months and 3,300 miles after setting off from Jerusalem, a thirty-eight-year-old parson's son from the west of England walked into the courtyard of the Great Mogul Emperor, Jahangir, in the north Indian city of Ajmer. A novelty in itself, as Thomas Coryate was the first Englishman to arrive in India with no thought of trade. But, as suggested by his rather bedraggled appearance and disintegrating footwear, Coryate had an even more unusual tale to tell than the other dozen Englishmen employed there by the fledgling East India Company. He had just done something no European had even attempted since Alexander the Great's infantry reached the Ganges 2,000 years before – he had walked to India.

The court of the Great Mogul was one of astonishing scale and splendour. Jahangir's annual income is estimated to have been about £55 million – and this at a time when most European countries could hope to turn over £500,000 in a good year. Even the cost of feeding and maintaining Jahangir's 30,000-strong menagerie of lions and elephants comfortably exceeded the total GDP of Tudor

England. And when the mood took him, he would up and leave and expect the court to follow – such was their mastery of the incomprehensible logistics that a 20-mile-wide camp for 200,000 could be erected from scratch in four hours. Rome wasn't built in a day, but if Jahangir's boys had been there it could have been.

I read about all this, and about the errant eunuchs being fed to the dogs while the women caught kissing them were buried up to their necks in sand, and then I imagined what must have been going through Coryate's mind when he first strode up to Jahangir's balcony, cleared his throat, and began to speak.

Only by recalling the nonchalance of the young man strolling up Montacute's imposing drive could I start to understand. In crossing the social gulf that separated the Phelipses from Odcombe's flyblown straw-chewers, Coryate had already made a journey that was in some ways no less exceptional. This, he probably thought, was just a whole new court to show off to, the grandest in the world, and, crucially, one which he could impress without fear of being sneered at on intellectual grounds.

And it seems that finally, as he'd hoped all those years ago when addressing the Odcombe church fête, performing orations had become his career. Travelling about with the East India Company boys, for whom the Mogul's patronage was also crucial, he cadged free bed and board but was too proud to ask for cash handouts. He was already competent in Persian, Turkish and Arabic, and once he'd added Hindustani he set about earning his keep – and in fact saving for his trip home – with a series of flowery impromptu lectures delivered to Indian noblemen all over the north of the country. That first speech, like those that followed an 'I am a poore traveller come hither from a farre country' -style affair, apparently earnt him silver rupees worth £10, flicked dismissively off the royal balcony.

Perhaps hoping for a further handout – Jahangir was after all comfortably the wealthiest man in the world, someone who alleviated boredom by weighing himself and giving away the equivalent in gold coinage to the masses at the palace gate – Coryate then began following the unwieldy court on foot as it moved around India on the Mogul's whim.

Preparing for a tough march from Mandu to Surat, a 200-mile walk along the Narbada River to the coast north of Bombay, he met Richard Steel, a maverick merchant–entrepreneur who had just returned from a royal-visit round trip to London. Steel had mentioned to King James that Coryate was in India; Coryate, feverishly excited to hear that the court knew of his epic achievement, asked what the King had said to this news. Choosing honesty over tact, Steel replied, 'Is that fool still living?'

'Which, when our pilgrim heard the news,' wrote one of Coryate's ex-pat associates, East India Company chaplain Edward Terry, 'seemed to trouble him very much, because the King spake no more nor no better of him, saying that kings would speak of poor men what they pleased.'

I'm afraid I took this personally. The strange hollowness in my head I sensed when reading this exchange for the first time was filled by an ugly clot of rage when I read it again. How could they? How *could* they? Tommy, Tommy, Tommy. What must he have felt as the King's words sank in? That Coryate could be infuriating was self-evident – I had just been reading of his new habit, when overnighting in Muslim towns, of waking up at dawn to shout down the muezzins from a rooftop opposite the minaret. But no one, no one, deserved to do all he'd done, to boldly go where he'd boldly gone, and be repaid like that by the man he'd most wanted to impress.

It seems as if this final and most crushing humiliation finally broke

Coryate's self-belief. No matter what his achievements, class and poverty would always be his undoing. He had, in the most literal fashion, gone to great lengths to gain the respect of his mocking betters – but the harder he tried, the more desperate he seemed and the more counterproductive his efforts became. Inevitably, he was doomed. Coryate's tragi-comic life is one of those where pride always came before a fall, and I suppose that even had he returned and written up his travels, he'd never have won over the court. They didn't want a cultural treatise tempered with incidents intended to demonstrate his resourcefulness, wit and religious faith. They wanted the artless, bawdy ramblings of a self-important buffoon abroad, preferably with illustrations to match.

Already weakened by his ceaseless wanderings, he stumbled into Surat, where the local East India Company rep immediately helped him to bed. Once there, he summoned the dregs of his strength to shout, 'Sack, sack! Is there such a thing as sack? I pray give me some sack!' His host's over-eager fulfilment of this uncustomary alcoholic demand ensured that these were Coryate's tawdry but memorable last words. He died on an unrecorded day in December 1617, aged forty. '*Sic exit Coryatus*,' wrote Edward Terry, one man at least who acknowledged the achievements that merited a suitably epic sign off. Thus much of Tommy.

No one knows who paid for the imposing domed tomb that still stands today on four sturdy pillars in a lonely plain near Suvali, just north of Surat. Its grand flanks are bare – no inscriptions for future Coryates to copy down – but the East India Company marked it as his resting place on its charts, and it is still labelled on current maps as 'Tom Coryat's Tomb'.

If you're ever passing that way, give his column a hug from me.

Bibliography

Arnold-Baker, Charles, *The Companion to British History*, Tunbridge Wells, Longcross Press, 1996.

Black, Jeremy, *The British Abroad: The Grand Tour in the Eighteenth Century*, Stroud, Sutton Publishing, 1997.

Chaney, Edward, *The Evolution of the Grand Tour*, London, Frank Cass, 1998.

Chaney, Edward and Mack, Peter, eds, *England and the Continental Renaissance*, Woodbridge, Boydell Press, 1990.

Chard, Chloe, *Pleasure and Guilt on the Grand Tour*, Manchester, Manchester University Press, 1999.

Coryate, Thomas, *Coryats Crudities*, Glasgow, James MacLehos, 1905.

Delaforce, Patrick, *The Grand Tour*, London, Robertson McCarta, 1990.

Facaros, Dana and Pauls, Michael, *Venice*, London, Cadogan, 1991.

Fleming, Fergus, *Killing Dragons: A History of Alpine Exploration*, London, Granta, 2000.

Hibbert, Christopher, *The Grand Tour*, London, Methuen, 1987.

Michelin et Cie, *Italy*, Clermont-Ferrand, Michelin, 1983.

Michelin et Cie, *Savoie*, Clermont-Ferrand, Puiseux, Boulanger et Cie, 1948.

Michelin et Cie, *Switzerland*, London, Dickens Press, 1965.

Michelin Tyre plc, *Switzerland*, Watford, Michelin Travel Publications, 1999.

Strachan, Michael, *The Life and Adventures of Thomas Coryate*, London, Oxford University Press, 1962.